Ab‹

In 2011, Heather Bandenburg moved to London with a degree in Gender Studies and a job in a call centre. While dealing with crippling anxiety and zero-hours contracts, she stumbled on Lucha Britannia, a group of wrestlers who train and perform under a railway arch in East London. Despite knowing nothing about wrestling and an almost heroic aversion to exercise, Heather had finally discovered something that she was good at. Six years later, she'd made a name for herself as La Rana Venenosa – the Queen of the Sewer, performing in London, and acting as a referee for two other leading UK women's promotions. Since then, her writing on women's wrestling has been featured in the *Guardian*, *DIVA* and the *Independent*; and she has contributed to articles in *Vanity Fair* and a variety of TV and radio shorts.

Unladylike

Unladylike

A Grrrl's Guide to Wrestling

Heather Bandenburg

unbound

This edition first published in 2019

Unbound
6th Floor Mutual House, 70 Conduit Street, London W1S 2GF
www.unbound.com
All rights reserved

ISBN (eBook): 978-1-78965-034-1
ISBN (Paperback): 978-1-78965-033-4

Cover design by Mecob

Illustrations by Jules Scheele

Printed and bound in Great Britain by Clays Ltd, Elcograf S.p.A.

MIX
Paper from
responsible sources
FSC® C018072

To the Resistance Gallery and the people within it.

And to Fraser, because without him I would have stopped long ago, like a sensible person.

With grateful thanks to Stu Alexander, Chow & Finch Fletcher, Jane Harper, Gianandrea Mamfredi, Ems Norton, Charlotte Passingham, Squid and Harry X for helping to make this book happen.

Super Patrons

Carl Denham
Dex
Emma Dingle
Amanda Dolphin
Will Donovan
Anthony Elliott
Greg Evans
Ray Filar
Betty Fox
Rebecca Fuller
Gemma and Russell
Julian C Giddings
Danni Glover
Izaskun Gonzalez
Linky Gray
Daniel Hall
Simon Hall
Ben Harding
Meg Hewitt
David Hicks
Havana Hurricane
Ana Iris Marques Ramgrab
Emily Joh Miller
Mark Joyce
Martin Kelly
Dan Kieran
Daisy Lang
Ann Legg
Benjamin Litherland
Benjamin Louche
Rachel Magdassian Dean
Lu Mason
John Mitchinson

Andrea Moore
Luke Morris
John Morrow
Ali Muir
Jamie O'Brien
Richard Phillips
Jean Luc Pickat
Justin Pollard
Rhonda Pownall
Tom Pratt
Steve Preston
Sophia Probert
Naghmeh Rajabi
Nicolas Roberto
Sochel Rogers
Roly and Maz
Michael Sachs
Belinda Seppings
Helen Smedley
Jen Smethurst
Johnny Stafford
Annabel Stark
Jessica Swann
Gavin Talbot
The Triskele
Jonathan Trout
Orrin Ward
P Wilding
Richard Winch
Leanne-Marie Withington

Contents

1

Queen of the Sewer

'You need to start a match like you start a book. If the first line of your book is boring, no one will read the first page. If you start your book with, "Dad walked in and was sick on the baby", then the readers are immediately gripped.'
– Greg Burridge, wrestling trainer, the London School of Lucha Libre

Before my first arena match, Greg's words of wisdom came to mind. This was because I had just almost vomited on a baby on the tube. I was on my way to the match, and I was still sewing sequins on to my leotard, trying to push my anxiety through each foil pinprick. My nerves were boiling over; I could feel heat on the back of my throat from bubbling stomach acid. I was crammed on to a seat with a pram beside me, the baby inside about three jolts away from bawling. In hindsight, trying to meditate while performing time-sensitive sewing on a swinging tube carriage was probably not the best way to prepare mentally for the biggest show of my career.

Like most wrestlers, I spent every spare moment daydreaming about my next match or what my ring gear would look like if money were no object. I was time-poor and constantly bruised, but at least I could jump off a ten-foot balcony on to six other people without batting an eyelid. With these skills being undervalued in modern London, I had no choice but to fund my Lycra and violence habit with a full-time job in an office.

On the day of my first arena match, I gazed into the space between Excel columns, trying to imagine what the sound of the crowd chanting my name would sound like. Would I be overwhelmed? Would I cry? Would I be sick on a baby?

When my boss asked me if something was distracting me, I answered, 'In about six hours I'm going to be risking my safety for the entertainment of two thousand people.'

'What? On a Thursday?'

'Yes, on a Thursday.'

'Well, make sure you don't drink too much.'

I think my colleagues assumed wrestling was just some weird fetish I had. A fetish that involved punching my boyfriend in the balls while others watched, all the while guzzling gin and drugs. I had stopped trying to change their minds as it was partly true. I liked gin and I had once punched my boyfriend in the balls in a match, but that's because he didn't move in time.

The tube I was on kept getting delayed by rush-hour traffic. When I emerged from Bethnal Green Station I rushed up the escalator in effort to make up the time. At the top – causing quite a stir among the queue of grumbling London commuters – were ten highly tanned men in tight t-shirts, with wheelie suitcases. Bickering in Spanish, three of them already had their masks on to protect their identity at all times. These were *luchadores*, celebrities in Mexico who would be headlining the show I was in. Here in London, they were mostly ignored by passers-by, who jostled them out of the way passive-aggressively, or who at most snapped them on the sly with their camera phones.

One of them recognised me, which led me to shake hands with them all – obeying the international law of being polite to fellow wrestlers. I gallantly led them to the venue – York Hall, world famous for holding boxing and wrestling matches. Three times a week I walked past this building on my way to practise, but that night I walked up the front steps and got past security with my name alone.

Empty plastic chairs waited for hundreds of wrestling fans. The year previously I'd got entry for free by selling t-shirts alongside the families of *luchadores*, watching only part of the show from the back of the room (though my Spanish did improve). Up close, the ring was at least a metre wider and higher than any that I had wrestled in previously. But now there was no time to practise; I was late and went quickly back-stage to get ready.

My wrestling family – Lucha Britannia – were all in a room in the basement, deep in discussion about which moves to showcase and how to keep the match slick. They tied up their boots, made last-minute sewing repairs to their costumes, and rubbed each other in fake tan. The ring girls – two burlesque stars in latex – admired my new costume. It was a tasselled, sparkling leotard, with a green chiffon cape and a new pair of Spanx. As the other girls did their foundation, I blacked out my teeth with eyeliner and rubbed red lipstick all over my face, finishing the look with the mask of La Rana Venenosa. Green skin, gold bulbous eyes and a permanent sneer fixed on a red, sparkling pair of lips. I stuck my tongue out in the mirror, growling at the face that was no longer me, but the Queen of the Sewer.

In one corner of the dressing room there was a photographer for a men's fitness magazine. To get into character I posed for

him – showing off my muscles, twisting my head like a possessed child. I dribbled water out of my mouth, coming so close
to the camera that the photographer stumbled back, purring
words of encouragement. As usual, the photos never materialised after the show. Rana was too weird looking for most
publications and, if I'm honest, I preferred it that way.

This ease with privacy is something that most outsiders find
surprising when they meet wrestlers. We are not only secretive
about our identities, but behind the masks we come from all
walks of life. Looking around the room, I could see a personal
trainer, a cash assistant at New Look, a landscape gardener, a
handyman, a stuntman, an events planner and a law student.
We only reveal these identities to each other, and our privacy
makes us as mythic to strangers as the 'real' *luchadores* upstairs
who, due to their fame in Mexico, are able to support their
families entirely through their wrestling wages. All of us are in
the sport for our own reasons, but we know that none of us
can say we're doing it for the money or the fame, as neither of
these is in large supply. The wrestlers from Mexico started off
the same; now if they wear their masks in public in their home
cities they're swamped by fans.

Tonight's show was the debut match for Muñeca de Trapo,
the Rag Doll. She paced the room, muttering under her breath,
trying to keep warm with a puffer jacket over her red bikini.
A blonde acrobat just under five feet tall, she had been trained
by a Russian ex-Olympian – before falling into the world of
wrestling with just as much surprise as I had. To try to calm
myself down I attempted to stop her pacing.

'Look, what's the worst that can happen?'

'I forget everything we went through and then fall off the
ring and break my neck.'

'First, the audience won't know if you've messed up; they

don't know who wins. If you forget, just do a backflip and a dropkick – that's more than I can do, and it'll make them pop.'

'Okay, but what if I die?…'

'No one here is going to hit you so hard you die – and we all catch each other, remember?'

'Are you nervous?' she asked me, her blue eyes glancing up through the skull holes of her *Día de los Muertos* mask.

'Of course I am and I can't even do a backflip – if I forget my moves I really am fucked…'

At seven, the doors to the hall opened, and we experienced a nerve-wracking hour as the hum of the crowd grew louder ahead of the show while we gathered in the wings. Ten of us would be competing in the same match; the winner would be the first to pin another for three counts. We muttered our parts to each other in a circle: 'Duck one… take a bump… come in and cut me off… then we go into the dives.' This preamble took the same pattern as for all of our shows – everyone in masks, muttering to themselves and punching the air like an opponent, and me, as usual, developing the sudden urge to pee.

Beyond the curtain I could sense the audience filling the seats, getting their first beers and plates of nachos. Then a sudden roar and we, the wrestlers, breathed in collectively. The announcer got in the ring and the cheering made my heart pound into my lungs. The sound was even louder than I'd imagined earlier, at work, yet I didn't cry. It was something I'd never felt before; my body began to buzz all over, glued to the spot.

The master of ceremonies introduced the show – 'The Spectacular of *Lucha Libre*' – the greatest *luchadores* all the way from Mexico. The stars of Lucha Britannia, who keep the Mexican tradition of *lucha libre* alive in humble, cold London, were about to amaze them with a '*lucha*-chaos' match.

'First to the ring is a fighter brought to this country as an egg in the pocket of a murderer. She grew up to become the most poisonous woman alive, the Queen of the Sewer, the kiss of death to all who fight her. It's... *La Rana Venenosa*...'

Then, the spitting guitars of my entrance music began; no more time remained to go through the match in my head, it was happening.

Through the blinding CO2 cannons and strobe lights, I strode on to the stage, careful not to trip down a flight of stage stairs, as the audience roared louder. The cheers turned to boos when I spat water at the faceless crowd, the front rows screaming in delight as drops fell on their heads. The energy was ecstatic as I aggressively cat walked around the ring. I glared into the faces of children, I roared back to those in the rafters. The thrill of getting the room to hate me, to understand that I should be feared and disliked, was a powerful thing to the girl behind the mask. The girl who spent the day on the phone with a smile forced on her lips to make her sound happier. Rana was the antithesis of this.

Climbing to the top rope, there was a moment where I had my arms open and felt the heat of the crowd hit me. 'La Rana Venenosa' was announced a second time, and then the spotlight moved elsewhere.

I was low on the roster, part of the ensemble, the first one out. In the summer night around York Hall, life went on as normal – joggers went by, people walked to the corner shop – but for the audience inside that world ceased to exist. Tonight, I was the first sight to pull them into another place; one where violence was dazzling, where good and evil were strikingly defined. The world of wrestling.

The other competitors entered the ring. There was La Diablesa Rosa, the pink demon, with the body of Wonder Woman, who had gifted me a pair of gold shorts for my

6

birthday the month previously. Then came Muñeca de Trapo, pulling out not one but about twelve backflips before she even got in the ring. El Nórdico Fuego, the Fire Viking, who had come straight from filming a period drama in Leeds, had a crowd of middle-aged women out of their seats. And finally, after the others, my teacher, Metallico, King of the Scrapheap, a veteran in British wrestling terms, entered the ring. He had previously told me that each time he wrestled it was like his first match all over again.

Rana eyed them all with fury as they took their places within the ropes. The girl inside the mask was bursting with pride at how they each commanded their own bodies. To the audience, we were the stars in the match – it didn't matter who we were behind our costumes, our real lives did not exist. To me, these individuals were my friends who I'd somehow grown to know through years of learning to kick each other in the head.

The bell rang – muscles twitching, fists clenching, death stares – then a ten-person brawl began. I took out Rosa with a swift kick and then strangled her on the ropes. She tried to move out the way and I muttered to myself, 'Right foot first', and jumped in the air, landing both feet on her chest. Rosa shook herself, dodged one of my punches and ran across the ring. She bounced off the ropes, throwing her whole body weight on me, knocking the wind from my guts and causing me to roll out the ring. I crawled around the perimeter as two wrestlers leapt over each other's shoulders and the crowd called at us like a firework show.

Whenever I found another wrestler outside the stage, I threw a punch their way. I chucked the Viking straight into the front row, knocking over chairs. Far from disgruntled, the audience was delighted, cheering as beer was spilt on their clothes. Seizing a moment just after Muñeca de Trapo had knocked over three opponents twice her size, I climbed back into the ring, leapt and swung my legs around her neck. She crumpled under my weight, her tiny body writhing in agony as I tried to force her shoulders on to the floor for three counts. I failed, and turning to the crowd to snarl at them for more encouragement, moved straight into the path of a kick to the head from behind – and fell over the top rope, out the ring.

It was painful, and it was hot. I was aware that even as I lay prone next to the ring that there was never a break in the action. As I struggled to my feet to attack a wrestler that had materialised at my side, he was knocked down again by the Viking somersaulting off the top-corner post. The ring was empty except for Metallico, so I climbed to the top rope, standing fifteen feet above the floor. As he turned, I jumped as high as I could, coming down with the 'cunt drop', my signature move, on his chest. The canvas made a huge crash as his body hit the springs. The crowd roared, and the referee counted to two before he pushed me off.

I turned around to face Rosa, who gave me a kick to the belly and pulled me over her back. With a shout she threw me to the floor, and I tucked my chin to stop my head hitting the canvas like a split melon. Rosa was on me, she held my legs and shoulders as the referee counted to three. I knew I had lost the match from the screams of applause for Rosa, her arms raised above her head, her championship belt returned to her as the crowd thundered.

After the ten seconds of shaking myself in defeat, I knew that only fifteen minutes had passed. I had been training for these fifteen minutes for five years. Those of us who were evil limped backstage, holding our sides, angrily cursing the audience all the way to the locker room as the crowd favourites were given longer in the path of the adoring crowd. I breathed deeply, the sweat running down my neck as I took off my mask and was handed a beer. A minute late, Muñeca de Trapo had burst in, thrown off her mask and was whizzing around, her pupils wide with adrenaline.

'That was so amazing! I want to do that every day for the rest of my life!'

Metallico was the last to return to the dressing room, his arm around one of the younger wrestlers who had hit the floor face first when he dived out. His mask was off and we made room for him, he'd taken a knock to the head. Wrestlers are used to concussions; even my cheek buzzed slightly from where someone had kicked me a bit too enthusiastically. But we also know from day one that wrestling isn't ballet.

The wrestlers around me unbuckled their masks – rubbing themselves down with towels, talking happily about the things they missed or apologising when a punch landed harder than it meant to. We all ached in those familiar places from old moves, putting cold beer bottles on the joints to ease the swelling. For our efforts, each wrestler was rewarded with fifty quid, paid in rolls of tenners, and Coronas from an ice bucket.

During the interval I went out in my Rana costume, thinking I could surprise my friends who had managed to get last-minute cheap seats. In the middle of the stalls, two English guys begged me for a photo. Rana Venenosa answered in her rasping frog voice, 'Okay, but one of you has to become my fourteenth husband.'

I pulled one of them into a sweaty, soft headlock. Seconds later there were twenty people queuing behind them to get a picture. Half were drunk British men, who would be sheepish as soon as they actually had to talk to me. There were also families handing me their babies and children so that I could hold them and do peace signs. All was forgotten about my frog's misdemeanours; they clearly didn't mind that my final move had involved knocking people out with my vagina. It was bizarre, exhausting, and uniquely lovely, to suddenly be

Rana the superhero made flesh. That night, the girl with IBS and bad skin behind the mask never did make it to see her friends.

For the rest of the show, I stood at the back without a mask, suddenly just a face in the crowd. Watching the Mexican fighters was like watching a master class in submission holds and disregard for their own bodies. They wore masks that were passed down through generations. Men who had trained from age fourteen, who learned to fall on concrete floors in order to prove their ability. Forty-year-olds with fake knees leapt over the top ropes. They left red handprints on each other's chests. The fights brawled out of the ring and into the crowd. To us, they were the pinnacle of success but a product of a completely different kind of dedication. I was humbled to have shared the same booking as them.

By the final match – a half-hour bout between two father-and-son teams – everyone was out of their seats; plastic beer glasses littered the floor; children stood on chairs. The good guys got the final pin, and the crowd rose with the heat.

As the stars gathered in the ring and the fans swamped them for selfies, no longer dressed as Rana, I snooped over to the merchandise table to greet the families I had met while manning the table last time. Weaving my way through the crowd, I spotted the Lucha Britannia t-shirts, stickers and mugs that we tried to push at every show. There was also a new addition of bootleg action figures – old toys painted to look like miniature versions of us.

My eyes shot to a spindly, dripping frog woman, her boobs different sizes and stuck on with FIMO modelling clay. I turned to a guy who had taken my place on the stand.

'How much for this action figure?'

'Twenty-five quid.'

I left it. We say that you've made it in the wrestling world if you get an action figure made of you, so I supposed it still mattered even if there was only one model on sale – and the guy who made it couldn't even recognise you out of your costume. Coming face to face with a charmingly inaccurate representation of me in miniature was one of the more bizarre, and equally affirming, moments of my life.

The arena finally emptied at eleven; one wrestler was concussed and another had had his shoulder dislocated. The *luchadores* had been promised a party which we all found out about as we were packing our bags. As with all *lucha* parties, it was held at the Resistance Gallery, the home of our training school, which was also a nightclub. Despite the peeling paint on the walls and stickered toilet seats, it was also our spiritual home where we held our shows every month. As we entered through the glittery curtain, I wondered if the *luchadores* had noticed the flyers for fetish nights and drag shows that were glued on the walls like a stucco montage of punk, queer London.

Vanderhorne, who owned the venue and who had refereed our match, had forgotten that the 'party' clashed with a medical fetish night. The jet-lagged, bruised *luchadores* sat on the stage and looked on with confusion as people wearing latex took it in turns to receive electric shocks and lie in various bondage contraptions. The music was a soundscape of medical sounds, and of screaming and terrifying child voices – so loud they couldn't talk to each other. To top it all off, a naked seventy-year-old man in high heels kept asking them questions about Big Daddy. We all ended up happily crammed outside in the smoking area in the muggy summer air, sharing stories about life as wrestlers.

For this is why so many of us are wrestlers – not for the action figures, nor the fame that a tiny fraction of us will attain

– but for the stories. We are, after all, just humans who decided at some point to become flying superheroes without a cause; to risk injury and to live a double life for the fee-paying public. Rarely are wrestlers able to talk about their lives outside the ring in the same sentence as their life within it. But together, we understand the rush of a crowd; the supportive resistance of muscle on muscle. To some, we are the leftovers of a bygone sideshow; to others the most versatile athletes in the world.

This is a book about the wonderful rebellion and escape we feel in doing something so fake, so bizarre and so difficult as wrestling. I am here to tell you truthfully about how we become wrestlers, how we earn the right to step in the ring, and how we find what we do almost sacred. I am here to tell you truthfully about how I too inhabit this double life, the life of an unlikely and unladylike female wrestler.

Like my creepy action figure, the purchase of which eluded me that night, I am not your average wrestler. I am a strange one-off that doesn't fit in to your archetypal wrestling persona. Read that as: I am not a large man with rippling muscles who has dreamt of fighting alongside the greats since the age of four. In the same way, this is not your average wrestling book.

There are certain things that a wrestling book *should* include – which is why I've just recounted one of the most startling shows of my career. I need to convince you from the get-go that despite not being a big, muscly man, I am a *proper* wrestler. The fact is, there are about fifty or so *proper* wrestlers in this book – but like me, you are unlikely to have ever heard of them. They perform purely for the love of wrestling itself, with an acceptance that they will probably retire in anonymity. Even if they don't wear a mask.

While fully accepting I will never be an international star, this does not take anything away from the fact that I am a *proper* wrestler. I want to explain why normal people, like me, are motivated to put on Lycra costumes and throw themselves around a ring made of wooden boards and elastic, for reasons completely separate from fame and fortune. Being a wrestler, to me, is about being a woman, and about being a badass, and being able to walk amongst the commuters of London, fully aware that I could lift up most passers-by and do ten squats with them. In fact, that has very much become my party trick.

This book is written for those people that I pick up – the general public who don't know anything about wrestling but think it's a worthwhile spectacle.

The wrestling industry does itself a disservice by not exploring the world of non-famous wrestlers – those individuals who, like myself, are happily relegated to the independent circuit of British town halls and underground night clubs. We are not all Amazonians, and many of us prefer the backstage banter and freedom of performance to spending every waking hour down the gym. Yet these are still people with stories to share, who can get a crowd out of their seats, baying for blood, without even touching their opponent.

I want to take you into the world that these performers inhabit. Built of sweaty mats, a passion for a weird hobby, and unladylike women.

Because, you see, women, no matter how skilled they are, are rarely considered 'proper' wrestlers. They are lower rated, lower paid, less respected, and very often completely absent from proceedings.

So, now I've established that despite being unheard of (and you should also know I am un-tanned, un-ripped, bikini-phobic), and of course, *female,* I am still a wrestler. I hope you can understand how unlikely my journey has been to get here; a journey that has seen me not only performing in front of thousands of people, on more than one occasion, but now writing a book about the experience.

I get asked a lot of questions about wrestling. For example, at my dad's wedding, a man who'd known me since childhood casually asked me how the mud wrestling was going, assuming that would be the only way that women could wrestle.

Now that we have established, I am, against all odds, a 'proper' wrestler, let's just deal with some basic assumptions you may have about wrestling.

Firstly, women can wrestle without mud being present.

Secondly, wrestling is not fake. You can't fake someone throwing their body weight at you so that it knocks you backwards. You can't fake being kicked in the stomach. It's more complicated than that. It's like saying acting is fake and not real either. But no, acting is acting. Just like wrestling, shockingly, is wrestling. You have to learn to pretend, you have to become a vehicle of the 'non-reality' that you are performing in.

To many, wrestling is a completely weird and unexplored world. As a concept it hums along quietly in the background, raising eyebrows in the press every now and again, like Marilyn Manson. You may have never watched a wrestling match but you know what wrestling is. It's a choreographed fight, so in this sense, yes, it is 'fake'. But the nature of wrestling is that it's about the characters and your investment in them winning or losing, rather than the violence itself.

In my experience, people focus on the pre-decided aspect of wrestling before they think about what it entails to perform. At the end of the day, even though it is fixed, the audience does not know the outcome, and the wrestlers only sometimes get actually knocked unconscious at the end. Wrestling requires the same determination, athleticism, commitment, sacrifice, friendship, brutality, creativity, shame, pain of 'not-fake' violence as boxing.

Like boxing, wrestlers are not enemies outside the ring. Unlike boxing, wrestling also requires basic sewing skills. Wrestlers perform aggression to tell a story, the ring is a separate reality, like a street in a soap opera – reflecting a fight in the world that we inhabit. Another reason that wrestling is often described as fake is because we use these overblown characters to tell stories, caricatures that are larger than life or 'gimmicks'. Telling a story through wrestling is an exercise in the suspension of disbelief: the audience knows that the violence isn't 'real' but like a play. If the characters are believable and the style is believable, they will respond like they are in a Roman arena. For a short time, the audience will truly feel that the forces of good and evil are at play in the ring. Wrestling gives people the chance to express themselves in this way, and to align themselves, simply, with storytelling.

Wrestlers fight in order to get the crowd to react, and they justify their actions through a character they inhabit, not for any reason within the 'real' world.

But like boxing, wrestling *hurts*. One of the main things that frustrates wrestlers about the 'fake' question is that it cheapens the years of back-breaking pain that wrestlers endure (sometimes literally) in order to learn how not to hurt their opponent. We hurt ourselves, but not each other. We are stunt doubles that double for no one. When a wrestler drops another wrestler on their head, we know that the person has a day job, a family. So, this means people don't get knocked unconscious at the end of every match, though they often appear to. We look after each other. And learning how to beat someone in a match while leaving them without even a bruise, let alone as a bloody pulp, takes years to perfect.

Very quickly you learn that bodies don't like being thrown around and picked up, and then smashed into again. Wrestlers sustain life-changing injuries; regular concussions and a whole plethora of other nasty and constant strains. There are muscles that I didn't know existed in my body until I tore them while learning to wrestle.

As well as physical endurance, wrestling involves psychological conditioning – shaping your mind to overcome bodily reactions, such as panicking, lashing out or freezing. Muscles have memories that learn how to defend the body instinctively from being destroyed, and wrestling involves overriding these. It is a mix of exposure and determination, so rather than wrestling being equated to 'hurting', you and your body just accept that wrestling and pain are similar but not the same thing.

Wrestlers, both men and women, are united in their knowledge that wrestling is difficult. Not just the training and the pain; but the put downs, the anxieties, the isolations, the fear of 'losing' the crowd in a match. To just dismiss wrestling as 'fake' ignores all the other hurdles and intricacies that it takes to be a good wrestler.

There's a name for the act of keeping schtum about how our hits, kicks and throws are not 'real' – it's called 'kayfabe'. Kayfabe is about *not* talking about the unseen forces within wrestling; keeping the story alive so the victories are believable. When wrestling is done well, it should be looked upon as if a fight has truly taken place.

In wrestling, traditionally, no nods should *ever* be made to choreography, or the lives that the competitors live outside the ring. I remember once telling someone, while wearing my mask, that outside the ring I work in third-sector administration. Later, someone who had overheard this conversation told me I had just killed my wrestling career.

Behold, three years later I am writing a book about wrestling. But I am still anxious about opening up this world to people.

I think it is important to understand kayfabe to understand the culture of wrestling: no one likes the person at the front of the magic show who tells you how every trick is done before you've even seen it. But I also think that by obeying kayfabe slavishly we will never be able to share just how much commitment wrestlers give to their art. Just because what we do is pre-decided, we are not phonies.

I hope breaking kayfabe this time doesn't destroy my wrestling career. Mainly because I think wrestling is an amazing art form.

The fact that it is not 'real' has meant that I can bundle all of my negative, weird energy into another character, a character who has the ability to do things that would make me lie awake at night deconstructing my every action if I did them without a mask. My body, rather than being this sack of muscles and water retention, becomes a tool to tell a story. I can make a crowd believe they are seeing a fight to the death driven by clashes of uncontrollable forces. Just by persevering in wrestling I feel like a strong, formidable woman both in an industry and in a wider world that would prefer me not to notice I have this potential.

To me, wrestling is an act of resistance – to resist the way we are encouraged to do things purely for money, or to achieve acceptable societal standing. Because the world is a mess, I have no mortgage, I don't have a successful career, and I have, unsurprisingly, not invented the cure for cancer. Despite this, I can be a visibly strong, weird woman who entertains crowds. This is how wrestling has become my main vehicle of feminist resistance – I am doing something that society deems worthless but which I know has saved my life and that, somehow, could save others.

Wrestling, in itself, requires you to be unladylike – to gain bruises, to make too much noise, to be grappled and groped, handled by people who are essentially strangers for the enjoyment of other strangers. To turn your weak, fecund body into a weapon is itself a feminist act. And perhaps that's precisely why women have been wrestling as long as men, but have also been pretty much written out of its history. In wrestling, you are always recognised as woman. Even if you don't want it to, it becomes both a personal and political fight for recognition if people use it as a label.

Through wrestling I learned to embrace the fact that I am unladylike. From a young age, girls are taught to be girls, we are expected to keep fit but not hurt ourselves; to be independent but able to be constantly emotionally available. Wrestling offers a way of using a body that is so different to what you are taught to do at school: to be aggressive, loud, to take up more space. To wrestle is to liberate what you have embodied for so many years.

There are no books for women about how to become an unfamous, unladylike wrestler – you need to be able to do it for yourself and write your own means of escape.

For that reason, this book is not just about how to wrestle, it's also for those seeking a personal revolution in the most unlikely of places. It's about investing in your own perseverance to find something you're good at. It's about being part of a dangerous and ridiculous performance that only succeeds if it sends an audience, sometimes of twenty, sometimes twenty thousand, home happy. Wrestling provides love that leaves you breathless, and it makes you hungry for more, despite arguments and resentments outside of that perfect square-circle of the ring. But wrestling is not a reliable lover – it is tough, unforgiving and happy to make you feel worthless or jealous. But when you are with it, you are part of its story, a story written by thousands of lives.

So, while this is not a story of a wrestler who you might

recognise at an airport, or who has had a supporting role in a blockbuster film, it is the story about the realities of wrestling. Tales from the front lines of a subculture that has been built on appropriation, but then appropriated and re-appropriated time and time again.

While learning to be a wrestler I have met a lot of interesting, inspiring and committed people. I have tiptoed around various delicate social situations that exist behind the scenes at shows, and I have been present at landmark performances that have left the crowds speechless. I still haven't learned to whistle but I've *finally* learned to tell my left from right.

2

Why Do You Make Yourself Ugly?

For the first twenty-three years of my life I was categorised as unladylike, and constantly searching for some meaning to bring together my very specific skillset. That is, being clumsy enough to withstand bumps and falls with little embarrassment or pain, being a sturdy size twelve ever since being ravaged by puberty, having unaddressed anger issues and, finally, having a love of bright costumes. Throughout my life, this combination has not been seen as valuable to wider society – particularly as it's joined with my overactive imagination. While it's not quite the making of an Olympic athlete, it is the recipe for a wrestler.

If you have ever read a book by a famous wrestler, you will see that they usually permit themselves the indulgence of telling their life story. And to be clear, a paltry number of wrestling books have been written about women wrestlers. I know this because when writing this book, I tried to find out if there was a reason why girls became wrestlers.

For example, the best wrestler ever, Mae Young, does not have a book written about her, despite having wrestled from the age of fourteen, right through to her retirement aged eighty-seven. She *literally* changed wrestling because she didn't do what people said or expected her to do. She was the first girl on her school's wrestling team. At her audition for a wrestling promotion, she body-slammed the experienced male wrestler who was supposed to knock her out so she wouldn't come back. Before the Second World War, if she was wrestling in US states where it was illegal for women to wrestle, she would fight alligators. In addition to this, Mae Young refused to sleep with promoters. She wore zoot suits in the 1960s, and she smoked cigars. She once even got herself out of a manslaughter charge after beating up a rapist. Aged seventy-six, she came out of retirement, something she was definitely *not* supposed to do, and wrestled on the WWF (which stands for World Wrestling Federation, later changed to WWE or World Wrestling Entertainment; they altered the name because of the animal charity with the panda logo).

To be clear, this does not reflect my career path in the slightest. The closest I got to combat sport before age twenty-three was knocking my friend out in a trampoline collision.

Then there are those others who had pasts like the stuff of wrestling fables – such as Luna Vachon or Charlotte Flair, who were both descended from great wrestlers. Told from a young age that they were girls, so this wasn't a family legacy for them, they nevertheless took it upon themselves to pursue their ambitions. Vachon ran away from home when she was only sixteen to train in Japan, meanwhile Flair took up the mantle when her brother, destined for stardom, died young. For most wrestlers, there is probably an event in life that steers them towards the sport. But one thing that female wrestlers have in common is that they often take up wrestling *because* they are girls, and they want to prove something.

From a young age, inadequacy gets whispered into the ears

of girls, or shouted in their faces from magazines. And some girls get through this by rejecting the delicate and the respectful. They find a path to being themselves by learning how to do a headlock take over and over and over again. Or at least that's what wrestling felt like to me.

Let's begin before I was born. I can confirm that in my family there is no grappling legacy in my bloodline. Allegedly, in my mum's childhood home in the Midlands, her earliest memory of wrestling is of being forced by her nana to watch it on TV on a Saturday afternoon. My great-grandmother would sit as close to the TV as possible and knit, booing the wrestling, my mum's pet budgie occasionally flying in and snapping at the wool (the budgie's behaviour being the main part of the story in the way my mum told it to me).

In another part of the Midlands, my dad had a similar experience, with my German grandfather insisting he took control of the TV every Saturday afternoon. Dad remembers the wrestling as boring – bouts were slow, a bit like a cross between snooker and boxing. Neither of my parents indulged in the belief commonly held in 1970s Britain, that wrestling was a great national pastime. As such, they would both go to their rooms and listen to David Bowie. I know that because he *did* feature in my childhood.

From what I gather, my parents' courtship was mainly pub based. At their wedding, Dad had to dance with every one of Mum's scouser aunts; they only had a chance to share the floor with each other during 'Come On Eileen'. In the mid-1980s, they moved to Suffolk for an idyllic countryside life and discovered that they'd landed in the middle of nowhere. To summarise the remoteness of my hometown, Bury St Edmunds, the headline in the local newspaper, the day after the Hiroshima bomb was dropped, was 'Donkey found Dead in Ditch'. My parents moved twice before they lived in walking distance of a bus stop.

In 1989, I was born so quickly that Dad was running down a corridor and my mum didn't get any drugs. I entered the world in my embryonic sac, which is supposed to be good luck. They christened me Heather after a hardy, highland shrub. (My middle name is Carolyn and no one knows why.)

My parents, my older brother and I lived in a house on the edge of a village ten miles from Bury St Edmunds, which itself was about ten miles from Cambridge – I did not have any cities in my life, growing up. A city is somewhere, perhaps, where the wrestling shows would have been; in Bury St Edmunds, however, there was no wrestling.

First I went to the village school, which had fifty pupils, during a time when there were only four TV channels. It's no surprise, then, that I had a pretty sedate childhood. I was rarely badly behaved and only if someone insisted that I was not equal because I was a girl – which, to be fair to my parents, was mainly done only by my peers. Highlights included expulsion from ballet class aged four when I bit another student (I was being a dinosaur).

I was also a bit of a creative liability. I was rushed to hospital for swallowing things out of curiosity – a loo block, a thermometer, a Polly Pocket. There were also the highly theatrical burial rites for the constant stream of hamsters that lived and died in my care. Headdresses and capes, messages to the afterlife, altars and my extensive monologues about animal heaven. I was already a showman, albeit a slightly unsettling one.

When I had to wear dresses to family gatherings, I would be told off for flashing my knickers when fidgeting. I regularly punched boys in the playground if they insulted the Spice Girls. I'm not sure this early aggression was a sign that I would later become a wrestler, but it certainly defined me as a feminist.

My earliest memories of wrestling are firmly imprinted on to the affections I had for my friend, Carys – the coolest girl in the village. Carys, like me, didn't really like being a girl, but she preferred it to the alternative of being a boy, like the ones she would beat in Take Down Bulldog. She had a Nintendo 64 and watched films with swearing in them. Whenever we went over to her house across the village, we'd end up staying up late and run around the garden while my parents got plastered. Carys would make us watch the WWE and could name all of the characters and moves. She and the other boys would pretend to jump off the sofa and land with an elbow on a cushion (hence why we often ended up playing in the garden).

I remember being puzzled by wrestling and not identifying with any of the big men on the screen – not dissimilar to my relationship with a lot of wrestling now. This was the mid-1990s: wrestling was as huge as it had been in the 1970s, but due to the advent of satellite TV, people watched American shows. This is referred to now as the 'Attitude Era': characters were all about the sex, the swagger, the offstage romances and drug busts. The zany side of wrestling appealed more to kids our age – characters could be clowns or undead vengeful spirits. There was also some less than okay content; for example, all the female competitors being contractually made to take part in a bikini competition during which Mae Young, the best wrestler ever, took her top off and exposed her 77-year-old breasts (something I thought I'd imagined in my childhood until I saw the footage again).

My parents had no idea what wrestling entailed when we were kids; they thought it was similar to the gentle matches of the 1970s. Watching back, it's clear that the wrestling of my childhood, despite its inappropriate content, was completely overblown in its cartoonish violence. These intermittent flashes, it should be said, did not make a big impression on my wrestling career.

Carys, on the other hand, had twelve action figures, a spring-loaded wrestling ring and a computer wrestling game. On the computer game you got to design your own characters – this was my job when there were six of us crowded around two controllers. I remember being told to hurry up as I tried to express complicated back-stories using the medium of digital boots and haircuts. But I wasn't allowed to play on the computer game, because one of the boys would always get angry. To get my own back I'd make their characters wear pink gear. The colour pink was a weapon of war used constantly in our childhood.

Based on Carys's influence, my brother and I began to watch the WWE occasionally on Saturday nights. This would be accompanied by a bag of pick 'n' mix sweets each, along with free rein of the TV until 8pm. The footage was always fuzzy because the signal was so bad in our corner of Suffolk.

My dad once came in and saw we were watching wrestling. He just said, 'Christ', and left again. Shortly after he left the room, there was a segment where the female wrestlers all took a new performer in to the showers and slapped her arse. I think my brother changed the channel because he was trying to see if he could predict the numbers on the National Lottery. In reality, we were both embarrassed and confused about why naked ladies and sex were encroaching on our cool TV show – it was almost as sacrilegious as the colour pink.

When I was nine, Carys and I watched with open mouths as Chyna appeared at a big WWE show, shooting flames out of a bazooka. Chyna was the first woman to hold a 'male' belt in the WWE and she could bench press 300 kilos. She looked like a superhero and she beat up men. For this reason, I instantly loved her, despite the boys insisting she was really a man. It was that night that I got the chance to play on the Nintendo 64 for the first time as Carys wanted a tag team of two Chynas. This proved difficult because you could only make male wrestlers. We settled for long hair and body suits.

Due to my inexperience, this backfired when I couldn't work out the buttons and kept punching her character by accident. Yet something unlocked inside my tiny child mind: 'I want to be that strong woman; I can be female *and* aggressive – this is the future!'

The following week, perhaps filled with the bravado of Chyna, Carys fought with another boy in the playground over a football and he gave her a 'Stone Cold Stunner'. This broke her collarbone and we had to have an assembly on the 'don't try this at home' message on TV and what it means. Wrestling was now strictly off the menu; Carys's action figures went to the charity shop and she couldn't play Nintendo 64 with her arm in a sling. Collectively, my brother and our friends stopped caring about wrestling and started collecting Pokémon cards instead. Wrestling and all of its glittering violence left my life for a while.

When I moved up to middle school, where there were a hundred kids in my year, not merely twelve, I floundered. I didn't have the right jeans and only listened to the Spice Girls or my dad's record collection – no one in between. Talking Heads weren't yet respected amongst my peers, neither were whatever clothes my mum had deemed fashionable for a nine-year-old (as long as it wasn't pink). I started comparing how I looked to pop stars in magazines and girls at school. Gone, suddenly, was the triumphant feeling that I was different to them and that I had rejected pink for many years; instead I felt inadequate, like they all possessed something I didn't have.

Puberty reared its head, and I changed shape. One day, when

I was wearing my new denim hot pants for the first time, a boy said that my legs looked like fat chicken drumsticks. This altercation led me to kick him in the shins. Feeling increasingly self-conscious, I walked home without my brother, only to encounter a car that slowed down behind me, with a man's voice asking me how old I was. He followed me for too long, saying nothing, and I could feel him watching me walk. A dog walker appeared on the other end of the pavement and the man drove away. I stopped wearing shorts for roughly seventeen years.

My brother and I were both weird kids. My brother was obsessed with Kraftwerk (I am proud of him for this, in hindsight) and was freakishly intelligent. I spent hours in my room writing books about vigilante gangs of orphans who could talk to animals. I was bullied at school, I cried a lot and grew B-cup breasts seemingly overnight. Being the uncool girl with glasses and three friends (Carys still a stalwart) was not aided by also being the only girl in the changing room to have a bra and pubes. I remember stealing tampons from the bathroom so that Carys and I could study them in horrified silence.

I was so anxious about people not liking me that rather than spend time making new friends I would hide in a cupboard in my form room over lunchtime. This was also around the time I decided I fundamentally hated exercise – I was always picked last for netball and football; basically anything that involved forming a team or running. (I was twelve, so of course I didn't have a sports bra no matter how much I needed one.) In addition to this, my parents were keen fell-walkers, and the majority of our family holidays involved the daily punishment of being woken up at seven to the sound of drizzle on the tent, knowing I would be walking uphill in it for hours. I wasn't raised to be competitive, and I was told that my greatest strengths were inside my head; as a result, exercise became redundant.

My hatred of exercise took on new meaning when I discovered rock and roll, or specifically, Nirvana. Through music I finally began to make friends; we would hang out in droves of black boots, long hair and holey jumpers. You were in if you liked Nirvana, and for me that was enough. Aged thirteen, I met my best friend, Becca. We both had facial hair, wore black and had tipped-over imaginations. She was the greatest friend a girl could have met in a small town.

We would imagine ourselves outside of the world of Bury St Edmunds, where we didn't have braces and could get the records we wanted – somewhere where people would value us. I dreamt of indie discos and boys who read books. At least twice a month, I'd go out with Becca in our Dr Martens to gigs at the Bury Corn Exchange and dance to the music they played in between the bands, which included Pulp, The Clash, and The Libertines. We would also use this time to stalk Seymour Glass, the bespectacled lead singer of local band Miss Black America, who had an earring, rode a bike and was the local poster boy for tragic youth. John Peel, who is buried in Bury St Edmunds, said that during this time it was the Seattle of England (having been to Seattle, I can confirm this is wrong, but I get what he means).

With the background of all this, what can I tell you? I was a lucky teenager; I didn't get into ketamine or get pregnant early, like many people around me did because there was so little to do. Suffolk can hold on to people who don't feel like leaving their village. Music had the opposite effect on my life; it could make me think of those endless people outside the house, outside the village, and outside the town. My walls were splattered with images of women who stood out – Janis Joplin and Courtney Love. They were who I wanted to be.

Music brought wrestling fleetingly back for one night in my living room. On Channel 4, at about two o'clock in the morning, my favourite band, British Sea Power, were filmed backstage at Reading Festival fighting with Mexican wrestlers. There wasn't even a ring, just ropes around a piece of grass, but the random nature of featuring some *luchadores* in their stage show aligned me further with alternative music. My brain went, 'Oh yeah – wrestling! Anger!'

Instead of pursuing a wrestling career, I forgot about this epiphany a week later, and instead went on to form a band with Becca. We played a total of three gigs over two years, but practised almost every Saturday. We played at venues we couldn't legally drink in, putting as much Kate Bush on the jukebox as we could afford as our warm-up music. Once I almost knocked her out onstage while I was tuning my guitar – to this day, Becca still has the scar.

By seventeen, I had gained several social and physical anxieties; mainly because I got my heart broken a lot of times, probably aided by listening to a lot of very good but very sad music. But I was only a year away from finally being able to leave Bury St Inbred (that was a name of one of our songs). My overthinking of everything in my quiet life in Suffolk wasn't helped when, in the space of a year, my parents had a messy divorce and all my friends went to university. I was stranded in Suffolk without being able to drive and faced endless evenings alone in the middle of nowhere, playing 'Morrowind' on the computer.

All of a sudden I was pretty angry about everything. But it was a kind of guarded, written-down anger – I read a lot of things in the news that made me angry. I started calling out people who commented on my body, often aggressively – though I still couldn't bring myself to wear shorts. I ate carbs to gain weight purposefully as an act of defiance against the girls my age who were already going on diets. My prized posses-sions were the ugliest dresses I could find in charity shops, put together with my grandma's homemade scarves. In the final year of school, I remember someone asking me, 'Heather, why do you make yourself ugly?'

Why? Because my poster girls were all women who did the same thing – Frida Kahlo, Janis Joplin, Peaches – they chal-lenged what they were told they had to be. I wanted, more than anything, to wear myself with pride, and I mostly wasn't able to. But I knew there was a huge world outside the con-fines of my small hometown. My friends who weren't straight-down-the-line hetero were closeted, when I knew they could shine. The BNP came calling door to door around council election times. It wasn't skinheads, but worse – smarmy, mid-dle-class people in suits, who knew every door that opened to them would have a white, British face.

During that last year in Suffolk, I would visit Becca at uni-versity in London. I was sneaked into the bars, people compli-mented me on my clothes. Upon my return, on the Monday mornings when I was on the bus on the way to school, I would hold on to this 'other' place that existed like a talisman. I would physically count the days until I left Suffolk and could be free to do what I wanted.

What has this all got to do with wrestling? It shows that even before I left home, and without any real reason for it, I had already developed low expectations about my body and my own imagination, about exercise, and about relationships.

I'll admit that many wrestlers come from harder grit than me.

All I suffered in my hometown was hatred of a small town mentality, and a determination to do *something* different.

Aged eighteen, I moved to Brighton. I studied anthropology – essentially a degree in people-watching – having lived somewhere so small that I wanted to throw myself into everything weird and wonderful about humanity. I was armed with two pairs of Dr Martens, a cache of vintage dresses, green hair in a messy bob, enough posters to cover a one-room flat and a pack of twenty Camel cigarettes.

The first day I arrived, I met about twenty people I liked just in the smoking area. I danced all night and woke up with a hangover, and someone that I could go and get a fry-up with – a fry-up in *walking* distance.

In reality, growing up somewhere so quiet and gentle, and dreaming of the fast city life, had made me naïve.

In Brighton, there was suddenly an abundance of boys everywhere. My sexual experiences to date had been either subject to judgement from my entire school, or made up of secret rendezvous in fields, sometimes even when it was drizzling and dark. It dawned on me that I could have sex with anyone I wanted, in a *bed*.

Within six months, the count had definitely reached double figures of people whom I'd met, fallen into a starry-eyed embrace with, and who then insensitively dropped me (some more sensitively than others, I should say). My self-esteem became intrinsically linked with whoever found me attractive. On a whim, I decided to take up life modelling to earn extra money, and within a few sessions I could feel myself liking myself more. Unfortunately, though, shortly after finding my confidence I was raped.

Surely being raped isn't something that is related to wrestling? Well, for me it is, and this is my book.

Wrestling made me realise, much later, that I had been raped. It hadn't just been some sort of unfortunate scuffle that hurt; it made me hate everything about myself. I should have been less passive, less polite; I should have realised what was happening. I should have thrown that fucker out of his house and paraded him through the streets.

I didn't, of course. Instead, I went to a boy's house, it happened, and I got the bus home and didn't tell anyone. Aged nineteen, whatever self-esteem I'd managed to muster was stripped away. I didn't get it back until I was a wrestler – but I'm glad, at least, that I got it back.

One of my best friends was raped around this time as well, and she didn't tell anyone either, because it was a similar situation – there were lots of boys-who-read-books walking around without any notion of consent in their heads. It was only ten years later we admitted to each other we had both been raped around the same time. We used to have baths together, we even shared a flat for a bit, but we still didn't mention it. We kept hold of it alone, normalised it, blamed ourselves – and carried it for years. We go through these situations and we internalise them.

I wish, now, that I hadn't normalised it and hidden the violation away like something that could not be fixed and which therefore had to be kept quiet. Loved ones started to notice I'd gone off the rails a bit, but how could I have told them?

It was the first time in my life where I lost a lot of weight due to stress, and people commented on how much better I looked for losing my 'puppy fat'. I don't think that helped. In November 2008, I found myself at a party, unable to shake a feeling of utter worthlessness. This feeling was not new to me but was stronger than ever before, and I returned to my house and tried to kill myself.

Forty-five minutes after the initial attempt, watching my wrists bleed, trying to clean up as the blood started to leak everywhere, thinking about my friend who would have to clean it all up, I called an ambulance.

Okay, suicide and rape, in the space of one page. There is a point to me telling you this.

It was strange that life had got me here: I was the product of a society that told me the things I was experiencing were normal, yet I just didn't expect them to happen to me.

I was letting life get the better of me. After that day, I started to take myself a little less for granted. I had therapy, took medication, avoided relationships for a while. But the rape didn't come into it. I didn't speak to anyone about my suicide attempt, apart from a few 'yes' and 'no' answers to my GP.

Like the rape, I was embarrassed about my suicide attempt. Rape and suicide are made out to be these huge, revolting, messy things. What had happened both times was a quieter, more suburban version of the definitions I'd been taught to recognise. So I just internalised it, but the damage it did to me was messy.

I survived, through good friends I got my footing back and I wandered. I visited America and Europe, blasting away my student loan. In 2010 graduated with honours, then got a job in a shoe shop because my rent was only £30 a week.

I spent a summer going around all of the music festivals I could in Britain, including Glastonbury. On the Saturday of the festival, I was with someone who was gloriously strung out. We stumbled into a clearing full of Mexican eateries and an arena. Inside the arena, there was a wrestling ring.

A man who looked like the MC from *Cabaret* twirled in to the centre: 'Ladies and gentlemen, just a reminder that the stars of Lucha Britannia, the UK's only *luchadores*, will begin in twenty minutes. Sit tight and be prepared for nudity, violence, mayhem and men screaming in little tiny pants. Don't go away…'

In my brain, the memories rushed back: 'Wrestling! Chyna! Excitement! British Sea Power!' I wanted to stay and see some live wrestling, something I'd never experienced before – hell, maybe I'd even have a frozen margarita. But the friend had a self-induced migraine and wasn't interested, so we left to go get chips. Yet again, wrestling came and left my life in an instant.

But this time, it wasn't for long. Aged twenty-one, many people in the wrestling industry have already had their first match – some are even signed to the WWE. Most wrestling books will pretend that for many of us the journey to the ring is something we know from the first moment we see wrestling, but it isn't. We are all from different places. Maybe it's because little girls aren't told they're going to grow up to become wrestlers, or anything big and tough. It's beyond the remits of what most of us can imagine.

After living in Brighton for five years, I had doused myself with new, often uncomfortable experiences and had survived them. I finally left in 2011, after walking down Kensington Gardens one day and seeing four of my ex-boyfriends.

I had moved to Hackney with the same boy who wanted chips instead of wrestling. The fantasy of London – diverse, buzzing, full of new friends and opportunities – was far from the reality I found myself in. Unsurprisingly, for a girl who grew up in a village without a street lamp, and who then lived for five years in a city you can walk across in two hours (and is mainly Regency sea-front) – I was not street-wise. I got pick-pocketed twice in the first month and regularly called my boyfriend in tears because I had taken the wrong bus to what felt like another town altogether. Every three days my bags were packed, ready to go anywhere else but London.

My dreams of making it in the city were also skewed by a generational problem: I had a degree that didn't guarantee a job. After trying first to work for charities, then for trendy shops, I ended up in a call centre. It was a zero-hours contract, with low hourly rates and it was entirely target-based. Within only a few weeks of starting, my long-standing respect for the charity sector was diminished by having to cold call the elderly and read to them a script about children dying of hunger, or stories of cats being put in microwaves. I'd be answered with anger, tears or racist comments, depending on what time of day I was calling.

In hindsight, this is probably one of the worst jobs someone with fragile self-esteem, and growing anxiety issues, could do. But I had a nice telephone voice, apparently, so it didn't occur to me that crying at work and drinking four beers a night wasn't a healthy version of normality.

All of my co-workers were in the same boat. The work force was overwhelmingly made up of graduates unable to get a 'proper' job. At one point there were six of us working there who had all graduated in the same year from the same university, which made shifts pass more quickly but ultimately didn't help resolve the feelings of inadequacy. Around me, though, there were also a large number of musicians, actors, writers, trainee tattoo artists, PhD students, stunt men and eccentrics – all waiting for their big break. We would spend our earnings on pints at the Wetherspoons across the road, and I was finally making friends even though we were held together mainly by our hatred of our job.

Becca, on the other hand, had been living in London since she was eighteen and had become part of the city. She would take me for bagels on Brick Lane, and invite me as her guest to her comedy gigs in back rooms of pubs. One day she performed at a club under a railway arch called the Resistance Gallery.

The Resistance Gallery is a place where you would walk

past the door if you didn't know the number. Inside, it was a cross between a motorbike garage and a Las Vegas strip joint. You walk through a dark cubby room with a Lynchian antique hotel desk, and posters smeared everywhere for fetish nights. You then find a balcony made of scaffolding, a spiral staircase to the rafters, and a bar surrounded by fairy lights. To this day, the Resistance Gallery is as it appeared the first night I entered it – slightly smelly, but a bit like the Bronze club in *Buffy*.

Becca performed a free-form poem about wine and failing her life dreams, and then we did our usual overbearing friendliness act at the bar to try to get ourselves a free drink. The bartender gave us a beer and started talking about his wrestling school. His name was Vanderhorne, and he was short, with a ponytail and unseasonal sunglasses. On this first meeting, he whipped out his phone and showed us a photo of himself – unrecognisable in green *luchador* tights and a mask, throwing another guy through the air. I had a moment of realisation: 'Wrestling! Childhood! Chyna! Margaritas!'

Luckily I re-phrased that to: 'Wait, were you wrestling at Glastonbury last year?'

They were. Vanderhorne had also wrestled British Sea Power at Reading Festival all those years ago when the event was beamed into my rural adolescence. When I mentioned I had not actually seen a wrestling show, he immediately invited Becca and me not to a show, but to his training school.

This is also not normal, I should add. Most wrestlers will seek out their own wrestling school, as part of making a determined decision to see if they have what it takes.

But Vanderhorne's secondary form of recruitment was finding likely candidates in performance artists and other weirdos who were drawn to the gallery, where he offered them a free trial session. Both Becca and I laughed at the mere suggestion we could train to be wrestlers. Us – the beer-swigging, angry, self-deprecating, lapsed actors.

Vanderhorne said, to his credit, 'Everyone has different strengths and, sure, you may not be the fastest and the strongest at first, but you're already big personalities. You're funny. What's the point of being able to do every move in the book if you have no character? Wrestling is more about characters than physique... also we need more women.'

I remember walking home through Hackney that night with a Polish beer in hand, my brain obsessing with ideas of how I would be a wrestler, what my mask would look like, and how the crowd would cheer. I'm not really sure how accurate those images were, having never really seen wrestling – but there were a lot of noises, and a lot of people enjoying themselves, and me in an outfit straight from *Thunderdome*.

Unlike any other wrestler who has written a book, I can proudly proclaim that I took up wrestling based on a drunken idea that I couldn't forget about.

After Vanderhorne had given us the initial invitation to attend the London School of Lucha Libre, Becca and I actually put off going for about two months. We said it was hard to find a Tuesday when we were both free. But there were also at least two instances when we would meet up and end up going to the pub instead, blaming it on Becca's tendinitis. We also rewatched the episode of Louis Theroux's *Weird Weekend* series, where he attends a wrestling training session in America, and they make him exercise until he vomits to teach him respect. It's safe to say we were both terrified of exercise, and were both also weedy intellectuals, just like Louis Theroux.

In the run-up to Christmas, Sh!t Theatre had a gig at the Barbican in an immersive drag show about the recession. Becca got me a job as one of a crowd of Santas who walked around silently and peeled potatoes, looking depressed and drinking cans of Coca Cola. Also working on the show was a French performance artist who had just started wrestling as 'La Tigressa' at Lucha Britannia under the coaching of Vanderhorne. When she found out we had not taken up Vanderhorne's offer, she made us promise we would go the next week, and through the fug of free Prosecco and Santa outfits, we agreed.

She also made us meet beforehand so we couldn't back out. After a seven-hour shift at the call centre during which I had earned the charity £3.50, I was ready for a change of direction in my life.

I remember the look on her face when we turned up in our 'work out' clothes. Neither of us owned a sports bra, and the closest we had to trainers were a pair of mismatched Converse (for years Becca and I owned seven odd Converse between us which we swapped every now and again). I was also wearing a pair of Becca's dad's pyjama bottoms, and she had the leggings from a bee costume, the sting still attached.

My first lesson was not how I'd imagined it would be in the weeks preceding it. I didn't walk in and suddenly take down a guy twice my size due to the pure feelings of misandry in my body. I didn't execute moves so perfectly that there were startled whispers: 'That girl is so good that one day she'll write a book on wrestling!'

No, of course not. I was terrible.

But everything I learned started with that first session, and it began with the hardest part of becoming a wrestler – walking through the door. In this case, down a back alley to the humble Resistance Gallery.

The Gallery has always existed below the noses of everyone around it. It specialises in performance art events, BDSM and queer discos: the wrestling school was just how it was occupied on weeknights. As part of a railway arch, the Gallery used to sit next to two garages, a sari warehouse, a greasy spoon and a pub with bowls of peanuts on the bar.

We entered the Gallery, finding it transformed from an intimate performance venue to a wrestling gym. It no longer had the dim-lit grungy vibe of the Bronze from *Buffy*, but was lit by strip lights and smelled of testosterone and old rope. There was a huge metallic noise and a rhythmic creaking from the wrestling ring, which took up most of the room. Two huge men were running around in it at a terrifying velocity, while other people leant against the ring, chatting, like it was just part of the furniture.

Tigressa barely looked back as she moved off into the room, where she was greeted warmly by the wrestlers while we stood in the doorway, feeling very out of place. One particularly large tattooed man, with piercing blue eyes and a cockney accent, came over. Rather than shout at us like the man in the Louis Theroux documentary, he was very polite.

'Can I help you?'

'We're here for the wrestling school.'

'Oh right, I'm Greg, I'll be teaching you, and Vanderhorne is over there.'

Greg indicated to a floor covered with mats where a man in a white leather mask, presumably Vanderhorne, was lying on his front while another man walked over his back. He was groaning in ecstasy. Becca continued to stare at Vanderhorne, while talking to Greg.

'Yeah… he said we should come for a taster session; we haven't got much experience.'

I think that might have been obvious. Greg looked down at our pyjama and Converse outfits but smiled and shook our hands.

'Well, that's okay. Just go upstairs and change into your gear and then say hi to Vanderhorne.'

We said 'thank you' and went up the steps to a mezzanine level, which was covered in a jumble of half-open kit bags, discarded clothes and Tupperware, with what I assumed were special wrestler meals in them.

Becca took off her coat. 'What do you think he'll do when he realises this *is* our gear?'

'I don't know, but I suppose they won't make us do it in our pants in the first session; though maybe that would be more appropriate for wrestling?'

Back downstairs, Vanderhorne was rolling around with another person on the mats. As I had only really watched wrestling aged eight during the fuzzy Channel 5 years of the WWE, it looked a lot more painful and complicated up close than I remembered. Vanderhorne put a foot in the back of his opponent, who was a young Asian guy with spindly arms. He moved his arms and then rolled him up like a pretzel, but they were both laughing. Immediately, I was struck by how wrestling was much more homoerotic than my eight-year-old brain could have realised.

He dropped the trainee and got up to see us. We got kisses on the cheeks, like drama luvvies, which I suppose we were. 'So, you only took two months to arrive, but here you are! Do you have gym gear?'

'This is our gym gear...'

'We don't go to the gym,' added Becca, helpfully.

'That's all right, I don't go to the gym either – horrible places, really boring.' He smiled. 'Okay, well, first thing is whenever you enter a new wrestling environment you go and shake hands with everyone in the room. Because it's polite, and also it makes it less awkward later when you've got your face in their tits.'

I was pleased that manners were important. Louis Theroux made me worry that I would come out of my first wrestling session shaken and with stories of hazing rituals. (Spoiler: I'm still waiting for the day when I walk into a wrestling environment and think, 'God, all of you are wankers.')

The independent wrestling world is a small and close-knit community – manners are key to people remembering you well, and to recommending you for bookings and hire. Those who might have a beach body but an ego to match may be remembered as arrogant, stand-offish and, as a result, are not spoken of fondly. In short, humbleness in wrestlers is seen as a valuable quality. Also, it does make wrestling a little more fun when you like the person you are fighting; if nothing else, they're less likely to drop you accidentally on your head.

Of course, having only met one wrestler between us, Becca and I didn't know this. But as we were from a small town we knew how to be jolly; going round the room and shaking hands with complete strangers was something you never usually got invited to do in London. There were about twenty trainees, ranging between giants with rippling biceps to scrawny men downing protein shakes. We happily told all of them we knew nothing about wrestling and were both very proud of the fact that we couldn't run for a bus or do a press-up.

We were taken under the wing of the two female trainees – Chow Mean, a Canadian–Chinese accountant, and McBitch, a Scottish woman with a terrific barking laugh. Chow welcomed us with the comment, 'Yay! More vaginas to add to the family!'

This was the kind of eloquence we needed in order to feel at home, as both Becca and I had been regularly told off in PE lessons for being the slowest, the least enthusiastic and the most cynical. Here people said 'vagina' like it was a good thing.

Unlike most sports you do at school, wrestling is not competitive; in fact, it throws competitiveness on its head. But of course I didn't know I was lucky to have fallen in with the London School of Lucha Libre (LSLL), which was, and remains, an unusual wrestling school in its openness. It welcomes people from any background, and at any level of wrestling skill. Some places will expect you to pay in advance for a set number of sessions; you must audition or qualify, or be of a certain level of fitness. There's nothing wrong with that, but that is not Lucha. It had an open-doors policy that was both admired and despaired of by the rest of the wrestling community.

At the time, Becca and I sensed that everyone seemed happy to be around each other, there was little posturing, and no one seemed to notice us. It was ideal: anti-gym, no mirrors, no gym bunnies and no joining fee. We were ecstatic. LSLL took new recruits in any shape or form, which was a relief considering that Becca and I had assumed everyone would be horrible. Stupid Louis Theroux for vomiting! It was all for TV!

Our optimism remained for about fifteen minutes until the actual exercise began. Then we knew Louis had not been pretending.

What we didn't realise is that fitness isn't always reflected in ripped muscles and skinny waists; wrestlers need to be at a level of fitness that surpasses simply being slim and eating well. Our intellectual, wine-addled brains couldn't imagine what this brand of fitness might entail. Wrestlers need to have peak cardio, reflexes, rhythm, coordination, gymnastic ability, body control, flexibility, athleticism and ridiculous core strength. (Note: I definitely still do not possess all of these.)

Wrestlers are expected to put their opponent gently on the floor while looking like they have just driven their head into the floor. You are expected to be able to keep enough breath during fifteen minutes of action to be able to be heard by those in the cheap seats. You should be able to lift and throw your own body weight from anywhere from six to ten feet off the floor.

In simple terms, you need to be as ripped as a boxer but

have the charisma and endurance of one of Beyoncé's backing dancers, or ideally, Beyoncé.

Luckily, LSLL had found that making this 'fun' could be achieved in a less intimidating fashion than usual, with structured and varied lessons. However, if you haven't run further than around a block of flats in twelve years, there is no way to make exercise not horrible. And Becca and I, at our first training session to become professional wrestlers, were pure examples of this.

The start of the dreaded 'exercise' began when, suddenly, booming gym music started and everyone robotically formed a circle – like they were part of a fitness video we had crashed. Becca and I made eye contact and moved as far to the back of the circle as was possible. The lights went off and the Gallery transformed into a semi-lit dance floor. As someone who could never dance well but enjoyed it, I suddenly felt a lot more comfortable under the cover of relative darkness.

The trainees shouted along with the pumping music, which had no lyrics, so lots of 'duh duh duhs'. Greg and Vanderhorne entered the middle of the circle, and we copied them with star jumps, lifting our arms above our heads. I was sweating already, but I was able to keep pace with the music. It was a lot less tiring than moshing to riot grrrl music at least, and I was accomplished at doing that until at least six in the morning.

My smugness was short lived. Someone shouted, 'Plank!'

Everyone dropped to what I could only understand as the most painful part of doing a press-up – I say 'understand' because at that point I only knew the theory of doing a press-up as I'd never yet completed one. Becca and I hurried down to our hands and knees to try to copy whatever this 'plank' was.

Chow helpfully pushed my bum down so that whatever I was doing hurt more. She smiled cheerfully. 'Squeeze your arse – it's supposed to hurt.'

43

I lasted for about ten seconds before I lay on the floor groaning. Another thirty seconds later everyone was told to relax and they all collapsed on the floor with a sigh. Vanderhorne seemed to enjoy the masochism. He could even talk at the same time – about how we were working our arms, our 'core', our glutes, our legs. I could only assume that this meant I had none of the above. I looked around to see everyone in the room gritting their teeth, shaking with strain, beads of sweat dripping off their noses – and I felt the need to vomit. I cursed myself forever for doubting the endurance of Louis Theroux. But at one point we sang 'super plank' to the tune of *Superman*, which did improve everything.

After another four sets of planking, Greg told us this would give us 'abs you could lose your keys in'.

Abs (i.e. abdominal muscles sticking out in an attractive way) are an obsession of wrestlers: everyone wants a stomach so flat that you can see through the skin. I assumed I had an ab in my stomach somewhere, but after the planking torture, I felt as if I had ingested whatever muscles were left in there.

Because apparently we hadn't suffered enough, we started doing squats to the music, with the trainees counting in time with each other. I stopped keeping count after twenty-five. Instead, I moved at half pace, trying to be inconspicuous. I glanced at Becca with a look of suffering and she laughed at me, and no one else even looked up. Despite the fact I was woefully unfit compared to everyone else (excluding Becca), no one seemed to care about anything except their own bodies. During my short-lived experience of attending yoga classes, I had felt like the fat bird at the back, but here, we were all blowing out of our arses, and no one was acting superior.

The lights were turned back up to full strength and the mats were covered in dark patches from sweating bodies. The other trainees went upstairs to change out of their clothes. Becca and

I just sat there feeling clammy, particularly as we'd noticed we were the only women in the room, which was mostly men. We suddenly felt self-conscious – back in our bodies, surrounded by strangers. Vanderhorne must have sensed this, because he came over and asked us how we found it.

'More fun than PE,' I said. 'That was the most exercise I've ever done in my life.'

Vanderhorne congratulated us on not being sick or giving up. They had been so much nicer to us than the Americans had been to Louis Theroux that we assumed the hard part was over – but of course we'd not done any actual wrestling at that point. Then again, neither of us were sure what that would look like when it happened.

What I'm glad I didn't know at that point, was how much wrestling hurts. Because if I had, I would have just pegged it out the door.

Wrestling requires sleights of hand, ways of falling and dis-plays that make things 'look' like they hurt. But that only comes when you've got used to putting yourself through strange and unusual forms of punishment. An example of how wrestlers prepare themselves for this is bridging.

Bridging is a time-honoured tradition of wrestlers: building up your neck muscles to reduce the risk of breaking your neck or getting concussion from constantly being thrown on your back. You push your entire body weight up from your shoul-ders to your head, using your neck. Kind of like a backwards crab but without using your hands – your back becomes a bridge with your feet and head on each side of it. Ideally, a wrestler should be able to hold a bridge while somebody stands on their stomach. One of the trainees demonstrated this and Becca just stared at the wall above them in dumbstruck terror.

With the help of Chow, we managed to do a basic bridge, where we rolled our heads on the floor in a painful way. When

I asked her if it stopped hurting at any point, she just smiled, which made me worry I had joined some kind of cult.

We tried to do some of the basic moves the trainees were drilling – the bumps, the rolls, the throws – but Vanderhorne saw that we were probably going to kill ourselves. He admitted he'd never actually taught two people as 'new to wrestling' (i.e. terrible) as Becca and myself.

'When we opened the school we wanted to have new people, people from all backgrounds. But because most people don't actively seek out wrestling unless they're already a fan, the students would turn up already knowing what a "bump" was; or being able to name moves. I guess with you guys we'll just have to think of some baby steps to get you to their level.'

Eventually, he told us we could then practise the 'easier' bumps. We were taught by Fraser – a short guy wearing, without explanation, a giant squirrel onesie – who, despite seeming to spend most of his time flailing around, was a precise and encouraging teacher. Becca and I took it in turns to be tripped up and fall to our knees and forearms. This came to us relatively quickly because once tripped up, we had to make a comedy scream like we'd broken our noses. Pretending to be hurt is called 'selling'; Becca and I spent the majority of the session happily falling over in slow motion and screeching. Selling was definitely our strong point.

Occasionally, we couldn't help but be mesmerised by the trainees in the ring. They moved with such speed and purpose – as if wrestling were a dance they had all mastered. Tigressa shone like a warrior queen. She grabbed the head of a man running towards her, spun around his shoulders, and threw him to the floor. As if it hadn't been beautiful and fluid enough, she did the same move again, three times, on different opponents.

McBitch climbed to the top rope and threw her entire body weight at Chow, who caught her and threw her to the floor.

Although the shouts and boom they made on the canvas made our mouths drop open, they were quickly told it wasn't correct, and had to go and practise using a crash mat.

We couldn't tell what they'd done wrong – I had never seen anything I had wanted to do more. People flipped and threw themselves on the ring canvas, making it shake with the impact. They were so spectacular and strong.

I remember looking at the clock and it was quarter past ten: I had been exercising for three hours and I hadn't given up under duress – possibly for the first time in my life. We joined the other trainees at the end as they sat around in the ring like a sweaty, adult story time (that doesn't sound good written down, but that's what it was like). Vanderhorne and Greg told us we had all progressed that session, and they also made a point of welcoming Becca and me. We got a heartfelt clap from the aching strangers around us, who had cast a spell on us while they practised; now they all ached, some held ice to their joints, after three hours of drills. We'd forgotten half their names but hugged all of them goodbye, saying that we would definitely be back next week.

Becca and I walked to the nearest tube station together, via the local, the Dundee Arms, the aforementioned pub with peanuts on the bar. We were not put off by the fact both of us struggled with the exercise, instead fantasising about what our wrestling characters would be. Perhaps a UN smackdown, where I could be Kill-ary Clinton, and she would be Angela Mer-kill. We made a promise we would return the next week and actually improve our forward rolls. I got home after midnight to the flat that I shared with my boyfriend. We smoked and watched *University Challenge*, I talked about wrestling constantly, and then, when the light went out, my body buzzed silently with endorphins and images I had never experienced before.

The next day when I opened my eyes, every single part of me hurt – my sides ached with muscles I didn't even know were there. I didn't have work until twelve so I stayed in bed till eleven. I dreaded the moment that I would have to get up and go down the stairs because all of the squats had made my thighs feel like fiery lead. I had bruises on my upper arms that were the exact measurements of Becca's fingerprints, from where she had been throwing me around the night before. There were also these pains down my side that I was concerned were linked to my kidneys, until a colleague reassured me they were muscles called 'lats' best known for making men on the telly look triangular.

I didn't stop hurting until a week later, and I'm pleased to say, I went back.

3

The London School of Lucha Libre

On making the decision to do contact sport, a sensible person would have probably invested in some better gym gear, but this didn't occur to me. I had no money to go to Sports Direct. It's a testament to the London School of Lucha Libre that despite my hating exercising and still not really knowing what wrestling was, I returned a week later, in my pyjamas.

I expected wrestling to be all about large, unfriendly men, but if I had to compare it to anything, I'd say for the months to come it was more like the bar in *Cheers* whenever I walked through the doors of the Gallery. My new friends – Chow Mean, McBitch and, of course, Greg and Vanderhorne – were all happy for me to be there. I was also happy to pay up my £10 per session even though ten minutes into the warm-up I was fighting the urge to vomit again. This was because wrestling had started to play to my other strengths.

Firstly, to be a wrestler, you have to be *noisy*. As someone with a problem controlling my own volume, being told to make as much noise as possible was like Christmas. As you perform, you need to amplify every sound and every movement you make. If I hadn't found the fact I was unfit embarrassing enough, this became somewhat heightened by shouting words like 'buttock' and 'clunge' at the top of my lungs among a room full of strangers during the warm-up.

There were limits to my success, though. In my third session, Greg announced that we were going to do 'character work'. As I had been a show-off since a young age, I thought I was ready to emote 'grieving widow' or even 'coked-up soldier', but it turned out the characters he meant were actual wrestlers who I had no idea existed.

When Greg shouted, 'Stone Cold Steve Austin', these words made no sense to me, but I saw everyone else begin to scowl at one another, and walk as if they couldn't bend their knees. 'Hulk Hogan' made everyone start yelling 'brother' and flex their muscles. I suddenly realised that this was turning into a hazing ritual where I was trying to hide my nervousness by cackling under my breath – unfortunately, it didn't have the same effect without Becca there.

Greg roared: 'Undertaker!'

I went to pretend I was carrying a coffin, whereas everyone else stood completely still and stared straight ahead. I was the only one moving.

Vanderhorne looked over and said, just loud enough for others to hear, 'Heather, don't you know who the Undertaker is?'

'No, but I've been practising my forward rolls.'

This was partly true, as I'd demonstrated that weekend to some friends when I'd been drunk in the park.

Vanderhorne didn't ask me to leave for not knowing who the Undertaker was. Instead, he just shook his head and smiled in disbelief. 'That's incredible, that's like not knowing who Arnold Schwarzenegger is.'

'I know who he is!'

I should note that the extent to which I knew Schwarzenegger's films was entirely dependent on whether *The Simpsons* had referenced them, but I didn't mention this.

But I wasn't completely put off by making a fool of myself. In fact, getting on a stage and shouting nonsense was something I excelled at. There were trainees who had muscles you could see from a mile away on a dark night, but when they needed to embody a character – in other words, 'pretend' – they floundered. Wrestling, you see, is silliness. Since everyone knows wrestling, to an extent, is fake, it seems short-sighted to pretend every match is grounded in reality.

The tricks, the jokes, the characters, the appeal to the collective memory of a crowd. These are the fun bits of wrestling that don't hurt, and which we do because it's part of the performance. Too much seriousness in wrestling – posturing and aloofness – can lead to boring matches and inflated egos. If you make money throwing people around while you're wearing tights, you need to accept that the silliness is not a sacrifice but a privilege.

I think it was the single reason that I found my first foray into wrestling so much better than any exercise I had done before. I couldn't yet do a dropkick, but in my third session I could make an audience boo or cheer me in three sentences (even when pretending to be a box of fried chicken). I felt I had at least *something* that warranted my keeping going, even if I couldn't tell my left from right.

The left and right thing has always been an issue for me. At university, I was told that I probably had dyspraxia and could take a test to find out. It turned out it wouldn't guarantee me a free computer or anything; it just meant it'd be less embarrassing when people asked why I couldn't ride a bike.

Wrestling training requires building up something called 'muscle memory'. You can't just learn moves by watching them, or reading them in a book (sorry). A lot of wrestling is about drilling the same moves until you can do them perfectly. In a match, you have seconds to react to things, and you need to make it look unrehearsed. The only way to do it is to repeat those moves again and again, using the same motions. For me, because my body couldn't grasp simple concepts like left and right, and balancing on one leg – even when I remembered things with my muscles – I was left second-guessing everything.

At the school, they were adamant that I had to learn the most basic fundamentals so that my body was prepared to do the more exciting stuff. Safety is key in wrestling, and until your body is conditioned to do this instinctively, you're at the bottom. In wrestling, a lot of this involves learning to roll off an impact instead of taking that impact directly into your body. It is for this very reason that at the London School of Lucha Libre everyone has to be an A-grade roller. Unfortunately, it turns out you still need to be able to tell your left from right, even if you become a rolling wizard.

Eventually, Becca came back with me. Vanderhorne asked us if we could do forward rolls. Becca said she absolutely could, and so he gestured to the mat we were standing on.

'Show me what you've got.'

On command, Becca did a forward roll that exactly matched the ones we did at primary school, resulting in her sitting on her arse. I followed her, managing to get to my feet at the end, albeit in an ungainly manner, like an albatross landing.

'Not bad,' said Vanderhorne. He then completed a forward roll that was a thing of beauty, making no noise and fluidly getting to his feet. He turned as soon as he got up and did another one. 'Try and make them more like that.'

Rolling from standing is not something you learn in Playschool 101. To improve, I had to squat and roll forwards, like a Weeble. I did this six times in a row until I had to stop. Becca could get herself over but whenever she tried to stand up, she would end up rolling to one side, landing on her back like a dead sheep, all while snorting with laughter.

Vanderhorne didn't point or laugh; instead, he just commented, 'I've never seen someone do that before.'

Although I was praised on the small amount of progress I made, it became clear how far I had to go when four students took to the mats. They rolled in perfect synchronisation in a space ten feet square like a well-oiled wrestling machine. I was so impressed by the first eight people I'd seen rolling that I assumed that they must be fantastic wrestlers. When it was my and Becca's turn to go on the mat, we managed to do one set of rolls and only collided with each other twice because we still hadn't mastered rolling in a straight line. Greg explained that we shouldn't get upset about this, even though it would mean we would be unable to learn anything more complicated for the time being, due to the likelihood of our bashing into another person.

By session five, I could complete eight forward rolls in a row, successfully getting to my feet upon completing each one. I had even figured out how to turn left or right as I stood up, with a sixty per cent success rate. Though I still seemed to be unable to roll in a completely straight line, and remained the slowest roller in class, I was increasingly ending up where I needed to be.

The constant repetition – along with the pressure of constant encouragement, and the fact my body was slowly becoming used to being thrown upside down – meant that I was eventually able to do a shoulder roll. In the next session, I learned how to lie down while holding someone's shoulders, and throw them over my shoulder. They would roll out of my clutch and make me look like I was strong, that I'd flung them six feet.

The reality–unreality of doing it was a rush.

Next time Becca threw me and I rolled to my feet, I got a 'lovely' from Greg or Vanderhorne and all of me soared.

My body was starting to amaze me, because it was improving at things. Having spent my life to date calmly giving up and laughing at myself rather than persevering, my body was actually starting to remember things for me.

For example, wrestlers are also expected to be able to jump as well as they can roll – be it over another person or up to the top rope, which stands five feet from the floor. I dreaded anything that involved jumping, because I seemed to be able to get maybe an inch of height, and then as I landed, I could feel my body jiggling with the impact.

At wrestling, I was made to jump up on to a stage, and then over people's backs, leapfrogging without the use of my hands. During my fifth session, despite believing I couldn't, I tried and succeeded in jumping on to somebody's shoulders from a standing position. Sure, that person was only five feet four, and he definitely squatted very low to help me, but I felt so thrilled at my achievement that once I was up there I forgot to hold on and promptly fell off.

Becca didn't have as much luck. She came to one session during which we learned 'side bumps' – a move a bit like someone fainting on *Dynasty*. You sort of crumple to the floor, but because it's wrestling, you have to hit the floor hard. I found them uncomfortable and my hip hurt after three attempts. Becca threw herself on the floor and her head knocked backwards and forwards. There was no noise from the mat, her head had taken all the impact; she got up slowly.

Poor Becca – she went home with 'weird diamond refractions' in her peripheral vision, and by bedtime she thought she was going blind or something. The next day she went to the hospital; she summarised: 'They implied I'd concussed myself because I have an overly large head and a weak neck.'

Becca's performing partner sensibly persuaded her to stop training. But I couldn't do it. A week later I went back to the Gallery without Becca.

My body, having previously always been this curvaceous sack of fluid, was now able to stand on the top rope and do ten squats without falling to its death on concrete. When it came to planning a match or doing anything that you would actually use in a wrestling show, I would freeze and doubt my own knowledge, but my body seemed to know how to stop itself losing balance better than I did. Muscle memory was quietly defying my own self-doubt.

There was one thing that I continued to struggle with, and that no amount of practice made any less punishing – and that was bumping. I was introduced to this concept with a soft, babystep bump in my first session. Alongside being able to jump and roll, I needed to do other things that were just as vital to wrestling, but a lot less fun to learn.

Bumping refers to when you are hit with a move, and you learn to fall from the impact safely. No one cradles you to the floor or quickly throws a mattress under you – you have to toughen and train your body to make it look vicious while doing it safely. I'd seen the trainees throw themselves on to the canvas with a terrific thud so many times, and had been pleased I hadn't progressed to 'that' level, but then one day I was told it was impossible to continue without learning this technique.

Vanderhorne went to the centre of the mat and without so much of a blink threw himself backwards on the floor, hitting his hands down hard and getting up again quickly, holding his back in pain. As soon as he was on his feet he did it again, and again, completing ten identical falls to his back, getting up completely unscathed.

'That's bumping: it hurts the first few times but when you understand how to do it, you can bump all day long. Bumping is what allows wrestlers to carry on their careers without ending up in hospital. You need to learn to love this because it's our bread and butter.'

Like rolling, bumping is part of the illusion of wrestling. When you fall backwards, it is vital to tuck your chin to your chest: this protects your head from concussion. You should also kick your feet high off the floor, which will raise your lower back so that as much impact as possible falls on your upper shoulders. Ideally, you should also throw your arms out and hit the floor at the same time as the impact: this disperses the force away from your back, head and abdominal organs and also makes a cool noise.

First I had to practise falling over from crouching into what I referred to as a 'crotch to sky' position, so I could get used to falling and tucking my chin. I felt more like I was in an antenatal class than becoming a *luchador*. And considering it was just an early step in learning the art of bumping, I already felt winded on the first three attempts – ending up on my back, raising my crotch at the last minute, every bit a turtle capsized. But Vanderhorne kept me at it for half an hour. Once he was convinced I could fall over from a crouch, he disappeared up to the balcony. A minute later, I heard him shout, 'Move!' and all the students parted way as a crash mat was thrown down ten feet into the middle of the floor. Now, I had to practise falling from my feet to my back from standing, with this big mattress to break my fall. This might sound easy but imagine standing up right now, and throwing yourself backwards like you've been punched in the solar plexus. What do you do first? Put your hands down? No, that way you'll dislocate your wrists, elbows or even shoulder blades – all your weight will go on your squishy arm joints. Do you sit on your arse and roll over? No, because it looks terrible, and the bounce of the ring will go up through your tail bone and spine; you could end up paralysing yourself. What you have to do is throw your legs in the air and land on your upper back, the place that can take the most impact. Not easy.

After another half hour of bumping, I got the real test – they took away the crash mat. I tried to fall slower than physics allowed and ended up essentially bending over backwards, which Vanderhorne agreed was impressive, but not the point of the exercise. Eventually, I did a bump they were happy with – my brain still shaking in my head as I got up.

'Now you've done it right, do it three times in a row so you don't forget.'

I did this as quickly as I could, then I conceded defeat because my elbows were bruised, my head hurt and it was almost ten o'clock. Instead we watched some of the more advanced students put on practice matches. I sat open mouthed at how hard they could all throw themselves forwards and backwards, roll and get to their feet.

Before she left, Chow clapped me on the shoulder and said, 'If you come back next week, then you're in for life, kid.'

My first session of bumping was the most painful thing I'd done to date, and it'd made the squats feel like a basket of kittens. As I tried to sleep, my head hurt so much I couldn't relax. The next day I felt lightheaded as I showered, the bruises on my elbows turned a mottled purple, and this is not even mentioning my back, which felt like it had been trodden on by a giant. I was used to hurting after training but this was different. I probably had a mild concussion, because my brain thought I had whiplash, so it was filling my head with protective fluid.

The next week I went back, begrudgingly, and was welcomed warmly by everyone. When it was time to bump, I walked up and did three in a row – and it still hurt. I wasn't throwing myself down hard enough, so I had to spend another session bumping. But still, I came back.

And now, five years on, I can confirm that I still hate bumping. As recently as last month I didn't tuck my chin in a match and had a headache the next day. I also have related short-term memory loss. But all wrestlers do. I've known people to be knocked out for six hours after not tucking their chin correctly, or almost breaking their neck from botching a roll. But, still, in every training session, we line up and do three back bumps each, to try to make sure our body doesn't forget how to land safely on instinct.

Wrestling is filled with things like bumping; things that we dread. I still sometimes hide to avoid some of the drills we have to do. Like 'grapes' – jumping on the spot for two minutes while holding the top rope. Even worse are the 'set and goes', where you alternate between a lying and a fighting position, on command, for three minutes. Sheer determination to learn something is key to wrestling. You learn that the dangerous stuff is fun, but only worth attempting once you can trust yourself to take an impact. And the only way to do that is by putting your body through exhausting experiences.

This is all designed to make yourself so tough that you can withstand twenty minutes of having the crap taken out of you in front of hundreds of people under glaring lights. During a match you can't stop and have a breather; you have to keep going. Ultimately, wrestling is filled with the sort of repetition that is not medically advisable and entails the kind of training that is never fully complete. You are forever being told to push yourself harder, and you have to learn to love it, because we have a different kind of relationship with pain.

Wrestlers have the 'good' pain of an aching body after a great match or a muscle that's bursting at the seams. We also have 'bad' pain of headaches, shooting pains, or something wrenched out of joint. It's going to hurt either way, so we try to embrace it.

Despite the agony, to me, this sort of exercise was more rewarding than anything I'd ever tried before (or since). Better than those PE classes when you would end up playing netball instead of contact rugby. Netball: a game where you actually have to stand still when you get the ball, and wear a skirt. It was better than going to the gym, where men will give you funny looks if you are doing weights, and where they feel it's appropriate to come and tell you that you should be doing more cardio to lose weight. At least in my experience.

When I've asked women, aged between the ages of twenty-one and forty-five, if they fancied trying out wrestling, they would just instinctively tell me that they were too weak, without even asking what it might entail. I wanted to tell them, shout at them, that you never stay weak – you become stronger, and that's the point.

Once I had learned some fundamentals, McBitch and Chow Mean elected to teach me some 'chain', a type of wrestling that involves putting people in holds. It's not flashy or fast; it's about outsmarting your opponent. We did a wristlock, which is probably the first move all wrestlers learn – basically a Chinese burn applied to your wrist. As I stood looking at my wrist, McBitch told me to 'sell it'. I started screaming as loudly as I could (because big is best in wrestling, right?) and Chow stared at me. 'Dude, why are you screaming like that?'

'I'm selling.'

'All I'm doing is holding your wrist; this is the most basic move. Just look, I dunno, annoyed.'

I glowered at her and pawed at her face, while she moved

away and did something to my wrist that actually made me yelp and hold it.

'There you go, you need to pretend that I'm doing that all the time… it's called wrestling!'

Pretty soon I had learned how to put Chow in the same lock. While I did it, I had to look mean, intense, like I was *actually* trying to break Chow's wrist. She told me I'd got the selling part down, but now we needed to work on my footwork. I looked down at my pigeon feet and she said, 'See, like Bambi!'

I was trying to mesh all of this knowledge together, and then Greg called Chow and me over to the crash mat. Along with McBitch, we were the only three women there.

'Chow, can you show a hip toss to everyone, please?'

'Absolutely!'

I scanned the line of thirteen men, and all but two of them were over six feet. They looked embarrassed – and Chow looked pleased. Before I knew it, I had found myself at the back of a queue, lining up to do what looked like a jumping somersault on to a crash mat.

A hip toss is like a throw you do in judo: you basically trip someone over by sticking your arse out and flipping them on their back. Chow made it look easy, shouting this wonderful screech when she dispatched each guy. Greg occasionally roared, 'Jump!' or, 'Stop sand-bagging, you strawb!'

It was only when it was my turn that I got instructed on how much the move involved the other person, and not just the awesome strength of Chow. It also explained to me the general gist of how wrestling works. Rather than one person hurting another, it's about two people working together to make something look real.

At the same time as Chow pushed me over her hip, my job was to jump over her leg. Then I was to do a somersault and land on my back so it would look like she'd thrown me herself without my momentum.

The first time I did it, I just rolled straight on to my back. Like a hamster. I got a second go, where I jumped before rolling on to my back. On the third attempt I managed to do the jump *and* roll at the same time, before landing safely on my back. I was so stunned that I'd done it that I forgot to let go of Chow, who landed on top of me and kneed me in the face.

There was a bit of blood trickling from my nostril, Chow shouted 'JUICE!' and assured me it wasn't broken. I went back to practising wristlocks. But Greg and Vanderhorne said they were proud that I had tried.

'We usually wait until you've been here two months before we do hip tosses; we were just checking you weren't a prodigy or something. You did good, though!'

Greg and Vanderhorne had confirmed what we all knew – that I was *not* a prodigy. When I was alone with Chow, I felt I had to confide in her.

'Chow, I'm going to be honest, I don't think I've ever seen a wrestling match.'

'What? Not one? Not even on TV?'

'When I was a kid, but I was more interested in the costumes and couldn't name the moves.'

'Well, you did look a bit lost earlier when they asked you to be Macho Man Randy Savage and you started pretending to hump things… I mean I thought it was funny, but he's like a hero to some of the guys here.'

'So what do I do?'

'Put wrestling into Google… actually, don't do that. You'll just get porn. Try and watch some old WrestleMania.'

'"Wrestle mania"?'

'Yeah, it's the biggest show the WWE puts on every year. I think we're up to twenty-six – there should be some old ones on YouTube. Hey! I bet you'll see them do a wristlock and you can say, "Yeah, I can do that!"'

On Chow's recommendation, the next night, when I finished my shift at nine o'clock, I bought myself four cans of Polish lager on the way home. I remember my dad used to watch the rugby with a beer and a salami sandwich, and having never sat down in my life before to actively watch sports, I thought this was necessary preparation.

I typed 'wrestle mania' into YouTube – selecting 'Wrestle-Mania 1' as a reasonable sounding option, before noting that it was four hours long and broadcast in 1984. With a beer on my bedside table, I sat down to experience 'wrestling'. As soon as the show started with its '80s graphics and infomercial music, and in spite of the shots of the 20,000-capacity arena, I was already smiling to myself.

A voice on the TV constantly told me about how great the show I was about to watch was going to be, in a cross between auction patter and a home-shopping channel. I heard the words 'Hulk Hogan' ten times in his speech so that I remembered he was a big deal. It was like a trashier, American version of *Match of the Day*. I fast-forwarded the video twenty minutes.

I landed halfway through a match. At the time, I didn't realise it, but coming into a wrestling match part way through is just the same as doing it with a film – even something spectacular like *The Shining* is less impactful with the first hour cut off. A man was giving a headlock to another man, dressed in a homemade-looking mask. The ropes looked like they were made out of spaghetti, bending under the wrestlers' weight. It was slower and less cruel-looking than the trainees I'd seen at LSLL. Eventually one of the wrestlers hit the apron (the edge of the mat and the hardest part of the ring) and the bell rang;

the crowd booed. The commentators kindly explained that the loser had submitted so his arm wouldn't break.

After the match there was more talking, a man shouted at another man about respect, and then another match started with lots of men in it with names like 'Beefcake'. One of them used a wristlock and I was excited until his opponent punched him in the face – apparently the only tool in my arsenal wasn't a very formidable move. I watched the match all the way through. I enjoyed it, and I saw how the audience became more excited at what seemed like the right point. While the wrestling moves weren't flashy, they were neat and they looked real.

By the time I was halfway through my second beer I was having a great time – I laughed out loud to myself at the overblown orange men, and I shouted when a move seemed to come out of nowhere. But I could see how, as a child, I would have enjoyed it a lot more than I ever enjoyed a pantomime – especially when Liberace did a parade around the ring just because he was there. I had never been exposed to the rich pomp and glory of it all.

There was a tag match that was an East vs. West patriotism fest. The Iron Sheik, a spitting Iranian in a tea towel, was paired with a man doing a Russian accent, and they were beaten by the US Express: two tanned studs in stars and stripes unitards. Racial slurs littered the commentary. It made me wonder about how the Iron Sheik and the Russian felt about being so adamantly hated by the crowd; about being a tool of propaganda for the American war machine.

I was opening my final beer in time for the penultimate match, at which point I let out a cheer to myself, as it was a woman's match. Cyndi Lauper marched up to the ring accompanying a woman described as '100lbs of steel and sex appeal', Wendi Richter. Her opponent was an old woman in a glittery jacket called The Fabulous Moolah. I was lost in their characters; in the applause and seriousness the crowd were giving their fight. I didn't care how technically correct it was – here were two women beating the crap out of each other in front of thousands of people, and I loved it.

Over the next few days, I continued to watch wrestling in the same lost and random way. I searched names I'd heard like 'Macho Man Randy Savage', who was a jazzed-up guy in a hat, and 'The Ultimate Warrior', who had make-up on and loads of ribbons on his arms like a child's bike.

I understood, then, that you do need to watch wrestling to understand it. To see how all the moves you're taught in fragments fit together to make a match, and to be able to see when wrestlers make mistakes, and whether they cover them or flounder. With every show, you might see a move that you want to learn, or a wrestler whose style you want to emulate. But unless you know what to look for, it's a huge and formidable universe of knowledge.

A lot of me felt that I didn't belong in this world. I was saddened by the fact that women seemed to be missing from the collective memory of wrestling: in a list of the top ten best wrestling matches of all time, not one woman was there. I was also bothered by the stereotypes I'd seen in WrestleMania. All the characters that were non-American were villains – the venomous boos for the Iron Sheik came mostly from a crowd that sported numerous Confederate flags. The only person of colour who was not automatically villainised was Mr T.

In hindsight, I was also limiting my watching of wrestling to shows that were decades old, or plucked out of obscurity. I was in danger of viewing a whole subculture as problematic, based on my own, tipsy YouTube holes.

When I turned up at training the following week, I proudly told Greg that I'd watched WrestleMania 1, and without thinking that maybe I had overlooked something, I summed it up as 'a bit trashy and I didn't identify with the characters'.

Greg listened patiently, then said, 'What you're telling me is you watched one show and thought that's what all wrestling is. Did you not watch their moves, or their ring position, or how they got the audience to love them?'

'They love Hulk Hogan because he's a big, orange man.'

'No, he's one of the greatest wrestlers of all time. Maybe you don't like him but wrestling wouldn't exist today without him. WrestleMania made the industry huge worldwide, and every year they sell more tickets. You need to try to understand why people love him or else you're not going to get on with wrestling; maybe it isn't for you.'

I stopped arguing at this point because Greg clearly wasn't seeing our conversation as funny and touching, and instead I was insulting his passion. A barrier rose up between us: I was the middle-class feminist and he was the working-class wrestling legend. I tried to reach a kind of middle ground.

'Well, I want to learn to be a wrestler, but I'm never going to be Hulk Hogan. Are there any women I should watch? Or some more recent stuff?'

'Just ask people.'

Some guy then came over and showed Greg a t-shirt design he was selling at a show that weekend in Norwich. Greg turned away from me and shortly afterwards the warm-up began. I tried not to think about our conversation as I started to move around, and within twenty minutes my brain was so starved of oxygen from the exercise I focused elsewhere for the next hour or so.

But as soon as we started to bridge and roll, the imposter syndrome crept in big time.

Please refer again to golden rule number one of wrestling: wrestlers are nice people. Of course I'd upset Greg, and one thing I know now about him is that if he actually cares about you, he will tell you what he thinks. If he hadn't cared, he would have just nodded along until I stopped talking. I knew after two months at LSLL that 'asking people' meant that I needed to do my own homework.

That night, I knew only a couple of wrestlers who were there, which didn't help my feelings of inadequacy. But I got paired with one girl I hadn't met before – Zombie Janey. She had started training as young as sixteen and was the epitome of an 'unfamous' wrestler – talented, a career of ten years, matches all over the world, widely liked and respected. But she also didn't want to go to the WWE; she had a job she liked, and she liked to come training and wrestle once a month. She had the kind of temperament that meant she was happy to pass things on to others without expecting anything in return. She was also a badass.

To this day, if I hadn't met Janey that evening, I'm not sure I would have carried on being a wrestler. I think I would have taken Greg's words personally and given up. But as soon as Janey got me in a headlock, I could tell she knew a lot about wrestling. Her grip was soft, not vice-like. She was unhurried, she wore glasses and was five feet tall, and like all good experienced wrestlers, she gave me tips: 'Keep your head up and hold my head like I'm a prize, you need to be dominant... Hold your hands, see that I won't break out the hold... Put your right foot forward – see, now you look stronger... Wrap your arms round my waist and then it looks like you're struggling.'

Janey stuck next to me for the rest of the training session, taking me aside to show me how to do things. I kept out of Greg's way, and when I told Janey he was a bit cross with me, she nodded and said, 'He can be like that sometimes. Just work hard and he'll forgive you.'

Everyone was told to go and plan matches. There was no one at the same level as me, so Janey said we would plan a match but not worry about doing it. So instead we sat by the bar with a cup of tea each, and she explained how wrestling matches are stories – the reason why it is 'sports entertainment' is not just because of the fake violence.

'So, the basic structure of a match is like any film you see. First you have the introduction of the characters, we use these as entrances to the ring. This is where you show your character, show if you're a heel or face.'

'Heel and face?'

'So a heel is a bad guy and a face is a good guy… look at *Star Wars*, in the first few moments you know that Darth Vader is bad, and that Princess Leia is good. Just by the way they are introduced. In this match, I suppose you would be a heel and I would be a face.'

'Why am I automatically bad?'

'Because you're bigger than me and the audience always favours an underdog. But of course that's without knowing your character… let's not worry about that. So in *Star Wars*, what happens next?'

'We meet Skywalker.'

'Yes, that's kind of right… but we also get an idea of how cool the rebels are. You get Han Solo and lightsabers. In a wrestling match, the face does something impressive that makes the audience like him – so, some flashy moves. Then what comes next in *Star Wars*?'

'Umm… Darth Vader is more evil? No wait… they go in a big snake mouth in the desert.'

'No, that's *Return of the Jedi*, this is just *A New Hope*. But you're right, Darth Vader is *really* evil, like when he blows up Princess Leia's planet – in wrestling we call this the "cut off".

The heel does something to get an upper hand on the face – the audience wants the underdog to succeed. Then there's the heat – so that's where the face gets the shit kicked out of them and the audience gets angrier, more behind the good guy. They might have something called a "hope spot", where the face fights back but is then shot down again.'

'What's that in *Star Wars*?'

'Umm… I guess when they're trying to rescue Princess Leia from Darth Vader and then Obi-Wan Kenobi gets killed.'

'Right, but they get her back in the end, they fight Darth Vader and get medals.'

'Yes, so after the "heat" they have a "comeback", where they gain equal footing with their opponent. So, maybe you've been beating me up for a while but then I get up and fight harder… then we go to the finish.'

'The big fight at the end?'

'Yep, when they blow up the Death Star, and then there's the end. In *New Hope*, it's the bit with the medals.'

'So, the face always wins?'

'No, not at all. If you think about it, *The Empire Strikes Back* follows a similar story: good versus evil, the good guys win for a bit, the evil guys win for a bit; it looks like the good is going to win then – bam! – Han Solo gets frozen in carbon. We end on a cliffhanger and the audience are shocked; there's plenty of good matches that end that way… well, not literally but you know what I mean.'

Janey's *Star Wars* analogy made some sense, but it was when we watched the matches planned by the other students that I understood what Janey had been talking about. They were all like little stories. One match would start slow, another would start fast – depending on who the characters were – and it would set the tone for whatever happened next. But there would always be a portion where the heel would beat up the face, but then get their comeuppance in the end.

Each match would end, and the wrestlers would suddenly break character, sitting in the ring, completely out of breath. They would look up at Greg and Vanderhorne for feedback, always in a wrestling vernacular that I was only just starting to understand:

'You didn't have enough shine, you kept on him too long so I just accepted he'd lose, which he did…'

'You didn't hit her hard enough; I knew she was going to win because she didn't get knocked off her feet once. Respect women by treating them equally or it makes you both look weak…'

'You come in all guns blazing and then he just puts you in a corner and gives you a load of chops? Where's your fire?'

Before I left, I did what Greg had told me to do; I asked Janey what wrestling I should watch.

'Well, I don't want to sound unkind but the WWE doesn't really have any good female wrestlers at the moment. If you go back a fair way there's some women like Lita, but I think you should watch Bull Nakano. She's a Japanese wrestler and she had green hair, like you.'

I immediately fell in love with Bull Nakano; I found her first match for the WWE from 1996. She came out scowling, with blue cracks painted on her face and sporting a vertical green Mohawk almost a foot high. She wore a purple regency coat with a ruff, held nunchucks under one arm and revealed herself to be a rounded, short woman. Her hair wasn't just green, it was turquoise, bleached and slightly washed out like mine. She looked strong; I could believe she would win a fight.

In the match, she faces an all-American blonde, Alundra Blayze – a hero who came out to win the belt back from scary, unusual Bull. Their characters are established in their entrances. When they face off against each other, they are equally matched: though Blayze is faster, Nakano is harder hitting. Eventually she knocks Alundra to the floor and puts her in punishing locks and holds. Blayze comes back and throws herself off the top rope, knocking them both down. They get to their feet and Alundra Blayze hits a series of clotheslines, landing her arm across Nakano's throat and knocking her to the floor. Eventually Blayze is victorious with a dropkick off the top, and the hero wins the belt, and the crowd goes wild. The whole way through I saw how they each took it in turns to play their part in a story.

The next week, Greg was making us walk around like wrestlers again. I walked around like Hulk Hogan, punching my pythons to the sky. And when we were told to be whichever wrestler we wanted, I stopped, crouched low to the floor and scowled.

'Who are you, Heather?' Greg shouted.

'Bull Nakano!'

'Excellent.'

Now that I could name my favourite wrestler, and do at least three wrestling moves without concussing myself, it occurred to me that I should try to see a show live. However, tickets to see Lucha Britannia at the Resistance Gallery were £25, which totalled four hours work at the call centre.

This is the standard price for a wrestling ticket. It's an industry that is cash-poor – it's hard to make a profit from a show if you pay everyone, as a show needs about twenty people to run it. You have the wrestlers but also the sound people, the compere, the referee, the humble people at the front taking ticket money or flogging t-shirts. So, when I asked Vanderhorne if I could help out in exchange for entry he nodded and said, 'Of course, it's time you start paying your dues.'

I looked blankly at him and said, 'Have I done something wrong?'

He laughed at me. 'No, you strawb. That's what we call it in wrestling. No promoter will book a wrestler he hasn't seen or met before; it's just not the done thing. Turning up and helping out will get you further than you think. It does here, anyway.'

So, I started to be as helpful as possible at Lucha Britannia, mainly because I knew I was lacking in skill. At the end of training, I would pick up the debris of water bottles and empty glasses that littered the Gallery. When the mats needed taking up or down I would always volunteer, even though I was the least qualified, because the mats were always disgusting – covered in floor fluff, sweat, glitter, old gaffer tape and bits of skin or hair. However, I was never the only one who offered to do it.

By the end of October, Vanderhorne and Greg checked we were all coming to the Lucha show.

'You guys are training to be wrestlers so we are giving you the opportunity to come to the show on Friday. For you, it's a fiver because you're students. But be aware we're watching: to get a cheap ticket to a show that's sold out, and that you should all be working to be on – you'd be stupid to miss it.'

Friday arrived, and I skipped my last shift to go down to the show. I met Chow and McBitch outside, and we queued up as they gasped in disbelief that this was my first wrestling show.

'No way – well *this* is the one to see. Everything else will look shit now!'

Lucha Britannia happened every month at the Resistance Gallery, its floor clear of mats and with the lights down low. The other students were all there, grouped around one side of the ring. I didn't realise at first, but it was because they had to catch the wrestlers when they come flying out.

When about 200 people had been crammed in to the Gallery, *The Great Escape* theme music played and out came the same MC I'd seen at Glastonbury, Benjamin Louche, in a ruffled goth suit and with a terrifying blanched face. There were also two women in matching full latex wrestling outfits, and another striking woman dressed as a nurse, one eye and her mouth covered in gauze. The show was as far from WWE as I could imagine; I felt this butterfly in my stomach that I used to get when I saw bands live and an excitement, an anticipation that I hadn't felt for years.

'Adrenaline junkies and violence enthusiasts welcome to the one and the only Lucha Britannia! Tonight we will thrill and excite you beyond your wildest dreams, but first let me ask you three very important questions. One, do you like violence?'

'Yes!' screamed the crowd.

'Two, do you like nudity?'

'Yes!' I screamed with the crowd.

'Three, do you like big men in tiny little pants screaming like little girls?'

'Yes,' my voice carried out of my mouth, taken by the crowd.

'Then let us begin our first fight! This is a Lucha Chaos match! What are the rules of a Lucha Chaos match? Nobody knows!'

Three people got in the ring; they were all men in brightly coloured masks and tights. Each made an entrance when their names were thundered out: 'Lagarto Del Plata, the Silver Lizard' appeared with a huge, lolling green tongue; techno music boomed and out came 'Metallico, King of the Scrapheap'. Then followed a smaller, green-toothed 'Piranha' who told the crowd they were all just 'skinny men and ugly women' – we booed in delight. The lizard spat water at the crowd; the robot moved like his crotch was automated.

'And who indeed would face such foes as a lizard, a robot and a... fish? None other, ladies and gentlemen, than the country's heaviest light entertainers – they've wrestled Big Daddy six hundred and eighty-six times and they're your nan's favourite. Say "how do" to the Fabulous Bakewell Boys!'

A shrill 1940s war tune began to play and the crowd went insane as two large, broad men with braces over their bare chests, flat caps and moustaches, walked through the crowd patting people on the head. They waved genially then made to jump in the ring, the crowd egging them on, until in a bit of an anti-climax they just climbed in. One of them was carrying a paper bag; inside was a pie which he handed to the MC and said, 'You left this at Mam's.'

They squared off against the twitching, snarling, out-of-this world opponents, but they held my gaze; they were immediately my favourites. The match itself followed nothing I knew about wrestling: there were two, four, five wrestlers fighting one another, so close that I could see the sweat fly off their bodies. I was on tiptoes with excitement. I had to be pulled out of the way by McBitch when a wrestler hit the ropes and nearly kicked me in the face. There were flips, explosive dives; at one point all five wrestlers dived into the crowd. One of the Bakewells picked up another and spun him around as the crowd counted – then put him down so they both fell over, dizzy, and the lizard flew out from the sidelines and landed on them both. By the end, the robot won, and we were salivating for the next match.

The show carried on, with an open challenge – the barman, who I recognised as Fraser from training, ran out to accept. I followed the steps of the match: first he flew around, and then he was kicked around like a rag doll by his bigger opponent; a posh guy with a hittable face. Then he came back and did some kind of move that I missed when I accepted a drink, but which made the crowd cry louder than they had all night.

He lost in the end, and he looked so broken as he was carried out of the ring that I went to follow him, worried; but then he winked at me. This was perhaps the first time in eight years that a man had winked at me and it had been conspiratorial, not gross.

After the match, there was a burlesque act. A woman with a body like Jessica Rabbit removed her gloves and stockings like they were her own skin. I was mesmerised, and when the interval was called I gabbled to Chow about how this could be the best show I'd ever seen.

I was on my fourth gin and tonic by the second half, and I had my heart in my stomach, gasping and booing with the crowd at each match. There was one match in particular, where the 'girl wonder', Janey Britannico, who could only have been the same Janey from training, took down another woman, glowing gold and twice her size. I was glued to every second.

The final match of the show was a title match. The belt was held by an undead terror, Santeria, wearing a white suit and looming over his opponent at six feet tall. To take it off him was Freddie Mercurio, a lookalike in white trousers, a vest, a yellow captain's jacket and a glorious moustache who came out to 'Don't Stop Me Now'. The match was mad, with both opponents pulling out top rope moves, and I witnessed a hundred 'near falls' where I expected Freddie to lose. Eventually he did a somersault from the balcony of the Gallery and won the belt. There was a feeling of elation in the crowd as 'I Want to Break Free' played and everyone was encouraged to stay and get drunk with the wrestlers. Which I did.

That night I danced to the '80s classics booming over the sound system and spoke to many warm lovely strangers in the smoking area. At two, the lights went up and Vanderhorne announced the ring had to come down. I remember trying to lift the huge metal girders, and getting in the way as these big strangers kindly asked me to move. I found myself instead picking up gaffer tape, empty glasses and bottles, bungee cords and putting them to one side. The ring was down by three, and when I tried to light the wrong end of my cigarette I decided it was a good time to leave. I said goodbye to my friends and left.

When I came to training the following week, I tried to pay Greg but he waved my money away.

'Nah, you paid your dues on Friday, I saw you taking the ring down and picking up glasses when some of these guys were trying to chat up girls.'

Because of the humbleness it instils, I still love taking the ring down. I like the camaraderie that happens when we're all tired after a show, when we've had a few beers, and want to get paid. But we take off the ropes, coiling them to one side. We pull up the canvas, the mats, stowing them away under the stage. The metal corner posts are released from the pulleys that hold them together by tension. We lift the metal bars – 200lbs a piece – and lift them into the scaffolding area above the toilets. Your presence is always noted.

Within ten months of wrestling I had learned how to be a trainee. To become good at wrestling was something that held more and more meaning for me each week. I would come home after practice and ask my boyfriend to walk on my back, sink into a deep bath of tiger balm and sometimes almost fall asleep.

Despite this, sometimes I was still unable to follow a simple instruction like 'put your left leg forward'. I still refused to drink less and go out less, as if I would just gradually become a wrestler even though I didn't get out of bed before twelve most days and drank on average four Tyskies a night.

I don't want to bullshit you. Training was great, but I wasn't as good at training as I could have been. There was still something I couldn't get about wrestling; maybe it was the constant distance I put between myself and this vast industry I had had no idea existed. But I could tell something was happening to me. Those around me saw it before I did. They looked past the bruises and sighs when I moved, and they saw my arms taking shape, that I was quicker to move, to lift things, to run. My loved ones expected wrestling to be put on the pile of discarded projects – such as making music, life modelling, human rights law, pole dancing, yoga, busking. It seemed wrestling stuck. I was allowed to be noisy, brash, tough and clumsy. For the first time in my life I stopped apologising for being the person that I was.

4

The Birth of Heather Honeybadger

On 5 November 2013, I drank too much gin at Lewes bonfire night and fell off a small wall. Despite the fact that, at the time, I was inebriated enough to numb the pain, and limp around the chaos of fiery, medieval streets, when I woke up the next day it was clear that my ankle was very broken. I was quite cheery until I was discharged with a pair of crutches and I had to walk up the hill to the station to get back to London, in the rain. It turns out that wrestling had not given me the upper body strength I'd hoped it would, and apparently my pain threshold wasn't amazing either.

My injury was funny for about a week, and then it became horrible. Firstly, it was not a mild winter, the pavements froze and I had to wear my dad's old socks over my cast to keep my toes working. I had only recently left my boyfriend and moved in to a new house with a room of my own. My flatmates were lovely but I had to pay extra to cover the fact I couldn't do any housework or get my own groceries. Not being able to get to the pub, and having to get buses for the shortest journeys, left me feeling very isolated.

To make matters worse, I was still working at the call centre, and my life had become repetitive. I worked a seven-hour thankless shift, sandwiched between two drizzly, strenuous bus journeys that took half an hour each way instead of my previous five-minute shortcut on foot. I started to have panic attacks for small reasons – if I slipped over in the rain, or if my lunch went missing from the communal fridge in the staffroom. A number of shifts were cut short due to my boss sending me home because I was on the brink of tears, which wouldn't help sell charity. As it was a zero-hours, no sick-pay job, this just made my earnings decrease steadily.

My friends were rocks during this time – turning up to make me cocktails in bed, and going to the library for me. But I cursed myself constantly that it was only now that I had discovered what my body could do, that I was back to feeling like a lump of slow-moving emotions.

I didn't go back to training; I must have told them what had happened but they probably didn't expect me to come back. That happened a lot at the school: people would realise wrestling wasn't for them. Or at least break their ankle wrestling; whereas I had just drunk too much, again.

On a Sunday afternoon in January, Becca appeared on the doorstep. I threw down my keys to her so I didn't have to bumshuffle down the stairs to let her in. I had got pretty uninspired about dressing considering I rarely left the house, so I was currently eating a cereal bar naked in bed.

Becca stormed in with a bag of bananas. 'I'm taking you to a wrestling show that starts in two hours.'

'Wait, what?'

'The student show, for Lucha? I thought you were on Facebook.'

'Facebook is pretty depressing when your plan every evening is to stay somewhere warm without stairs.'

Becca started to root through my drawers, determined to find something that I could wear that wasn't jogging bottoms.

'All the students are going to wrestle and they get to do their own characters; and we get in for free due to the fact you've broken yourself. So we're going to wash your hair and put a fresh sock on your cast and… Wait, you better not be crying.'

The fact was, I was quite moved. I assumed that the wrestlers had forgotten about my existence. I'd stopped boasting to people that I'd taken up wrestling, as I felt embarrassed that my injury wasn't caused in the ring.

But within an hour we were out the door and in a cab. My heart was warmed, and as the confused cabbie dropped us off in the back alley of Poyser Street I saw the queue forming in the drizzle to get in to see the show. We walked straight in and, as the familiar smell of old sweat and canvas hit me, there were cheers from a number of people.

McBitch strode over, covered in blue body paint and wearing a kilt, like Braveheart's angry aunt, and hugged me so tightly I almost toppled over. 'I've missed having another woman about!'

Vanderhorne and Greg asked about my health, and also joked about Becca's whiplash, which had now subsided into her regular comedy routine. The students were in varying states of undress – a photographer had been sent upstairs to get some good shots of their characters. Becca and I settled on a sofa in the front row with a bottle of cider each. Vanderhorne asked everyone to come to the ring before the show started.

'Right guys, this is the first show for most of you. You all get to try and put what we've taught you into practice. I want you to take risks, to have fun, and to look after each other. Most trainee wrestlers don't get the chance to do this until they get a booking on a show.'

Greg interjected, 'On my first show I got thrown out of the ring and broke my leg because no one cared about me. I'm hoping that learning to do a show safely, in a nice environment, in front of your friends and family, will teach you it's about the crowd and giving them a great show, not about you. I already know a lot of you have what it takes to make it all the way – now is your chance to show me! So let's smash it!'

There was a little cheer akin to the start of a school production of *Grease*. This was my second ever wrestling show and it was about as far removed from a night at Lucha Britannia as you could get. Gone was the rockabilly soundtrack and stark lighting; the audience were families who had come to see their loved ones get smashed about. They paid their £5 and took their seats under full lights. The bar was stocked with Fruit Shoots and 50p cups of tea to tempt in the audience. Just before the show started, some of the reprobates that I'd come to know jostled in and hung out at the back, nursing beers. Eventually there was standing room only for the latecomers – a selection of gangly hipsters who had, reluctantly, each paid £4 for a bottle of Becks.

Greg and Vanderhorne presented the show like a pantomime. They were mid patter when some death metal music played and they pretended to be frightened. It was at this point that an enormous guy, who I assumed was new, came out of the toilets. He was dressed as a Viking, and was around six feet five, with what looked like a fur throw from Ikea over his shoulders. He climbed into the ring, and Greg and Vanderhorne were perfect pictures of shock and awe.

'Whoah! That frozen Viking we found when we were re-plumbing the toilets must have come to life, Vanderhorne!'

The Viking boomed, 'I am El Nordico – the ice

Viking! Bring me someone I can crush or I will destroy this building!'

'Oh, right, sorry mate… well luckily this is a wrestling show, so someone will fight you, isn't that right ladies and gentlemen?'

The audience cheered, and Greg called down an opponent. 'Careless Whisper' by George Michael belted out from the speakers, and the man who played Freddie Mercurio came to the ring wearing sunglasses and a mankini and drinking from a portable coffee cup.

'It's the bravest man in adult entertainment – Magic Moustache Mike!'

Magic Mike grinned winningly at the crowd, who cheered him despite the male stripper references in just about every element of his gimmick. The Viking roared and knocked the coffee cup from Mike's hand, then threw him across the ring. The match was a series of body splashes and the Viking chasing Magic Mike around the ring – the kids in the audience went crazy. The Viking, though it was his first match, looked like he was killing Mike, particularly when he withstood three dropkicks to the stomach in a row and stayed on his feet. Mike was doing everything he could to make his opponent look strong – even though just two months ago I saw him win the title for Lucha Britannia.

Eventually, Mike was knocked to the floor and the Viking pinned him for three. He strode out the ring shouting, 'The building stands – but next time bring me someone less puny!'

I was about to turn to Becca and explain how the match told a simple story and was a good example of how wrestling is more about the work involved than winning the match; hence the more experienced fighter happily agreeing to lose for the sake of his opponent. But Becca was grinning ear to ear, eating a packet of Pom Bears she'd found in her handbag, and I decided not to ruin the illusion.

Next up was a match between four different boys, all wearing trunks and different shades of leather jackets. One of them did a lot of flips, while the others just pretended to kick each other in the head (although it was obvious they were slapping their thighs to make the sound of impact). Becca leaned over to ask, 'So is that how they make the sounds in wrestling? Because they slap their thighs?'

'I mean, no one ever told me to slap my thigh.'

Near the end of the four-person match, one of the boys fell out of the ring and landed badly on his knee. He crumpled out of sight. The children looked for a second, and then were back watching the wrestlers in the ring. I watched as some students appeared and hauled the guy upstairs – it turned out that he'd broken his leg, and it was no one's fault but his own. The match ended with one of the trunk-boys dropping another on his head in a way that looked clumsy and unintentional, and the audience gave a polite clap. Vanderhorne seemed to have disappeared to administer first aid for an injured leg and possible concussion.

Meanwhile, Greg continued as though nothing had happened. 'Are you ready for a ladies match?'

Becca and I roared so loud I think it scared people.

'First to the ring, she's a seasoned wrestler who has wrestled all over Europe and the UK – welcome, Cherry Sourz!'

A woman who I hadn't met before slinked down the stairs, wearing a bikini and fluffy boots. She stroked the balding heads of the oldest men in the audience, and snarled in the faces of the women next to them. When she entered the ring she went through the bottom rope and stuck her arse towards the audience, then she leaned in the corner of the ring twisting her hair in her fingers.

Becca muttered, 'Is she really named after an alcopop?'

'Yes... But if she's wrestled all over Europe, I bet she's good.' Spoiler: she wasn't.

'Next to the ring, all the way from Japan, please welcome the happiest woman alive – it's Chow Mean!'

I crinkled my brow as some J-pop played and Chow came down pulling a peace sign at everyone in the audience, wearing red and yellow. She vaulted into the ring and hugged Greg and Vanderhorne; then she bowed to Cherry who gave her the finger.

'Oh dear boys and girls, Cherry must have something wrong with her finger!'

Why was Chow now doing a Japanese character? She was supposed to be a sadistic Chinese powerhouse, according to her descriptions at training. I was confused, but before I could come to any conclusions a third person approached the ring.

'Introducing our third competitor, all the way from the Highlands of Scotland, leader of a tribe of Barbarians. It's McBit... McBitter – Madame McBitter!'

Greg, I learned when I eventually had him announce for me, often forgot the names of wrestlers, so he'd make them up. A child-friendly version of McBitch came marching down the stairs, shouting in the faces of kids who shouted back; the crowd immediately hated her, this larger, blue-painted, ginger-haired woman.

Becca leant over. 'Can we cheer McBitch?'

'I guess so, but maybe don't shout bitch at her on account of the seven-year-old behind us.'

The match told another story: the two baddies teamed up on Chow, but whenever one of them went to get a pin, they would squabble. Eventually Chow outsmarted them and took them out with a cross body from the top rope. The match was better than the one before, and Chow was easy to cheer for.

Cherry seemed to not know any wrestling moves that didn't involve pulling her opponents' hair. There was also a weird moment where she said 'C'mon you chinky bitch' to Chow.

The audience booed her but Becca and I just pulled a face – wow, actual racism. Very quickly McBitch kept the crowd alive by calling them lily-livered southerners and getting huge boos in response.

An interval was announced and Becca concluded: 'Great! So far we've had a plethora of cartoon characters and a racial slur! It's like when Bury St Edmunds theatre does Aladdin.'

'No, nothing can be as racist as a Suffolk version of Aladdin.' We both shuddered at the memory.

The show built momentum after that. Fraser, decked out in silver pants and a green, homemade space invader mask, took on the zombie from the main Lucha show, 'Necrosis'. Greg referred to them as 'Zombie Boy' and 'Silver Pants' because he'd forgotten their names again.

Then, there was a three-way involving 'The Ozzie Explosion', Kurt, who hadn't lived in Australia for seven years but somehow managed to work a boomerang into his entrance piece. There was also 'The Conspiracist' who wore a hat made of tin foil and kept leaving the ring to point at the sky. Kurt did an incredible move where he combined diving into the ring with a sunset flip that both Becca and I lost our shit over. He also then seemed to buckle under the weight of The Conspiracist when he tried to lift him over his head – I found out later that it gave him such a bad back injury he was never quite the same afterwards.

Before the final match was announced, the school's protégé – the Aerial Assassin, Will Ospreay – appeared, calling the students 'minnows' and describing how he wanted a 'big fish'. He challenged Greg to a fight. They had a promo spot, in which they talked about respect and proving themselves, which was akin to the sound bites from some of the American wrestling I watched. But the audience were enraptured, except Becca, who just sniggered, 'This is amazing, it's like a soap opera with only straight men in it…'

Greg and Will both dropped their mikes and squared up, chest to chest, jaw to jaw.

'I take it back,' she said. 'It's a soap opera purely aimed at a gay male audience.'

I'd never seen Greg fight before, but I'd figured he'd be good, otherwise how else could he own a wrestling school? What I didn't realise was that he was a master: everything he did was simple, but he moved slowly, and with command. Eventually Will Ospreay got the upper hand and went for Greg's injured knee – the one he'd torn half a decade ago that had metal in it. Greg screamed, and Becca looked ashen faced, as Greg seemed to beg for Ospreay to stop, reaching to the ropes to break the hold. Eventually he appeared finished – and Will looked down to pin him. With a smirk, Ospreay climbed to the top of the ropes and pulled off a flip without five rotations in it, but Greg put up his knee and wounded him as he landed. Then, despite a limp, Greg knocked Will Ospreay off his feet with line after line, eventually pulling him into a complicated hold, making Will tap out in submission.

The match was nuts; I was even up on my good leg, cheering Greg on. Becca sat down beside me, looking elated that she'd found herself, somehow, charmed off her feet in order to shout at two men under a railway arch on a Sunday afternoon. All the students got back in the ring and were cheered, and then we went to the pub.

After that outing, I had a bit more gumption and started to leave the house more often, as if I could see the end of my sentence approaching. I even returned to the Gallery, though it was for a very different kind of night. The Gallery was also the home of a number of legendary queer discos – the original and, in my opinion, best, was called 'Bad Reputation'. It described itself as being for 'punks, queers and geeks' – music would range from Le Tigre to Beyoncé to Nirvana to Stevie Nicks. One Saturday night, shunning the fact it was Valentine's Day, a load of us went. I wore a black prom dress and about an ounce of glitter. I was wheeled there from my house in a stolen shopping trolley like a trash queen.

I was so drunk on gin that I only have vague but wonderful memories of that night. What stuck out was the friendliness and beauty of so many queer bodies dancing to music. With a knowing nod, Greg let me in without searching my bag, fully aware I'd likely have contraband on my person. By the end of the night – about three in the morning – I was onstage, naked except for my cast, screaming the words to 'Violet' by Hole before crowd-surfing to the bar.

Sure, Greg and Vanderhorne had seen my chuff and if they hadn't been the kind of people who run a venue for nights called things like 'Slap and Tickle' and 'Gimps Optional' I would have been embarrassed. But in the same way that riot grrrls, when together, feel comfortable dancing to anything, and stripping down to our nipples if we get warm enough, I felt comfortable showing them this side of me that, for months, had been constrained within the four walls of a bedroom or a call centre.

Before I left, Vanderhorne smiled at me. 'I think I know your character now, you're Heather Honeybadger – you don't give a shit.'

And like a beautiful pearl of angry, liberating joy, that was what I woke up clinging to the next day. Sure, I didn't have a character, or a costume, or the ability to wrestle as well as my fellow students, or even two fully functioning legs – but I had a name. Heather Honeybadger was born.

In February I was finally released from my plaster-cast prison. Meanwhile, at training my body had forgotten how to do pretty much everything, apart from the rolls. There's a term for it, 'ring rust' – you need to constantly move and practise as a wrestler or else your body will forget. It will forget when it's supposed to turn right to get out of a hold without breaking your arm; it will forget how to roll on to your feet, turning in mid-air to be ready to be knocked off your feet with a punch. Most of all, your body will forget how to bump safely so you are back to having slight concussion by the end of the night.

But my trainers were nevertheless impressed by my change in attitude. Greg said, 'It's like you've gone away and got better, like you've taken wrestling pills.'

'Wrestling pills' were the new form of praise from the trainers. They also had a new form of gentle punishment if you did something really badly, where you had to get on your knees and apologise to wrestling. As someone who apologised too much, and hated their previous form of punishment – fifty squats – this suited me fine. Weeks rolled past and I re-learned the basics of wrestling, and several other new things too.

By the end of March I could do a whole match, including a couple of body slams and a 'reverse STF' toe hold to finish (which is basically where you trip over your opponent and bend over backwards, holding their head in a lock upside down – it looks savage, but is easy if you can do a crab). One day, we were told that it was about time that we all had a gimmick.

Vanderhorne explained, 'If you can do a body slam, it's not enough to just execute it – you need to be able to do it in character.'

Thinking back to my first session with Becca, when I'd done a promo about how I intended to scare everyone's dicks, I decided to channel my inner femi-Nazi. This involved me punching Janey in the guts, calling her a gender traitor, and then screaming 'down with the patriarchy' before slamming her on her back, baring my teeth all the while. I got a holler of applause, and Greg Burridge shouted: 'Heather Honeybadger is in the house!'

I was delighted, and while we were changing at the end of the session, Chow came up to me.

'This is awesome! I bet we can tag team in the next match – big, evil bitches.'

'Huh?'

'Well, we're both big for female wrestlers' – we were both a size twelve to fourteen and about 5'4" – 'and we're both heels.'

'But, I kinda thought I was going to be a face?'

Chow laughed. 'Are you joking? Firstly, what you just did in the ring was ace. But mainly it's because the audience for wrestling is men – none of them is going to cheer a woman with hairy armpits; if anything, what you're doing is a gift for easy heat. I mean I became "Chow Mean", but no one boos me because I'm Chinese; they boo me because I'm a big angry woman.'

'But we're not that big…'

'Dude, it's wrestling, we're whales.'

I didn't want to be discouraged by my friend's honesty so I went downstairs to see Greg, who was giving a trainee advice for a strained groin muscle.

He patted my shoulder. 'Well done today, Heather, you're getting better every week.'

'Thanks. I just have a quick question. You know my character, Heather Honeybadger, is she a heel?'

'Yes, of course – she's a feminist.'

It was said without malice, just in a way that implied it was obvious. I had to avoid using the F word.

'I guess that's it, I don't really understand why I'm a heel. I mean, I idolise women who are badasses – like Courtney Love and Bull Nakano and…'

'Yeah, but you're not an average wrestling fan, are you? Sure, a character like yours could probably get over at a Lucha show at a push, but we're not like the rest of the wrestling scene, y'know?'

I clearly couldn't hide the fact that I had never seen wrestling outside the Resistance Gallery. He guessed correctly.

'Look,' he continued, 'you can't be a wrestler unless you know everything about wrestling. You need to get to other shows, see what else is out there.'

'But how?'

Greg sighed, but thankfully didn't say 'you buy a ticket to a show, you dipshit'. I'm now able to look back through his eyes and see myself as I was then. Earnest, out of place, wearing a neon leopard-print unitard (I had progressed to Lycra when my pyjama bottoms had split up the leg), I was investing a bit of my monthly pay cheque into some new paraphernalia such as kneepads, boots and a sports bra. I had a black eye fading to green from when I'd been kneed in the face last week, and I'd got straight back up again and carried on. He knew that I didn't have my finger on the pulse of British indie wrestling but he could tell I wanted to improve.

He made a snap decision. 'Right, do you know where Swanley is?'

'No, is it in London?'

'Yes, but zone five or something, it's basically Kent. I'm in a show there on Saturday. If you come down early and help out, I'll get you in for free – you have to sell my t-shirts, though.'

'Sure! Oh my God! Thank you!'

'Yeah, yeah, just remember you need to pay your dues, okay? You be the picture of respect and be friendly and polite like you are here. And no offence, you won't need to say much about feminism and that – you'll see why your character will be a heel everywhere else except *maybe* here.' Sage and depressing advice.

On the day of Greg's show I turned up at midday, as instructed, at a town hall in zone eight – and the doors were locked. Outside were two large men about my age, both with a duffle bag, and a bucket of fried chicken. The shorter, stouter one had his hair tied back in a wet perm akin to Meatloaf; and he waved at me.

'Ay up, you're a Lucha trainee aren't you?'

'I am! I'm here to help out with the show.'

'Well me and Jerry will look out for you, we're not on till second half.'

Jerry, the taller one, smiled and nodded his head, nobly offering me a bit of fried chicken, but I declined.

'Sorry, I'm trying not to eat as much fried chicken.'

This was a lie I told people to make myself feel better. The truth was I could do about three fried chicken dinners in the space of a night out, give or take how much beer I'd had – so I tried to turn it down when sober. It suddenly clicked in my head that these friendly, unassuming men were the Fabulous Bakewell Boys.

Steakley did a loud fart, then turned to Jerry conversationally. 'It's the same as last time, that chicken shop – it's a four-star meal but the farts aren't worth the twenty-five per cent extra free.'

'So should we downgrade it to a three star?'

'Two and a half, but will try again.'

'Fair,' said Jerry.

They continued their chicken-comparison double act, picking up their suitcases and taking me round to the back of the hall.

'Come in with us, duck, and they won't bother you.'

'Who would bother me?'

'You'll see.'

We entered the back doors, and walked into a room that was clearly a kitchen but today was doubling as a changing room. The ceiling tiles were grey and patchy, and while wood panelling covered the room, it was boarded with hasty chipboard replacements. In one corner, about 200 plastic chairs were stacked dangerously close to a blacked-out window. The place smelled instantly and recognisably of the dining hall at school. We walked past a few men doing press-ups or looking at their phones. As we moved through the room, Jerry and Steakley were launched upon by every large man that caught sight of them, with handshakes and familiarity. I also introduced myself to them, obeying the polite way of shaking hands with everyone in the room, and I quickly noticed Greg wasn't there.

A bald man came through the double doors, swearing into a mobile phone. Putting the phone away from his mouth, he shouted, 'Help with the ring please!'

Then he went straight back out the room. Wordlessly, the wrestlers around me followed him. The doors led us through to a hall, which had a 1940s vaulted ceiling and light green velvet curtains over a stage. The only sound came from our footsteps echoing on the hard wooden floor. It was big enough for 200 people, but currently there was just me, fifteen men – and no other women. A van had parked up outside the front of the town hall with its hazards on, and I could already see the first parts of the ring being handed out. Steel girders, fourteen feet long.

I walked towards the back of the van; the bald man was inside it. He looked me up and down, and said: 'Don't worry, love – you just help with the t-shirts and don't hurt yourself.'

'But I'm a wrestler, I'm here to help.'

'Oh yeah, who trained you?'

I could sense a quiet behind me; he wasn't the only person waiting for the answer.

'Greg Burridge.'

This seemed to satisfy him, as he picked up a six-foot piece of iron and handed it to me. I put it on my shoulder and heaved it up. I walked five steps before it slipped out of my reach and clanged to the floor, a small dog across the road barked at me, and I suddenly felt very weak, very female, and very out of place. I didn't make eye contact with anyone, as I grated my nails on the pavement to tackle the bar again, changing my grip to support the weight of it on my hip, where my hump could give me a boost from a centre of gravity. Not to be shown up in front of a group of strangers, I staggered with the 40lb bar into the hall, almost knocking an ornamental palm over in the process. When I got it through to the hall I felt hugely proud of myself. Until I realised that the ring had eight more of the 'small' girders, and that Steakley had brought in two, one on each shoulder.

I made eye contact with Jerry and he nodded me to where he was. I thought it was to be helpful, but then saw that I was standing, obliviously, at the centre of where the ring was going to go.

Jerry smiled and said, 'Don't worry about putting it up. Start putting out chairs and then you can help take it down at the end. Everyone is full of beans right now but they won't be after they've wrestled, been paid and the pubs are open.'

I walked to the changing room. Three guys were in there; only one was in a state of undress, but they turned at me like I was a thief. The guy in his boxers didn't feel the need to cover up. Instead, he turned and looked at me straight on; I could see the end of his penis wobbling. He had shaved stripes in his eyebrow.

'Hi, babe. Are you lost?' one said, unsmiling. He had laid out his gear over the chairs I needed to fetch.

'Er... no, I'm putting out the chairs. Do you mind moving your... costume?'

'Costume! What do you think this is, fucking Shakespeare? You someone's bird or something?'

The other men both sniggered, while I swallowed a ball of rage that usually would have led to me calling them all cunts and making an exit. Instead, I sighed and said, 'I'm putting the chairs out so can you move your things, PLEASE.'

'Who you paying your dues to?' said the one in boxers. Why was he still in boxers?

'Burridge.'

'Sounds about right, he loves the women.'

I felt myself blush, slightly, not enough for them to notice, but enough to make my stomach curl because they'd made me feel embarrassed. He did move though, and to prove a point I took five chairs under each arm and cheerily called back, 'I'll be back – you should probably put some clothes on!'

I waited until I saw the boys leave the dressing room and went back in to get more chairs. I placed the chairs out and watched as the ropes went on next. They were in a heap, tangled together like an octopus. There was one scrawny, tall kid in the middle who looked lost. I went over and asked, 'Do you want a hand?'

Like the rest of them, he looked at me, registered my gender, then said, 'It's okay.'

I walked back into the dressing room. Greg had finally arrived, and he gave me a nod of approval, but then went on to ask why I was putting chairs out when the ring wasn't yet up. 'I tried, but they told me this was better for me.'

He nodded, went to the main hall and walked straight up to the skinny kid with the ropes.

'Mogli, you strawb, I told you to find this girl and get her to help you. Why is she putting out chairs?'

Mogli said nothing but mumbled acquiescence; I grabbed the ropes and started heaving them apart. It was satisfying, like untangling a big ball of bendy necklaces. Within two minutes I had them untangled and separated into three distinct piles: top, bottom and middle rope. Meanwhile, Mogli had wandered off to listen to a wrestler who had just arrived – he wasn't putting out chairs.

Once I'd shown Steakley the ropes were done, I went to my bag to get a drink of water. In the ring, the bald man was tightening the ropes using a spanner, turning it through a metal spoke to add more tension. He tested them by putting his body weight on them. When satisfied, he shouted, 'Steakley, come run the ropes quick.'

Steakley climbed into the ring and ran full throttle at the side of it, but rather than bounce off the ropes, the top one snapped with a slithering sound. Steakley almost rocketed out of the ring backwards but managed to grab the second rope to stop himself. I could see him eyeing the hardwood floor six feet beneath him as he dangled mid-air, probably calculating whether it would be concussion or a split skull.

The bald man swore extensively, then ran out the doors, presumably to the van. He came back ten minutes later with a coil of blue nylon rope and four rolls of gaffer tape. Looking gravely at the snapped rope, he said, 'Right, I need someone to replace the top rope with the bottom one and then make a new rope.'

No one put up their hand, except me.

'Right love, no offence but have you any idea how to do a plait?' By this point, all eyes were on me. I knew that a few were sneering, but a couple of the men were genuinely concerned there would be no bottom rope in the match.

'Yeah, I mean, I can plait things…' I stopped before I said 'like friendship bracelets' but this seemed qualification enough.

The bald man smiled at me for the first time that day, showing me his gold front tooth. He growled, 'Good girl, now, er… Burridge can start you off.'

Greg cut the long piece of rope into three smaller pieces. Then I plaited them together and covered them in gaffer tape. Eventually I was left alone plaiting and taping because Greg had a match to plan. Half an hour later, I had a long coil of a plait that I didn't know what to do with, but luckily Tigressa had appeared at the doors. As soon as I told her what had happened she was looking for gaffer tape too, and we wrapped the remaining rope in the sticky plastic tape.

Each corner of the ring has a 'turnbuckle' – which is how we refer to the padded corner; although a turnbuckle is actually a threaded hook that pulls on the ropes to make them tighter, to form a square barrier around the ring. The promoter, which is who the bald man was, climbed into his ring like it was a machine he tended daily. He didn't speak to us as he tightened the turnbuckle at each corner into place; I could tell he wanted us to watch and learn. Eventually he stepped up on to the bottom rope, and it wobbled, sinking under his weight, yet it held. It had worked.

'That's what wrestling ropes were like until the 1990s. Jumping off the ropes was invented by the Mexicans, the boys need to learn to do without it.' He smiled at me and said, 'Well done.'

I remembered that I'd left my bag in the changing room so went to get it. When I entered, half the wrestlers turned round.

I made eye contact with Steakley who frowned slightly.

Pants boy said, 'Why are you still here?'

'I'm getting my bag,' which I did, promptly, aware that my

vagina had made my presence in this crowded room as welcome as a case of diarrhoea. As I left, I heard him, or one of the others, mutter, 'Ring rat.'

Tigressa had also come along to sell t-shirts, but for a tag team called the Bhangra Knights. Every t-shirt came with a free poppadum. I shuffled in next to her, and sold Greg's t-shirts until the five-minute start time was called and people began taking their seats.

'Tigressa, what's a ring rat?'

She responded in her French accented English, reliably honest. 'It's like... a slut, who hangs around wrestlers to try and fuck them. Why?'

I looked at the floor. I knew I wasn't a ring rat, I was just a woman who had made the mistake of treading in a man's territory. Never mind that I'd fixed their sodding rope.

'Did someone call you that?'

'Yeah, backstage—'

'Wait! You went backstage? Oh, okay, I see.'

'What?'

'Well, you're not allowed backstage even if you are a girlfriend; it's just not done. But hey, you're green, you wouldn't know.'

I looked at Tigressa, who I had once seen jump and take out three opponents, the same wrestler who had got a cheer louder than her male counterpart, the Bengal Tiger.

'So, you aren't allowed backstage?'

'No, no, I'm not booked on the show.'

'But what if you were a man, a male wrestler? Would you go back there?'

Before she could answer the music started and the crowd, which had swelled to about a hundred, started to cheer as the show got underway; and quite soon I stopped being angry. The matches were funny: Mogli came out painted blue, he got knocked out by the pants boy who had tried to do something complicated, forgot the bottom rope was loose, and had dropped his opponent on his head. I drank my bottle of Panda Pop happily.

The Bhangra Knights took on Jerry and Steakley, who were unrecognisable in their in-ring personas. It was autumn, so to 'celebrate the Harvest Festival', they had placed a bag of apples under the ring which they threw their opponents on to, and when they left there were half-broken cores everywhere.

Greg featured in the main event, but he was a villain and stalked around the audience, calling everyone a slag, before running away from his enemy and hiding on Tigressa's lap. He had a twinkle in his eye when the crowd clambered out of their seats to boo him.

After the show finished, I made a point of staying to take the ring down and put the chairs away. I took the ropes off, folded the canvas and carried the mats. The bald man was even friendly to me, thanking me for helping with the rope. Steakley and Jerry walked me to the station, and they almost bought themselves a family bucket of chicken each on the way, but decided against it when they remembered how bad their shits had been before going into the match.

While we waited, Steakley said, 'Well done, by the way, for getting on with it today. Sorry that you got stink eye when you went out back before the show, but things are quite old school here. Don't take it personally.'

'Do women ever wrestle there?' I asked, and Jerry shook his head.

'It's not that they won't have women, it's just they have to be good. That's the difference. Women get pigeonholed into being sex objects, and the ones that actually want to fight get told that's what the industry wants. It's not always been this way, but it's how it is now.'

I spent a nice hour chatting with the Bakewells on the way home. When I got back to the house, I was tired from lugging about heavy bars of metal and drinking all those fizzy Panda Pops. I ran a bath. I thought to myself that Greg wasn't wrong when he told me that I couldn't be a feminist face. I could now see that in this environment a woman was a rare sight, and that while you could hope for some kind of brotherly care, you would rarely receive respect on an equal level. I didn't walk in there expecting to be treated like an ambassador for gender equality, but to get those wrestlers to work with a woman, or even to get an audience to pay attention to a woman, felt like a challenge.

When I usually sat in the bath after training, trying to loosen my muscles, often with a tinny, I would imagine my character entering the ring. The guitars would blare music by Hole, I would come in like a burst of energy, snarling, and the crowd – made up of riot grrrls, punks, queers, my friends – would scream for me. In these weird fantasies I never needed to think about who I was fighting, what moves I used in the match – I was just Heather Honeybadger and I made an entrance.

I knew women could be amazing wrestlers. How could an audience not appreciate the same raw, untapped anger of a pissed-off woman? Could that not be something amazing in a wrestling ring?

On Monday at training, rather than feeling downtrodden, I was inspired – both by seeing Greg Burridge in action, and through my determination to shake up the kind of shows that UK crowds were used to. When I tried to pay for training Greg shook his head slightly and pushed my money away; it was like a little gold star of approval.

In the session, I moved myself through the usual motions, my body finally starting to improve on what it had learned and forgotten before. I could stay in the ring for five minutes, just wrestling on the fly, before not being able to figure out what to do next. My selling was improving; I got thrown to a corner and made it look like I had knocked out a tooth. I managed to do this to the extent that Vanderhorne stopped what he was doing to check I was okay. At the end, as a 'treat', we pulled out the crash mat. The room got divided between those over and those under three months' training, and for the first time I was in the advanced group.

That session I learned two finishing moves that I still use today. First, the fisherman's suplex: you kick your opponent in the stomach, then pull up an arm and a leg, tightening your grip around their body so you are holding their body weight up. You then bridge backwards, using your ab muscles as you launch your opponent over your head, landing with your shoulders off the mat, and the opponent pinned. Fraser let me give him three in a row and jumped high for me as I lifted him. I even got a cheer.

The second move was the hurracarrana. I hadn't attempted this before, but once I got used to the fact I would be jumping on to someone's shoulders from standing – which I had done before – the rest seemed so much common sense. Eventually I was able to bend over backwards, through the legs of my opponent, pulling him down into a pin. It was smooth, terrifying and my new favourite thing in the world.

At the end of the session, we sat down. We were told well done, and some theory was thrown at us to make the lessons seem structured – the usual. Then Vanderhorne said, 'We've got some great news: we're going to have another student show in two weeks' time, so tell your friends and someone make a poster. We don't know who will be on it yet, but a lot of you have impressed us recently so we have some people in mind. There is one person we want to be on it though, and that's Heather.'

A little cheer came up from McBitch, Chow, Tigressa, Fraser and all the other regulars. I felt myself turning red, and told myself I wouldn't cry because I was a big tough wrestler.

'Heather, for those who don't know, turned up in the autumn and we thought she was going to die because she couldn't tell her left from right. And she used to drink tinnies on the way home from training and didn't know who the Undertaker was. Then she broke her ankle and couldn't come for the whole duration of winter. And two months ago, she came back with a different attitude – and, well, we're very proud of her, because she shows that anyone can be a wrestler if they put their mind to it. So, Heather Honeybadger, we got you a little something.'

Greg had gone to the bar on the sly and returned with a paper bag, which he gave to me with a smile. 'We saw this at the car boot yesterday and decided it was a sign.'

Of course Vanderhorne and Greg go to car boot sales together on a Sunday.

I opened it, and inside was a comic. The front had a creature with a Mohawk and leather jacket, staring down some zombies.

'Honeybadger vs. the World.'

I knew this wasn't the place for an acceptance speech so just gave them both a hug. On the train home, I couldn't stop pulling the comic out of my bag and smiling at the pissed-off creature on the cover. The same, tough, snarling, constantly underestimated animal I was named after.

5

We Need to Talk about Stereotypes

This is the point in the book where I feel I need to talk about stereotypes.

One thing I had gathered so far in my welcoming but limited wrestling career is that in-ring characters are never subtle. They require a hundred per cent commitment from the performer not only to tell a story of good versus evil, but to portray this while doing something dangerous. The wrestling ring acts as an arena upon which the frustrations and joys of the audience are mapped. It is a spectacle that suspends disbelief. In the same way that we can accept that the violence in wrestling is fake, if it entertains us, we will believe a character is a person's real nature (providing they act engagingly enough).

Before you add the death-defying moves and the pomp of rippling muscle, it is the battle between 'good' and 'bad' that remains the most integral component of the performance. The audience must know which wrestler corresponds with which side of their moral compass, and this compass is intrinsically linked to the society around them. A wrestler portrays their goodness or badness through their costume, their music, their facial expressions, and even through the way they enter the ring.

They then have roughly fifteen minutes to tell a whole story so exciting that the audience are out of their seats. There is no script, there is no time to rehearse, and there is no editing suite. There is no time for the audience to reflect on the bad guy's abusive childhood and how this relates to him carrying the head of a bear into the ring. Nor is there time to explore the self-image of the woman in the gold bikini who high fives the kids in the front row. One is good, because she's pretty and happy; and one is bad, because he's tortured and deranged.

We need to talk about stereotypes because as soon as you accept their use in indicating good and evil, it becomes a slippery slope of assumptions.

Let's take an example: the voodoo witch doctor. This is a character that recurs again and again in wrestling – evil, mysterious and powerful – and usually with negative connotations of Afro-Caribbean culture. In the Gorgeous Ladies of Wrestling (GLOW), a women-only promotion in the 1980s, well-remembered for its problematic portrayal of, well, everything, one of the characters, 'Big Bad Mama', a 'voodoo priestess', blew dust in her opponents' faces. In the 1990s, the WWE brought in Papa Shango. These characters are both widely considered to be two of the most racist characters in the wrestling industry, though still remembered fondly by fans. Why? Because Papa Shango, with his skull make-up and top hat, is a 'relatable' stereotype of an evil black person written by, and for, a white male audience.

However, using these past examples is a bit like shooting fish in a barrel. What about now, in the lovely, left-wing, mutually supportive UK wrestling circuit that I inhabit? Well, to date I've seen three 'witch doctor' gimmicks:

1. Mogli: the white, skinny boy who got knocked unconscious at the show I went to in Swanley was, I was told afterwards, supposed to be a witch doctor. I should have got this when he walked to the ring to the sound of didgeridoos, talking nonsense and pointing at the audience with what appeared to be a curtain rail with some fake fur stuck to the top (the kind that you get for a pound a metre on the market). His entire body was painted blue. Throughout the match I was thinking, if he had walked out the front door into the streets of South London there would have been a full-on *Die Hard* moment.

2. Santeria: he wrestled for Lucha, and was there around the time that I took part in my first match. I started to meet him outside of his gimmick. It turns out that the 'monster heel' of the promotion would put on a ripped white suit, paint his face like a skull, and suddenly resort to smiling terrifyingly, instead of speaking. If you wanted to talk to him you had to do it before the make-up was on, because afterwards he became someone else. He would walk along the top rope and do flips, which considering he was almost seven feet tall was impressive to see. He was something undead, a bit like a zombie. Santeria seemed to be an outlet for his otherwise very normal life. He didn't speak in an accent or pretend to be something other than a terrifying scarecrow filled with evil.

3. Amarah the Voodoo Queen: I met Amarah a few years later, when she was on a show I was presenting. She was the whole shebang of occult fury, covered in white make-up and talc, her tongue pierced, with white contact lenses, and screaming into the faces of the terrified audience. I never asked her directly, but she told Italian *Vanity Fair* in an interview: 'Amarah is not a racial stereotype, I wear

the make-up of my mother's matriarchal village in Nigeria where women are revered. If people think that me representing this element of my cultural past is offensive they need to think about what they're saying.'

Amarah created her character based on something that she deemed to be a powerful reflection of her own identity. I think a woman crafting a character is very different to a person simply being given a character based on the colour of their skin. This is different, as well, to a white person deciding to just 'try on' voodoo for a cheap boo – although this is still how some gimmicks are created in wrestling. I know two promotions in the UK that are run by a woman. I know of none, however, that are run by a person of colour. Wrestling on the whole is written by one group of people: white men. The only way to change the problematic bits is to give someone else a go at deciding who the story is about.

This is why we need to talk about stereotypes. There are, of course, the extremes of racial stereotyping within wrestling, but then there's also gender stereotyping. If you are a woman in this industry you will always be a 'female wrestler', never just a wrestler. The stereotypes that befit a woman follow us as we try to create characters. This results in the ditzy, manic, pixie dream girl who the audience root for, or the slut who cheats to win. Women are encouraged to remain in these boxes to 'get more bookings'. In other words, women are encouraged to fit neatly into a storyline written by and for men.

But what happens when you create a spectacle in the ring that is not made by and for men? In those early days of my wrestling career, this idea was so radical it was unthinkable.

That's why I decided that if I was going to be a wrestler, I wanted to claim this in a way that was radically female. I wanted to do everything within my power to make women love me and make men's dicks scared, and to do it without relying on tired stereotypes or someone else's ideas.

This was going to be a problem when I still had such limited wrestling experience. I was constantly being reminded, too, that a feminist face was a no-go. In short, this made me feel I could not fully embody the character I was given. Heather Honeybadger was a caged beast, and I needed to figure out how to change that.

The next two weeks before the match flew by, and I tried to transform my mind-set as much as possible into befitting the snarling, evil monster I was pretending to be. Greg and Vanderhorne hadn't decided, yet, who my first opponent would be. I had a feeling they would make Janey go in with me – though she had the opposite issue to me. Because Janey was so small, the audience would automatically cheer for her, even though the characters she wanted to do were zombies and deranged schoolgirls. In the same way that I would never be a face, she was typecast to always be the underdog.

One day, on the way home from training, I noticed that Fraser was getting on the same transport home as me. It turned out he only lived down the road from me, and he was understanding when I told him about my dilemma. I was worried about which moves to do with my character and about how to prepare for a match against an unknown opponent. I was unsure of myself – so not really embodying a honey badger at all. He kindly offered to come round to my house and help on his day off.

He turned up three hours late, and I hadn't spent any time with him outside the Gallery. He burst into my room with the noise and energy of a fighter jet, albeit a cheerful one. First we talked about what moves I could do, but he kept saying I needed to be tougher and harder when I impacted things, because I was a heel. He decided to show me some old matches from the WWE, and rolled a joint. We smoked it together and I told him about my concern.

'So, I'm Heather Honeybadger, right? This strong, punk woman, who I think is rad – but everyone has told me that I can't be a face. Janey and Chow said it was because I'm not small enough and I don't have long hair. Greg and Vanderhorne just straight out said that no one would cheer for a feminist.'

Fraser took a drag of the joint, held it and looked confused, then said, 'I mean, no offence, but what is the difference between being a feminist and being a decent human? Like, I've never been called a feminist, but I think women get treated like shit, and I hate it, and I call it out. I think it's stupid that women aren't shown on TV wrestling well, because, I mean, look at Janey! She can wrestle ten times better than me, better than most guys I know, but she doesn't get booked 'cos she's a woman. So... what was I saying?'

'How can I stop myself being a heel?'

'Oh yeah, well... first thing is maybe just don't say "feminism", just be a woman with crazy punk hair who likes rock music.'

'Well, that seems easy enough to do...'

'And, well, just wrestle a man! Crowds *never* cheer a man beating up a woman, they always side with the woman.'

'Because she's weaker?'

'No... well, yes. Look, women are underdogs in life and in wrestling as well. The audience loves an underdog, particularly when they show that they're stronger than the heel. So, that's that. You just need to wrestle a man. Why don't you wrestle me?'

I looked at Fraser; skinny, the same height as me but definitely a couple of stone lighter. He'd always been slight, and recently he had been forcing himself to eat five meals a day of rice and tuna, and drink four pints of full fat milk to gain weight. He trained four times a week, but had spent much of that time teaching me moves because he was small enough for me to pick up. In fact, after Janey and Chow, he was probably the person I wrestled most.

I hesitated. 'I would like that, but what would Burridge say?'

'Burridge will love it. I can be a heel; I can say you were... I don't know... messing around on the BBQ; that feminism has gone bad; that all women in the audience should be at home. If you bring your friends, they'll hate that... plus, I would get to be a HEEL. I NEVER GET TO BE A HEEL.'

We agreed this would work, and now we could start to plan a match. He also started teaching me arm bars that afternoon, a basic hold that you should be able to get someone into from pretty much any angle.

I put him in an arm bar, and then this weird, difficult, strong feeling entered my chest. It was a sudden, and graphic, realisation that I had a massive crush on Fraser.

I hadn't seen the warning signs – he was the complete opposite of all of my former lovers. He wasn't a musician, he wasn't tall and skinny, with pasty skin and a cigarette constantly hanging out of his mouth. He was always smiling rather than holding in some complex secret I needed to know. But here he was, with his well-put-together body that could do back flips; with a kind heart that welcomed everyone.

He seemed completely oblivious to the fact that we were sat on my bed and I was staring at him, stunned, while still holding him in an arm bar. He just said something about Hulk Hogan and pointed at the screen – we were watching old videos; well, at least he was.

After he had gone, I told my flatmate Kirsty. They laughed that I'd actually fallen for a wrestler, when I had been describing wrestlers for the last six months as 'loveable dunderheads'. And I was fighting him.

'This is like something from *Friends*,' they told me, joyously.

'Don't fucking tweet about it.'

They sighed and put their phone down. 'FINE but it *is* funny. Hardboiled feminist invites man in to bedroom for "wrestling practice" and is suddenly shocked when she's aware she can have sex with him.'

'Don't rub it in, I have to pretend I don't want to have sex with him now, *all the time*.'

I can confirm that falling for someone you wrestle with is a total fucking nightmare. When you like someone and can't tell them, you become completely aware of their every movement. You might exchange a brush of their hand, a certain look; it's like being a teenager again, you can spend hours fixating on that slight touch. But in wrestling, you have to grab them around the stomach, drive their head into your tits in a headlock, stretch out their back muscles, listen to instructions and constantly try to forget who this person is. You are, in short, distracted.

Greg told me off twice for being dopey, and for staring off into space. I had to apologise twice to wrestling, and he told me that if I messed up again it'd be fifty squats. He didn't seem to mind putting extra pressure on me as I was the only person who'd been announced so far for the show. Things improved when I managed to have some kind of body or stationary object obscuring the line of vision between Fraser and me. This would last until, at some point in the session, he would inevitably bound up to me to practise a move ahead of our match and I would not be able to form words.

He would talk to me like a dude, and I thought I was going to burst into tears. It seemed incredibly unfair that I had made this important decision to be a feminist character, a face, to beat up a *man*, and had then ended up accidentally wanting to have sex with said man. Talk about stereotypes: I tried to be all holier-than-thou with my gender politics and now it felt completely forbidden to tell anyone how I felt. Why? I didn't want to be a ring rat. I didn't want people to think I was just wrestling to meet *boys*. In fact, it occurred to me that this was one of the only things in my life I had ever taken up just for myself, without any underlying intentions of finding romance.

I managed to filter these frustrations into a constant snarl on my face and banshee screams whenever I struck him. It turned out that sexual repression helped me embody my character more than anything else.

As well as finding the whole episode both intriguing and hilarious – that I was 'wrestling' my crush – my friends were incredibly enthusiastic about my first show. Kirsty and all my flatmates, as well as Becca and my dad (Dad being the only one who didn't know who Fraser was), all made a trip to Bethnal Green to see the match. Becca sat with Dad, with strict instructions that under absolutely no circumstances were they allowed to mention the 'sexy-fake-violence' that they would be witnessing.

On the day of the show, there were still no matches announced except between Fraser and me. All the trainees who thought they were match-ready were told to be at the Gallery for noon, sharp. Anyone late would not be on the show. When I arrived, there were almost twenty people there, including the Bakewells.

'Petal, we hear you're wrestling the monkey here,' Steakley said, indicating Fraser. 'We wanted to say congratulations, and to please treat him like a delicate flower.'

'Yep, we don't want a repeat of Comicon,' added Jerry.

'What…?'

'I got knocked out once for six hours, these guys put me in

an ambulance and then Chow had to stay with me in hospital while I kept asking the nurse for ketamine,' said Fraser, grinning proudly.

We talked through what we would do in the match. Fraser was excited; he spoke at about three times the speed that I could retain in my head, and I told him to slow down, to keep it simple. He wasn't frustrated, though.

'Sorry, I've never taken someone through their first match. It's like taking someone's virginity, there's a lot of pressure to do it right.'

I blushed a shade of beetroot, and I think he noticed this time, but said nothing, and instead just gave me a punch on the arm 'like a bro'. By the time Greg arrived, we had the whole match planned, including a hurracarrana finish, which Fraser was confident I would be able to do.

Greg told the others to line up like action figures while he figured out matches. In the end, there were seven bouts because there were so many people – anyone who had shown up was awarded a spot – and we were on second. There was an hour to go before the doors opened, and we didn't get a chance to try anything in the ring apart from the hurracarrana. I failed twice to jump up to Fraser's shoulders, possibly because I was scared about putting my vagina right into his face in case it lost control and tried to eat him. Once I was up there, I bent backwards through his legs, holding on to the knees, and as if by magic, he rolled us through to the correct position.

I pushed him off because it was all a bit too intimate and he laughed and said, 'Remember to pin me for three or else I'll just have to give you a brain-buster and win instead.'

We went upstairs, and there was a horrible empty period before the show started, a bit like before the school play, when you're in your costume but have nothing to do except wait. But unlike a school play, there were twenty sweaty bodies in a dressing room roughly the size of an en suite bathroom. I wasn't accustomed then to the crowded dressing room at Lucha – with no windows, one mirror and a lethal spiral staircase that led directly down to the ring. I would soon get used to it, however. The hushed chaos while people taped up their injuries; remembering the key stages of their matches by muttering to themselves in the corner; one guy painting his face like a Japanese kendo mask while someone held a torch to light up his face.

I found some space and put on black lipstick and eyeliner. I tried to backcomb my hair as big as it would go although it drooped with all the body heat from the wrestlers around me. Peeking through the curtain, I saw my dad between Becca and three of my flatmates, and they all seemed happy enough. Clearly my dad hadn't had to use the toilets yet; only one locked and only three flushed, meanwhile the urinal was completely open and not actually plumbed into anything.

After what seemed like hours, eventually the *Great Escape* music started to play, the same music I had heard on that fateful night when I'd first seen Lucha. Now I was in the show, even if it was in a small way; yet to get here had taken an unbelievable amount of hard work, perseverance, uncomfortable situations and learning about myself. I breathed out shakily as I tried to be proud of what I'd achieved, and not give away how I actually felt – effing terrified. Fraser saw me, grinned and gave me a hug.

That didn't help my nervousness. Greg and Vanderhorne gave their usual commentary to the 'boys and girls', acting like the Gallery was their living room, which reminded me that this was not, in fact, WrestleMania. In fact, for many of the more experienced wrestlers, it was just an opportunity for a laugh and some free ring time.

The first match was a four-way that included Jerry, playing

a new character and sporting a blue silk dressing gown. He was up against two boys who wrestled in full goth make-up, but who seemed only to do super kicks. There was also 'Peace', a very shy but strikingly beautiful wrestler, who could do a standing moonsault but couldn't turn left. Yes, like Zoolander.

Within seconds of the match starting, Peace had not ducked a punch and his eyebrow was cut open, blood streaming down his chest. He carried on regardless, as was expected. I tried not to worry, and told myself I would duck every move like my life depended on it.

Next, before I had time to realise it was happening, Fraser smiled and said, 'See you out there.' Then he disappeared down the spiral staircase as 'Parklife' by Blur started to play and Greg introduced us.

'The next match, ladies and gentlemen, is going to be a barnstormer. It is a battle of the sexes. We here, at the London School of Lucha Libre, accept people regardless of gender, and we are proud of that, but—'

'Shut up, Burridge, you nonsense! Women shouldn't even walk through the door!' shouted Fraser, as he came to the ring. The audience turned and booed as he grabbed the mike off Greg. I could see that he'd been wanting to be a heel for years, and this would be just as much a first for him as being a face was for me – and he loved it. He launched into a tirade directly aimed at my friends, with whom he'd shared a pleasant cup of tea when he'd visited my house the week before. They were grinning ear to ear and baying for his blood.

'Stupid women, they can't wrestle! And you know what else? They can't barbecue! My opponent this Heather Honey-whatever – this *woman*...' – at that, the crowd cheered my name, or at least familiar voices in the crowd did – 'Last week at the annual London School of Lucha Libre picnic, she tried to take over *my barbecue*. That is a *man's place*! It's sacred! I'm here to teach her, and all you women, a lesson!'

The boos were enormous, particularly when he pulled off his grey polo shirt and threw it at Becca, yelling, 'Wash that!' I'd pointed her out to him, but didn't mention she was sitting next to Dad, who was hit full in the face by the top.

Greg took the mike back, and said, 'Okay, Rowdy Simon, if that's your real name!' It wasn't – Greg had forgotten that Fraser was supposed to be Ferocious Fraser. 'Well, I know your opponent, and she isn't a normal woman. She's... frankly, she's terrifying. And this is her first match so you better pray she goes easy on you, because she's been building up that rage for *yearsssss*. Ladies and gentlemen, please give it up for the fearless Heather Honeybadger!'

I heard the first three chords of 'Celebrity Skin' and launched myself down the steps, screaming at the top of my lungs. As I came into view, the crowd cheered and I punched the air; a little kid smiled and high fived me. I went into the audience, got another round of high fives from strangers and a kiss on the cheek from Becca, and a swig of her beer, and then I climbed into the ring.

As soon as I was in the ring, Fraser was on me – a 'jumpstart' we call it; he went to punch me but I spat beer in his face and punched him into the ropes. The bell rang in my ears as the match officially started. I didn't even notice the ref, or the crowd, or anyone except my opponent.

Fraser had given us simple things to do. First up were strikes, and then he kept getting me in a wristlock, and I found more and more impressive ways to reverse it, eventually climbing up the turnbuckle and jumping into an arm drag. I followed this with three more arm drags and then we stood facing each other.

There was a cheer to show that I had bested him, and I

realised how much I loved being a face. Particularly as Fraser was an incredible heel: he shouted at the audience, told the ref I was cheating, and eventually he went for a 'test of strength'. The audience cheered me to accept the challenge, which I did, but was then swiped clean across the face by Fraser and pulled down with an RKO – a jump that pulled me facedown on to the mat. Fraser then sat on me and went at me with his fists: we had started the heat. The 'heat' was an opportunity for the heel to beat down on the opponent, which would make the audience pity the face even more, so that their comeback seemed all the more spectacular. It felt like it had been three seconds but we were already almost halfway through our match.

Taking heat is easy enough as long as you look consistently like you are being hurt. I can imagine it looked pretty nasty, what with Fraser hitting me, and me selling everything to the max. The booing reached peak crescendo and then he told me to come back. I got up slowly from a hold, broke through by punching him three times in the stomach, and then bounced off the rope into a spinning neck breaker. It got a pop from the audience, with both of us lying on our backs for five seconds, and then I slowly got to my feet.

I screamed at the top of my lungs, taking Fraser out with two clotheslines and a drop elbow. He kicked out of a pin, and then gave me a suplex, which I kicked out of. Eventually he threw me to a corner, picked me up in the vag-to-face position and took me to the middle of the ring as if he were about to throw me down to the floor. Finally, I rolled through with the hurracarrana, and we bumped heads. Everything was going round and round, but I held on for the count, and eventually heard the bell and then the cheer.

Greg held up my arm as a victor. I was grinning from ear to ear, the hottest and most out of breath I'd ever been in my life. I stayed in character, kicking Fraser out of the ring so that he ran away. A member of the crowd passed me a beer as I limped up the stairs. Fraser grinned and hugged me, and I felt normal for a minute and then lay down on a pile of bags and tried to make the room stop spinning. It took at least half an hour.

The rest of the show went without a hitch, and I slunk down at the end. My dad hugged me and looked like he was about to cry with happiness. He took Becca and me to the pub, and insisted that Fraser joined us 'for looking after his daughter'.

I'm not sure how pretending to punch me is 'looking after', but the fact that I got up and walked away was evidence that we had both done a good job. Next ensued a very pleasant couple of ciders where Becca, Dad and I – and Fraser – sat in a leafy pub garden in the first warm March afternoon of the year. They waxed lyrical about how good I was, how strong, all while I was ready to tell them at least ten things I had done wrong.

A little later, Dad had to go home so he hugged me, gave me a tenner for another drink, and said, 'All those times you fell over as a child – who knew that would lead you to do this one day?'

Becca had to go as well, and as she hugged me goodbye she muttered, 'He's really cute, and really nice… just sayin'.'

I looked over at Fraser, who was waiting for me to finish, but who was now distracted by a friendly Staffie tied up outside the pub, talking to it and letting it lick his face. We had been told that the other wrestlers had gone to another pub, but we decided instead to head back to one that lay between our houses. And after several more pints we went to sleep at my house and woke up naked and in a secret, meaningful, wrestling-based love affair.

Honey badgers are, decidedly, the most fearless creature on the planet. They live in the plains of Southern Africa and are scavengers, mainly. Their name comes from their love of honey, but this doesn't cover the fact that they will burrow, face first, into a bee nest and take the entire wrath of a hive without really giving a shit. They also eat venomous snakes, sleep off poison that would level a human, and wake up feeling a bit hungover. They live in monogamous pairs and they are notoriously hard to keep in captivity because they will literally work at an exit for days, non-stop, trying everything necessary to get out. They are never sated by a meal; they just wander about, getting into fights.

To be compared to a honey badger within a wrestling context was a huge compliment from the get-go: it implies resilience, intelligence and toughness in the face of every opponent. I suppose, because of my feminism, it also gave the impression that I could take down any man, or just didn't care what they thought. The problem was, though, that being a honey badger was very much a stripe painted on me. It was a character that I wanted to embody so much, but inside this exterior that Greg and Vanderhorne had planted on me lay a lot of insecurities. And within wrestling there is no room for insecurities; in fact there isn't room for a lot of things, only wrestling.

The fact is that wrestling is hard not just because of the physical pain, but the time it takes away from normal life. Just to get my first match had taken almost two years of training, and at least once a month I would work unpaid at Lucha for entry.

I was also training so often I barely saw anyone outside Lucha.

Those friends who had seen how I had become more confident through wrestling supported me in it, but there were plenty of people that just didn't get it. That was because I lived in a bubble of young, over-educated, broke, queer, angry feminists. When I first moved to the house it had been dreamy, the rent was cheap and I could have communal baths whenever

I wanted. There were Freddie Mercury posters and a mouse problem – justifying the adoption of two cats. We had so many varieties of tea, we had to have a list stuck to the cupboard door. We also had a weekly house meeting where someone would always get upset about the washing-up. We had also agreed that at all times there should be a less than ten per cent quota of men in the house.

This had all been reasonable when I was anxious, had no routine and, quite frankly, was done with relationships with men.

But, ironically, the creation of Heather Honeybadger began to take me away from this world – this bubble of feminism. My exposure to a world dominated by men hadn't changed my wish to make things more equal, but it had meant that I realised not all men were scum. And now that I had a fully-fledged new boyfriend visiting me almost every night, I was not obeying the ten per cent quota.

The tension grew, and I felt that I couldn't wrestle with Fraser any more at training, because we were still trying to keep our relationship secret. Meanwhile, my flatmates felt I spent too much time at wrestling, and berated me for never cooking communal meals.

Despite the fact they barely acknowledged him, Fraser liked my flatmates, and he happily washed up and cooked meals. They complained that his voice was too low and voted that he could only come round twice a week. No one else's relationships were ever discussed, only mine. This was because I was suddenly 'the straight one' as I had chosen to side with the enemy. It apparently wasn't relevant that my relationship was with a small man, an underdog who got emotional about animals, and with whom I shared a love based on the purest of things – boning and wrestling.

The stereotyping, it seemed, worked both ways. I was showing to the machismo world of wrestling that feminists could be nice, normal people, who could learn to be wrestlers in their own rights. My friends, who had at first supported me in doing something violent and aggressive, did not like the fact I wasn't changing the industry around me enough. I wanted everyone to meet and have a chat about our mutual ground, but instead I just got stuck between two worlds. The fact was that I needed my community of femmes and queers to come see me wrestle, to get invested, to help me change things, but they didn't. I needed love and community because I was feeling alienated from my own ideology, and wrestling was there waiting to hold me up.

But amongst these challenges, I realised exercise was good for me. My arms, which I had always covered up due to their being loose, flabby things, merrily on their way to becoming bingo wings, were suddenly not wobbly. In fact, in photos you could see that I had *guns*. I had started training with the 'pros' that wrestled at Lucha. We did drills and drills of fireman's lift relays to make sure this happened. There is a satisfaction that cannot be named when you can successfully pick up an 18-stone man and carry him across a room to the cheers of your comrades.

The gender imbalance was still quite pronounced at Lucha, but then one week two new people showed up who changed everything. One was a very skinny, very naïve, nineteen-year-old boy who worked in New Look; he would one day become Cassius the Neon Explosion. The other was a woman my age, who had decided she no longer wanted to be a professional dancer, after spending six months touring care homes and being told to lose weight. She had spent her childhood obsessed with wrestling and wanted to get to the top; she soon became La Diablesa Rosa.

When Cassius and Rosa started, even though I wasn't very

technically advanced, I jumped in with enthusiasm to show them the basics. Both of them already had good physical fitness, and they trained three times a week. Within the space of a month they were both right there with me, learning suplexes and dropkicks. To teach someone how to do these moves, I had to learn to *take* their moves – to make them look incredible by throwing myself around after them; lifting them in the air when really they should be the ones spinning around my body. When we planned matches, I found myself offering moves that they could do to me to make them look good. I went to being a 'base' who could lift up others to tell a story.

By Spring 2014, I was no stranger to the working conditions at the Gallery and worked there every other weekend for some extra cash. The rules were simple: help yourself to the bar but don't get drunk; if someone is rude be rude back; and fag breaks are encouraged. As I served drinks at the array of queer discos that happened monthly, the faces of the acquaintances began to blossom into fixtures of a new underground life. The burlesque dancers and drag queens who did Lucha shows began to know me by name. I was the one who got friends on to the list, the one who could get them a free beer, who would go outside and have a fag with them because they didn't want to go out alone into the street dressed as a sexy lobster, for example. I spent less and less time in my house, and to be fair to my flatmates, I was using it like a hostel – to sleep in, do my washing and to have sex in. The Resistance Gallery became my home.

As I was the absentee of the house, it became increasingly easy for others to blame me for any mess or problems. In hindsight, the main problem was that one flatmate didn't like me and wanted me out so they could have the bigger room. It all erupted in a fight that culminated in me, with my bag packed, getting the bus to Fraser's place. I was homeless and, at that point, at least, felt friendless.

There was a rough month where Fraser and I shared a box room in a house in Catford with ten people and one bathroom. His room had no windows except for glass doors that opened directly on to the living room, where another person was sleeping on the sofa almost semi-permanently. Greg and Vanderhorne could see I was having a hard time and told me not to worry about paying for training. So I dealt with my feelings of stress and abandonment by endlessly bumping on to canvas, and playing 'Zelda' on the Gameboy.

Fraser and I moved into our one-bed flat on the day before my birthday. We got it cheap, as there was no furniture, just white goods and a chest of drawers. But out of the window you could see all the way to the Shard, and opposite there was a park with parakeets, and also a pub next door. The first night we slept on the floor, and ate a takeaway using our hands because we only had one fork between us. We celebrated by drinking cheap Prosecco out of jam jars, and I woke up feeling the happiest I had ever been on my birthday. I was twenty-four.

Lucha had a corporate gig at a tattoo convention in Alexandra Palace and Vanderhorne had insisted we attend as his guests. After a breakfast of bacon rolls and black tea drunk from our jam jars, we set off across London, on a bank holiday Sunday – which meant the journey took about a million hours. As we arrived, Fraser put on his gimmick – a mask in the shape of a space invader – and I pulled on a black and gold bee mask that had been gifted to me from the Gallery's lost property.

We were waved through security, and were about to ask directions, but then saw the ring was already up and the Bakewells were having a fight. The crowd was already about

200-strong, all as bewildered as we were as to what wrestling had to do with tattoos.

Fraser began to strip to his black pants and was suddenly on the apron, ready for anything. He fought in a ten-person match, while I hung at the side with the ring girls, wearing my new red birthday dress. I felt more a part of the show than I ever had, and it took us half an hour to get back to the dressing room because so many people were taking pictures.

As soon as we were through the doors to a green room the size of my new flat, Greg took off his Metallico mask and scowled at us. 'So, where the fuck were you?'

'It's Heather's birthday and we moved house yesterday so we were a bit late starting off.'

Greg looked at me. 'I knew it was your birthday, where's your gear?'

'Well, I didn't bring it, I thought...'

'Always bring your gear!' echoed Greg and Vanderhorne, who had turned up behind him.

'This was gonna be your Lucha debut, we were a person down; poor Greg had to wrestle, didn't you, bud?'

'Yeah, I was just here for a tattoo, but I always have my gear in my car.'

'We don't have a car,' I said, unhelpfully, and then started covering my tracks. 'Please, wait! I'm sorry – of course I want to wrestle; I'll do anything, I'll go to Primark now and get a leotard—'

'No, we'll have something here. You can just be... Birthday Girl. When people know it's your birthday you'll be over as fuck.... If you forget your kit, you have to do it in your pants.'

I was wrestling in a tag team with Tigressa, and we would be fighting Janey and Zombie Necrosis; he was training to be a piercer and body modifier, but I'd seen him cry with laughter at a video of a corgi stuck in a bush. They kept the match simple, and I hadn't realised that when you tag in matches, you do half the work. As I was so green, they agreed I would take 'the heat' – which meant all I needed to do was some flashy moves at the start, get beaten up for five minutes, and then lie down until I did my finisher. They also agreed that I would win the match, because it was my birthday.

I learned a lot that day – some wrestlers drink before shows, some do not; some wrestlers plan every move; some do not. Some will play a game called 'lemon dick' where you try and catch a lemon in your trunks (which apparently isn't 'sexist, as women also have pants'). Some will swap clothes with each other and try to see if anyone can tell the difference once they're in their masks. Some will just sit on their phones or nap.

Eventually the time arrived where we had to walk in a convoy to the ring, past all the stalls alive with buzzing of tattoo needles and stands of taxidermy. As promised, I wrestled in my pants (well, someone else's pants). I borrowed a 'sensible bra' from one of the burlesque dancers so I had pumped-up cleavage but they were held in place like concrete. Then I borrowed Vanderhorne's Y-fronts because they had a unicorn on them, with tights underneath. I wore a leopard-print jacket borrowed from Cassius, who had decided he was just going to cover himself in glitter rather than accessorise. And the pièce de résistance was a mask handmade for me by Tigressa, which was covered in a comic strip – another birthday gift.

I learned a lesson as soon as I was announced as Birthday Girl, to the sound of 'Girls Just Wanna Have Fun'. Commit to something a hundred per cent and people will think it's intentional. The crowd's faces lit up, and I was handed beers to sip from to congratulate me on my birthday. All I did was smile and shout 'it's my birthday' at them but I was already a fan favourite, and it was enough to get me through the whole match.

Tigressa was first, and offered a load of complicated chain wrestling and some beautiful arm drags, each move followed by an expression of her character with a turn to the crowd for a cheer. I was tagged in and I ran at Necrosis. I ducked clotheslines; pulled out a dropkick; a flip off the top – I could hear the crowd cheering but it seemed a fake echo because I was moving too fast. Janey distracted the ref and then I was sent down with a huge headbutt from Necrosis, which, even though I knew it was coming, seemed to arrive too soon.

As I was given heat, Janey muttered a number of times, 'Stay down!' I didn't realise that I was making her look weak by getting to my feet whenever she knocked me down. It was only when I stayed down and kicked out of a pin on a two count that the audience started to get behind me. I looked up, thinking of Tigressa, and tried to reach to tag her. The zombie pulled me back and into a savage arm bar. The audience chanted for me, giving me the strength I needed to roll out of the bar, hit the ropes and give the zombie a flying neck breaker.

I tagged in Tigressa, and then lay down and listened to the cheers of the crowd as she hit her high-flying move. I lay down on the side of the ring, trying to be ready to break up a pin Necrosis had on Tigressa. I was there too soon, shit.

I kicked off Necrosis, who grabbed me around the neck and muttered, 'Kick me in the balls, then sit on my face – we'll go into the finish.'

Necrosis and I had joked at training that I could have a face-sitting finisher – the cunt drop – that would knock out my opponents. I had practised it once, jumping up and landing with my legs either side of my opponent's head; it looked savage, but always descended into laughter.

I kicked Necrosis in his right thigh, and he sold out massively to the audience, falling over backwards and flopping around. I stood over him, and as predicted the audience cheered when I jumped, landing perfectly on his face, and the ref went in to count the pin. As Necrosis raised his arms off the mat at two counts, I realised he'd just said, 'Go to the finish.' The finish was the hurracarrana; before I started to worry about how to get into it, I realised that Necrosis was lifting my entire body weight until he was standing with me on his shoulders in the vag-to-face position. I flailed my arms around like I wasn't expecting it – which was completely correct. I then took a deep breath and bent over backwards, through his legs, grabbing the knees and ending up in that magical position where I had the final pin.

The audience screamed for me as I won; I ran to the ropes and climbed them, though quite unsteadily. Afterwards, I stood at the side of the ring to watch the final match, which had *all* of the moves in it – backflips, standing moonsaults. The crowd was growing with every cheer.

The Lucha family were given a drinks token each. I was given two, due to it being my birthday, and we sat in the May sun looking out over London with pints of cold cider. Snake Fervor, a sword-swallower who was one of the ring girls for the day, was discussing her phobia of ants – which seemed completely at odds with the fact she held four world records for fire breathing. Fraser and Necrosis shared a spliff behind a wall, while Tigressa told me about her ex-boyfriend. Greg said he was proud of me, and Vanderhorne told me I could keep his pants.

There was this little hole in my heart where I thought about my birthday the year before – a house party full of my nearest and dearest rather than an unpaid gig with strangers. But I told that voice to be quiet, and to focus on the rolling urban hills below me.

The month after my debut, Cassandro visited. Cassandro's

reputation preceded him: he had been a champion and a veteran of the ring for over twenty-five years, and was respected by *luchadores* all over the world as a founder and a teacher. He was also the first openly gay wrestler to win a title, let alone survive and sustain international stardom. He had been there at the start of the Lucha school, and was always keen to teach the students proper *lucha libre*.

The first night I met Cassandro, I remember being nervous in the knowledge that I'd be training under him. I walked in and saw him on his own. In his photos, he'd wear fifteen-foot capes; pink and silver body suits, and eye shadow that matched. My first impression of him in the flesh was of a short man wearing a lot of hair spray. He was standing in the corner, on his phone and chewing gum, wearing black leggings beneath which I could see he had smooth, unmarked legs. As with all wrestling training, we would be shaking hands, and I waited patiently until someone I knew went to greet him so I could go along and introduce myself. He smiled with his perfect teeth, a Hollywood smile, and immediately called me 'honey' and talked about how tired he was from the tube. He then went out for a cigarette as we started the warm-up, and I heard him tell Vanderhorne he was just going to 'do his cardio'.

It wasn't until after the warm-up, during which Vanderhorne made us do 130 squats to show off to Cassandro, that he was formally introduced to us by Greg.

'When we first set up this school, the only person who was proud that their culture was being taken out of Mexico and taught to non-Mexicans, was Cassandro. He is the fairy godmother of the London School of Lucha Libre – and also my wife.'

'You wish, Greg; you are *my* wife.' Then, still chewing gum, Cassandro muttered, 'Follow me' – and without a thought, we obeyed. First, we did standing leapfrogs around the room, making sure we could jump and land on the exact same spot, and clear people twice our size. Everyone stumbled. Next we moved around the ring but, if we spoke, Cassandro would glare at us for silence. We had to follow exactly what he did: a forward roll, a backward roll, a shoulder roll, and even walk on our hands out of the ring.

I took my time, getting as far as I could walking on my hands before falling on my face. I laughed in a huddle on the floor, and as I began to get up, Cassandro said, 'Do it again, from the top.'

This time I did it with more fluidity; I hesitated when I went to stand on my hands, falling over again. He said, 'Okay, this time just the hands. When you do it, look up, straight at where you're going. Where your head goes, the rest of your body follows, even if you're upside down.'

That's when I learned to walk on my hands.

The drills got more complicated. The rolls got replaced with kip-ups (where you jump to your feet from lying down – I've never completed *one*); with walks along the top rope with only a hand to hold; we began doing 'planchas' – a cross body into a shoulder roll. There were no trials on the floor, and we all had to leap up to the top rope in one bound and then throw ourselves off it before Cassandro was satisfied.

If someone did it wrong, they repeated it; if someone did it without making a sound, they were called a *cabrón*, which definitely was not a good thing, and made to repeat it. Cassandro was endlessly patient, but he would only offer words of wisdom if we got stuck.

'The only way to learn is to push yourself, and then you get up and try again. If you can't learn by watching, you aren't watching hard enough.'

Everyone ended up getting injured when learning Cassandro's tricks, even the pros. Steakley, who was usually a joker when it came to wrestling, was deadly serious when faced with Cassandro. It occurred to me that I'd never seen Steakley jump off the top rope, but he could, and he did it perfectly.

'See, even big, beautiful men like you can fly; never let them tell you that you can't.'

For all of us, it was '*cabrón*' if he thought we weren't trying hard enough, although I got 'atta girl' when I did something right. By the end of the session, we were all feeling better about our ability, but I had never ached so much in my life. My head swam with the combination of new information and knocks to the head. He sat us in the ring and talked to us, while we held cold beers to our joints in order to ease the swelling.

That's when I really found out about Cassandro:

'They call me the Liberace of *lucha libre*, that's right, the glitz and the money and the mansion – the teeth and the hair and the cloaks. Sure, I am as glamorous and openly gay, *unlike* Liberace... but I came from nothing. We were dirt poor. I always say that I never came out the closet because we were too poor to have one. Where I grew up, if you were Mexican and poor, there were just three ways to get out: the army, drugs or *lucha libre*. It's still the same.

'I was trained by Rey Mysterio. I learned from aged fourteen, as the others bullied me. They raped me, they beat me up, they were harsher on me than anyone else – but I pushed through it, I just decided I would be the best. And you know who taught me most? Women. *Lucha libre* is so machismo, that's not me, so I learned from Japanese female wrestlers and *luchadoras*. Only they could understand how hard it is to be doing something so masculine when that just isn't you.'

Cassandro told us about his struggles, including his addiction to drugs and alcohol, his suicide attempt, and his leg injury. He told us how *lucha libre* is both a gift and a curse from God –

if he could not wrestle, he would die. The room was silent as he spoke; everyone was amazed at this small guy in his forties, who was still able to tie up guys half his age with impeccable skill. He told us about how in Mexico, things were still hard, how he'd been at a *lucha* show only a month earlier where he'd had to take cover because of a gunfight that killed eleven people.

'So you know, this shit still happens, I am lucky. Sure I have my PMS sometimes – poor me syndrome – but I pull myself up. You have to learn in life, "your ego is not your amigo", and especially in wrestling, because as soon as you stop being humble you will struggle. That's why I travel, and why I am so hard on you guys when I train you here. I have so little time to teach you all, and you are all so lucky to have trainers that support you and offer you such a safe space to train in. You must *all* stay humble, and you will see what I mean, you will learn better and be stronger...'

He enraptured us all, and towards the end I got his autograph and he told me that he liked me, but that I needed to push myself harder. I started to tell him I was going through some stuff, and wrestling was where I found salvation; and I realised I was crying.

He listened, then held me and said, 'You need to *toughen the fuck up*. Believe that you are strong and everything will follow.'

I did need to toughen the fuck up. The sense of abandonment I still felt from the friends I had lost seemed to be helped by meeting Cassandro. He proved that wrestling could have role models who weren't macho men; he had broken the stereotypes where he found them. On the way home, Vanderhorne sent me a text saying that Cassandro had asked personally that I sell his merchandise at a big show in York Hall, the 'Spectacular of Lucha Libre'. I jumped at the chance.

At York Hall, it dawned on me that I wanted to wrestle on a stage that big. And also that I was going to be expected to sell a lot more t-shirts than I'd sold in Swanley. In fact, as soon as I mentioned I was there for merchandise, the mostly Spanish-speaking *luchadores*, all in their masks, became very enthusiastic about making sure I knew their pricing structure. Luckily, a seventeen-year-old guy in a Jim Morrison t-shirt came up and helpfully interjected in English, 'You don't speak Spanish, do you?'

'I can say *gracias*.'

He laughed, then spoke to a wrestler who seemed to not have noticed that I had stopped watching him laying out his t-shirts. There were now three other wrestlers who were also laying out t-shirts and scribbling price lists.

The young guy introduced himself as the son of Hijo de Santo.

'Right,' I said, 'you're the son of the son of the saint.'

'Yeah, and that's my mom.'

He pointed to a woman who was beautiful and terrifying, and who was covering the table with pictures of her husband, wearing a silver mask with grey tights – every piece of merchandise in vivid technicolour. Mrs Hijo de Santo was very nice, but strict on pricing. I had to remember that the big plush toy of the wrestler was a minimum of £40 because they were handmade; that the t-shirts couldn't be sold for less than £15; the key rings were £1 each; and the iPad covers were a tenner.

After five minutes of pointing and giving each other thumbs ups, the families of the world's most famous *luchadores* and I were faced with a sudden stream of around 2,000 people. By the time 8pm rolled around and the show started, I had made the *luchadores* about a grand, and I felt like we were friends.

By selling merchandise to the crowd, I was able to see about two thirds of the crowd were Mexican, and knew exactly who their favourite *luchadores* were. They bought the t-shirt and the signed photo. Then, there were the British, who bought masks without caring who they belonged to. They wore sombreros and downed shots of tequila by the trayful. I thought about stereotypes again, and I thought about whether I was part of the problem. I asked the son of the saint what he felt about people putting on his family's legendary mask like it was a costume.

'Hey listen, you know those old ladies selling tacos – do you know how much they're making, serving here tonight? Do you know what it's like to work for something you hate? What if you are proud of what you make, and you want to show the world? I guess wrestling is the same. Yeah, it's a stereotype, but it's also an honour and it's a great thing to be doing something you love. Everyone will leave tonight thinking that *lucha libre* is skilled and amazing. That's what's important.'

The show started, and I watched through the back doors as my Lucha Britannia family wrestled at the highest level I'd seen any of them perform, swept up in the atmosphere. It was a hot June night and the place was boiling with sweat. The beer was flowing, there were children running around everywhere, there were whole families with Mexican flags, and the matches were announced first in English, then in Spanish.

Cassandro was in the final match, tagging with Hijo de Santo. He entered to 'I Will Survive' by Gloria Gaynor, and he moved perfectly throughout, getting up even after being thrown into the crowd, knocking ten people from their seats. He finished with a dive into the ring from a thirty-foot balcony.

I came away feeling exhilarated. Cassandro had offered me a revelation about wrestling. The crowd saw you as a superhero, the person inside was both destroyed and saved by this love. It was hard to be a wrestler for a reason – and that reason was because it is a way of life, not just a hobby. I was starting to understand that.

As I was saying goodbye to people, Vanderhorne came up to me. 'You'll be here with us next year.'

'Yeah, sure…'

'No, in fact, you'll be starting with us next month.'

'What?'

'I want you to be a frog woman, *La Rana Venenosa*, the poison frog. Get some gear made and we'll debut you next month.'

I didn't think it was possible the night could get better, but that news took me to a new height. As I tried to sleep, a smile rested on my lips, even though my brain repeatedly asked, how the fuck do you wrestle like a poisonous frog woman?

'Gear' is what wrestlers call their outfits. It is more than something you wear: it needs to be immediately recognisable as yours, and people should know your character from just looking at you. What's more important is that it needs to be something that enables you to immediately transform into someone else the moment you put it on. The wrestlers I knew all had several sets of gear, and they were all custom-made.

A friend volunteered to help, and considering she was doing a degree in costume design, I leapt at the chance. First we Googled poisonous frogs, and the colours popped out of the page – these tiny, poisonous creatures with flashes of yellow down their legs, or bright red like a strawberry. We decided on a poisonous tree dart frog, bright turquoise with what looked like gold legs. We spent a whole day on the roof terrace of my friend's flat, with the London summer buzzing around us.

I didn't want a bikini; what I wanted was, essentially, a

Power Ranger outfit. Leggings, a leotard and long stockings to cover my boots, complete with green feet at the end. There could be panels cut into the side to show off a bit of skin, and it could be low cut, but I wanted it to look non-human, non-sexy – slimy.

The mask took the longest to make: first, we had to make a hood to fit my face, and then we sewed a bra to the top of it to make bulbous eyes. The lips were bright red, and my nose wasn't visible, giving me a strange, mutant profile.

As soon as I put on this first version of Rana, I could feel something move inside me, like I was looking into the eyes of someone else. I sent Vanderhorne a picture: 'Meet Rana Venenosa.'

'It doesn't scream frog to me,' was his response.

I took a minute for this to sink in, before I asked what it was supposed to look like. He responded with a picture of Kermit the frog.

'So what,' my friend said, 'he wanted you to be a sexy Kermit?'

With some mixed reviews, Rana got the thumbs up. I would be new to the roster this month, along with two other debuts. I tried to improve my move set, but was then told to focus on hitting and kicking, because I would be a heel, naturally, with the high-flying moves reserved for my opponents.

The day before the match, I was at work when I got a one-line message that I later learned Vanderhorne had sent to everyone he knew: 'The Gallery has burnt down. Please help.'

6

It Ain't No Beauty Parlour, Honey

If anyone ever complains about the Resistance Gallery – its dodgy toilets, the clutter hidden under throws upstairs, the lighting that is basically a coral reef made of extension cords and dead fairy lights – I like to remind them that it burned down once. Most people don't realise this, and it therefore seems to add to the club's legend. It became even more precious to us once we'd faced the reality that it might be the end of the wrestling school, the wrestling promotion, and to be honest, the end of Vanderhorne.

As soon as I heard the news, I rushed out of work and went straight to the Gallery. I turned down Poyser Street and found a huge pile of blackened debris that filled up one half of the road. With dismay, I saw Latrice, the female mannequin that we used to practise promos on, still standing but with her face and arms melted off. Two cherry-red leather sofas, which we used to joke about because they had electric sockets in the arms, were now ripped and blackened. One of the Bakewells came out, covered in soot and wearing a protective mask; he threw pieces of shapeless plastic on to the heap of what were once pieces of art, but which were now charred remains. He nodded to me, as if to say, 'Yes, it's as bad as it looks.'

The fire had been started in the bins that leant against the articulated door that led into the archway – the bright idea of someone with nothing to do on a summer evening. It had begun in three dumpsters filled with glass and cardboard, spreading up the outside walls until it broke through the window glass at the top of the arch. Luckily, the barman, Bryan, was having a nap in his car outside and was woken up by an orange blaze that lit up the entire street. It took the firemen five hours to put out the blaze.

The dressing room went up immediately, due to it being filled with old costumes and dustsheets, and the fire spread from there. The heat inside was so intense it melted the steel girders that covered the roof; they were the first thing I noticed when I entered – the stalactites of jagged metal.

Inside, the Gallery was a hive of activity, though no one was talking louder than a whisper. There was no electricity or water, just one strip light that revealed Janey knelt on the floor, scrubbing soot from the crash mats. Shockingly, the ring was still standing; the canvas was black and the ropes hanging in shreds, but there it was. Greg once told me the ring was worth about five grand and they'd been able to get it completely by chance. Not only this, it was the biggest asset Lucha had, and my stomach dropped when I realised that it had now melted together. The careful engineering of ropes and tension had been made useless, which meant it was just an unstable steel square.

I found Vanderhorne talking gravely to Gary, who was a gaffer. They were discussing what to do about the changing room – whether to take it all down or to try to fix it. Thankfully the balcony had survived, although it was filled with detritus. Vanderhorne reached over and patted me as he carried on talking to Gary, then winced.

'To top it off, my back's gone. I'm on more tramadol right now than the Queen at Christmas.' He sort of laughed, but I didn't. We didn't know what to say to each other, because it just seemed too real to discuss.

'I'll help with the carrying if you want...'

'No, I need you to wash the mirrors, to clean the bar. I need to see how much can be salvaged from the fire damage. Also, we're out of smoke-inhalation masks and legally you can't go up without one.'

I nodded, went round the corner to the caff where you could get a full roast dinner for a fiver, and they lent me a mop, a bucket and a pile of used J-cloths. I stripped out of my work clothes to my underwear, because it was now about 29°C inside, and started to scrub away the dirt. The mirrors weren't cracked under the dirt, but it would take another four washes with clean water to get the smears off them. I scrubbed at the bar that I had always loved, with its collections of unusual liquors – all the bottles now smashed. Vanderhorne's collection of rare action figures had all melted into little black piles, with the odd plastic arm or laser gun sticking out. It was heartbreaking, scrubbing away at somebody's treasure, all now unrecognisable though displayed proudly for years and years.

From this wreckage, all I was able to salvage was a metal crown, a woman's head painted with a *Día de los Muertos* face, and a pair of pliers. The rest went in black bags, apart from the scraps of the action figures, which I put in a box, knowing it was a decade's worth of car boot sale treasure. We worked until ten, ordered pizzas, washed our hands and faces with baby wipes and had a can of beer each. Someone said: 'What about tomorrow?'

It hadn't crossed my mind that my debut was supposed to

be the next night. It was probably the longest I had spent not thinking about it all week. I'd been so numb, pulling apart the carcass from this weird place that had become my home. I found myself looking at Vanderhorne, all of us were, and we waited for a response.

'Well, let's be honest, the only thing that's survived this is the ring. The firemen said that we can't move it but it's stable. I mean... fuck it. This might be the last chance for us to put on a show, let's do it.'

'You can't be serious, we'll get arrested if we have a show here,' said Tigressa, always sensible.

'No, we won't, and if we do I don't care. We'll announce it and offer refunds for people who don't want to come, but we can have fifty people in here.'

I waited for someone to say that this was stupid, dangerous; that there were no lights, no dressing room, no ropes, no chairs, no speakers; even the till had been melted shut with a couple of hundred quid incinerated inside. But everyone, I suppose, felt the same. Fuck it.

This place was ashes, not dust. For Cassandro's first show, there had been a wooden board on the ring, not even mats, and he still put on the best performance he could. We would do the same.

Fraser and I travelled home on the train, both aware that we stank so much of smoke and dust that people moved away from us. We talked endlessly about the future, and what would happen next. Did they have insurance? Probably not, it wasn't that kind of place. What about the discos, the queer dance parties – where would they now be hosted? How would we train, and would people come back? Would people just give up?

We shared a shower to save on cleaning the bath afterwards, lay in bed, sleepless, holding each other. Terrified that we would have to go back to our normal lives, our lives as notwrestlers. For me, the next night could be the first and last chance to do what I loved.

The next morning, we both called in sick. I also woke up realising that we'd turned our sheets grey from the soot that was still on our skin. I spent an hour in the shower; shaving and exfoliating, terrifyingly aware that I'd be in body-clinging Lycra in front of a crowd later. I had no idea who I would be fighting, which was not unusual, as the card – the list of wrestlers taking part – would be decided about two hours before doors. I spent the day listing on paper the moves that I could do reliably, with Fraser reassuring me that I'd probably use two, and that as a heel I would be expected to leave all the shiny stuff to the faces.

We arrived at the Gallery at four o'clock, and the stink of smoke hit me like a blast in the face. Aside from the lingering smell, we had entered a place that had been transformed by a small army of people who had been working all day to make it at least passable as a safe building. Where yesterday there had been muffled voices and emptiness, now the air sang with hammers and drills as the balcony was reinforced and the broken pieces of metal sawn off. There were three new strip lights, begged and borrowed, and an amp on a shopping trolley, covered in old rave stickers, which was blaring out Madonna.

In the ring, Greg was making a new set of ropes, sorting through a pile of rusted and blackened metal hooks. He saw me and asked me to help by taping up the rope. I took the gaffer and proceeded to wrap up the long snakes of elastic. I got through two rolls before going to the bar to find more. There I found Viva Ruin, one of the ring girls, sipping a beer and cleaning the Lucha Championship belt with baby wipes. The belt – its leather cracked and frayed, its brass buckles grimy – was still a thing of beauty to me and something to covet.

Viva smiled at me: 'We won't have to wear so much make-up, as there won't be any lights. It's your first show tonight, right?'

'Yeah, it's cursed!'

'No, this makes it even more special. Tonight will be legendary, even if there isn't another one.'

An hour later, Bryan the barman turned up and we all went to his van to unload crates of beer cans. Someone brought in a bulk bag of decorators' masks that we would have to wear backstage so that we didn't get blackened lungs. We all changed in the ring, and there were no lights on the balcony. The voodoo witch doctor painted on his face and Greg bound up his injured knee in three supports; it was surreal that this was happening at all, even more so because I was there too.

My made-to-measure Rana costume had never been worn in public before. As I slipped into it, my legs shone turquoise and reptilian in the strip lights. I wore two bras to keep from a nipple slip and felt proud of my cleavage probably for the first time in my life. Tigressa got dressed next to me, and advised me on finishing touches. A touch of gaffer tape was applied on the straps of my leotard to make sure it didn't slip down to reveal my bra. She also lent me black nail varnish and green eye shadow. Looking at my reflection in her compact mirror (as all the dressing-room mirrors had been tarnished by the fire), I decided I looked too pretty. I took a finger of black grease paint from Santeria, and rubbed it on my teeth and gums, making them look rotted.

As I gurned at Vanderhorne, who was looking old, destroyed and distracted that evening, he grinned. 'Beautiful.'

We all ran upstairs in our gear, except Freddie Mercurio, who insisted on wearing his pants until the last minute, because his gear was white and he at least wanted it to stay that way until he did his entrance. I was tagging with Janey against Tigressa and La Diablesa Rosa, who was also making her Lucha debut. We laughed whenever we caught each other's eyes while we were getting ready. La Diablesa Rosa was putting pink extensions in her hair, perfecting her eye make-up, and finishing up her fake tan. Meanwhile, I was making myself into a monster.

We kept the match simple. Janey told me she would just tag me in for heat on Tigressa, with Rosa winning with a double missile dropkick from the top rope. The only moves I did were a fisherman's suplex, and a power bomb – my other moves being 'too face' for this match. We had to whisper as we ran through the plan for the fight, as the audience had begun to file in – the speakers had been turned off to save power for the show and they might overhear the finish. After all, it was still a wrestling show, and we had to make it real for them.

Benjamin Louche welcomed the eighty dedicated fans, thanking them for their support, and telling them that by pulling off this show, it would offer a reminder of why the venue existed in the first place – because of the resistance and strength inside it. Next, the Bakewell Boys came out and sung a heartfelt rendition of 'I Will Always Love You' before getting knocked down by a clown and a lizard wielding metal chairs. The show was just like a normal Lucha show, but everyone was trying to animate it a bit more vividly. The crowd were extra loud, and many had brought their own booze with them because the bar had run dry within an hour, and without a fridge the beers were lukewarm.

Upstairs, the women and I started to tie up our wrestling masks. I was so nervous that I could feel my heart pounding. Rosa complained that she really needed a wee – this, we found out, was just something that would always happen to her before she ever got in the ring. At the same time, Janey was reassuring us that all we needed to do was be slow, give a lot of character and have fun.

'Remember, if you mess up, just pretend it was intentional – no one out there knows what we have planned. Make it seem real and they'll love every minute of it.'

Janey went out first; a couple of months previously she had done a turn as a heel, and her character 'Janey Britannico, the Girl Wonder' had gone from being a teenage baby-face to a deranged, terrifying zombie child. The crowd loved her even more, chanting 'Zombie Janey' and cheering as soon as her music began to play. She would claw through the crowd, crawl to the centre of the ring, and bleed from her mouth, but it just made the cheers even louder.

'And next, ladies and gentlemen, making her debut tonight comes a creature who has been spawned out of the ashes of these very arches. The most poisonous animal on the planet is not a spider, or a snake; no, ladies and gentlemen, it is a frog the size of a teaspoon. She creeps in the dark, she slithers to you now, but don't kiss this frog or she will strike you back. Welcome to the ring, La Rana Venenosa.'

Then, there was the sound of spitting guitars, music I had never heard before, and I waited for a drop in the intro that didn't come, so instead I just ran down the steps like a deranged beast. The audience cheered me, and taking a leaf from Janey's book, I knew I had to change that fast or the pace of the match would be a mess. I grabbed a beer from a trainee's hand, downed half of it, and then climbed across the apron and sprayed the crowd. The roar and boo was tremendous. I rolled into the ring, turning and writhing until my name was said again. I continued to roll around until I remembered I had to get out the way, and crept over to Janey on my back legs.

She said quietly, 'Great entrance, but move less in the match, okay, or else you'll mess up.'

Janey was right – I'd only done my entrance and already I was out of breath, 'blowing out my arse', as we call it. With the heat of the audience's standing bodies, stuffed between the stuffy, smelly walls, the sweat was already building up behind my mask. The lights were hot and blinding to look at, and so I made myself still, crouching in one corner, occasionally leaning into the crowd with a sneer as someone took a picture.

Tigressa entered to 'Eye of the Tiger' to huge applause. She back flipped into the ring gracefully. La Diablesa Rosa then came in, swinging her ponytail around at the crowd, with her perfect smile and long legs. At over six feet tall, and with biceps that could knock a man sideways, I knew already that she would be booked into every show from here on in. I was right.

My match, as always, passed in a blur. I suppose, because it involves every part of your body, every ounce of concentration in doing or remembering or planning, the adrenaline doesn't let you slow things down around you. I know that it started with some chain wrestling, where Tigressa did some beautiful reversals including a cartwheel and a backflip, and I ended it all by punching her in the vagina. I tagged in Janey and took a minute as I watched her beat up Tigressa, the crowd baying for her blood.

I was panting and sweating; I'd had no idea previously how disorientating the mask would be. I had done one roll and ended up somewhere else; I almost got kicked in the face because my mask had moved, covering my eyes and obscuring my vision. I was happy for a second that I had time to recollect my thoughts, but then Janey tagged me, and my mind went blank, with me ending up just sitting on Tigressa and pretending to pull off her mask. The crowd hated it, but luckily she could tell I was lost and said, 'Do the cunt drop thing, just do that.'

I threw her to the floor, taking my time to get to my feet. I gave the audience the finger and then sat on her face. I could tell she only just moved her face in time, but the audience roared with disapproval as I almost pinned her for a three count. When she kicked out, I dragged her back by her hair to the corner where Janey waited, who said, 'Keep choking her on the ropes when the ref's back is turned.'

She then did the oldest cheat move in the book: running to her opponent's corner and slogging Rosa off the apron. The crowd roared as Rosa struggled to get back in the ring and exact her revenge. In the meantime, while the referee was distracted telling Rosa to get back in the ring, Janey and I laid into Tigressa – with the crowd literally shouting 'behind you' as the ref's back was turned.

All I did was hug Tigressa's neck to the turnbuckle, but she kicked her feet and writhed around to make it look like I was doing something intentionally painful. I had nothing else planned so I was relieved when Janey tagged me in and said, 'Go home.'

I pulled Tigressa into a corner. I ran in with a back elbow once, twice and then, all of a sudden, on the third run she leapt on to a rope, span around my head and threw me to the floor. We both struggled to tag our partners. I went too quickly, so had to writhe in pain until Janey gave me the signal by turning her palm up; then I leapt to her and tagged her in. The crowd exploded as Rosa jumped over the top rope, with Janey running in, ready for a clothesline. I had just got back to my feet when Rosa knocked me back as well.

Rosa did a body slam on Janey, and I threw myself over to break a pin, suplexing Rosa, and pinning her for a two count. Then I stood up, outraged, just in time for Tigressa to leap from the top rope and knock me out. Janey ran in and threw Tigressa out of the ring, and we both got to our feet and turned to see Rosa standing on the top rope. She jumped horizontally, kicking us with a foot each – one each, placed firmly on the tit

– and took us down. I lay back and let her take the winning pin. Suddenly it was over.

The match had lasted eight minutes.

I rolled out of the ring, kicked by Tigressa, and fell straight to the concrete and bashed my elbow. I limped up the stairs a bit too quickly for someone who just lost a fight, but I needed to breathe and get the mask off. The boys upstairs all patted me, and told me well done. The other girls came up and we all hugged one another, and said thank you.

Suddenly, a wrestler came up behind us and said, 'Great match girls – just a few pointers…' He then listed everything we had done wrong in the match, as we were still panting and trying to get our breath back. We stared at him, speechless.

Vanderhorne overheard and said, 'Are you actually just doing this? Let them get their breath back, you twat… That match was great, girls, well done. I was very happy.'

Of course, all I could concentrate on was what the guy had said: how my entrance was all over the place; how I should have had more of a defence against Tigressa because I just stood there and took her moves; how my heat was too short, my strikes were weak, and that there were a few times where I wasn't a frog any more, I was just standing around like a normal woman. My character was amazing, but as soon as I started to wrestle, I was told, it fell away.

Someone sent me a video they'd taken on their phone, and watching it back now, it wasn't a terrible first match. The guy who sent me the clip did so because he thought I was great and different, that I wrestled in a way no woman he had seen had done before.

'You disgusted the crowd – you had no bikini, no make-up, no hair; you were all elbows and spite. It's your first match but you had your own style: hold on to it.'

Frog style: technically sloppy but horrifyingly engaging.

I didn't mess up, I know that now; I did what a wrestler should do – make their opponent look good. Considering it was my first time wrestling in front of a loud, drunk, Lucha audience, in a burned-out building – and I'd never worn a mask before – I did pretty good, I think.

I also hung on to what Janey told me: 'Wrestling isn't about moves, okay? That's for the good guys. You need to be hate-able. You can't do that if you're better than the person who beats you in the end. You did exactly what you were supposed to do, and no one knew you forgot anything; in fact – you didn't, you did well.'

Rosa had done better than well, executing a handful of moves perfectly, and she was enjoying her well-deserved time in the spotlight. I didn't resent her; in fact, this was a quick lesson in the interdependence that wrestlers have on each other. We can't afford to be competitive. My job was to be part of the happiness she brought to people. I went on to fight her more times than I can count, and every time she beat me, I felt proud that I was fifty per cent of that victory.

After the match, I didn't stay in my gear. It was so hot that I just put on a black swimsuit and boots and went downstairs for a smoke. Some of the regulars who I had met over the course of my time serving drinks and selling t-shirts at past shows were delighted to see me up in the ring. It seemed everyone there knew me without the mask, but there were no secrets at the Lucha show; the whole building had burned down, and we were all there to enjoy the ashes.

After the interval, Snake Fervor, the ant-fearing sword-swal-lower, performed a defiant fire-breathing act. This was just a couple of hours after I'd seen her use up four cans of Flame-Guard on the ring and walls before the show had started. The night ended with a title match between the Britannicos: two high-flying wrestlers from Essex who were usually a tag team.

That night, their repertoire was limited to quite low-flying moves because there were still bits of metal hanging from the ceiling. Instead, they brawled into the crowd, and spilled outside on to the street, diving off dumpsters and car bonnets.

Eventually, when the fight returned to the ring and the winner held their hand up, all of the wrestlers put on their masks and returned to the ring. The ring creaked uncertainly under the weight of twenty people, but its collapse would have merely been the final stroke in an evening that celebrated destruction, defiance, and most importantly, resistance. Vanderhorne was handed the mike, and it was the first time I'd seen him at a show without his mask on.

'Thank you, everyone here tonight. The last few days have been hard, but we've been touched by all the love and support we've had. This place was a husk yesterday and these people around me, these wrestlers, came and cleaned it, and made it possible for their own show to go on. We don't know what will happen now, but we will keep fighting, because we are the Resistance, we will keep fighting.'

We stayed drinking until the generator powering the lights ran out. I watched the doors bang shut and Vanderhorne lock them and limp to his car. Everyone else walked in the opposite direction, back to our homes and our other lives as non-wrestlers. I've never quite got the smell of smoke out of my Rana mask from that first show; it still lingers four years later. It's become a reminder to wrestle every match like it's my last.

Within a couple of days, a crowdfunding page had been set up.

Just two weeks later, the Resistance Gallery had raised £15,000 to pay for the rent and the rebuild. It was no easy feat raising that much money, and it took a lot of work from everyone to ask for people's spare change.

Thankfully, we discovered that the fetish nights and vampire club nights that the Gallery had hosted for over a decade had some surprisingly wealthy clientele. Money often hides in debauched basements, after all. Bethnal Green was more convenient than Soho for plenty of bankers and they still needed a place to be choked out by an oil wrestler (interactive female oil wrestling being just one of the earthly delights on offer at the weekends). There was also the skin-suspension club, as well as the Japanese rope bondage society; all of these groups who could only do what they loved in the Gallery because it was a place that accepted the weird and the perverse.

So, while the Gallery had been saved, it was another story for the wrestling ring and the mats. The ring was not covered by the budget, and we couldn't afford new mats. During that time, we would turn up to training, only to spend another night cleaning the crash mats and walls. But as soon as the money went towards a new sound system and we had lights again, the wrestling school was back on. What's more, the ring used to be a treat only once a month, but now it was up all the time, because Vanderhorne wasn't convinced that it could be taken apart without a steel grinder.

The fire got Lucha Britannia a lot of publicity, particularly when pictures circulated of the wrestlers, against the odds, putting on a show in the burnt-out ruins of the building. Bookings started to fly in, and there was a demand for us to do more corporate gigs and Christmas parties. As I was now on the Lucha roster, I was involved in all of these activities, which marked an even starker difference between my life as a wrestler and life as a 'muggle'.

I had left the call centre earlier that year, and by the autumn was working in an auction house, doing their itinerary and answering the phone; it was fun, scuttling amongst the taxidermy and measuring furniture. A typical day in the winter of 2014 meant going to work in the freezing auction house in my thermal underwear, sometimes running on the spot to get warm. I would walk in circles between lots, clocking up about three miles a day. Then I would leave work at six, buy a cup of coffee, and walk along the canal to Mare Street. On my walk, I would look into the windows of the lit-up houseboats, marvelling at the yellows of the clouds in the sky, which were a haze of light pollution.

The Gallery door would always be unlocked, and inside could be found a group of people constantly working to improve the place in some way. At first I would help by making tea, but soon I found myself painting walls black, or helping Fraser with his pet project of wallpapering the toilets with comic books. I began to love the place even more, as I became accustomed to being on my knees beside the grossest toilets in East London, trying to rub symmetrical panels of back copies of *Love and Rockets* next to adverts for a Spiderman watch. My hands would go numb from the cold wallpaper paste, but at least I wouldn't have to pay for training.

When the warm-up would start, we wouldn't put the heating on to save money on petrol for the generator. I can remember our breath freezing, clouds of steam coming off the backs of all of us as we did sets of fifty squats.

The Gallery's focus was the fire, the struggle and the need for money and, as a result, we were seeing no new people joining us at training. The need to pull together made our numbers dwindle, as we knew that we would leave the place with all our clothes stinking for days, and that the coaches would usually be too tired to plan lessons well. We relied on teaching each other, and this kept us humble.

The club nights at the Gallery moved to other venues, as they had no choice. For three months there was no sound system, no lights, and the venue couldn't legally be open past twelve, when in the past we would sneak our way through to three or four. Whenever I spoke to Vanderhorne, he would complain about money, how he was up shit creek, and I would only be able to nod and listen, and try to say something hopeful.

If anyone ever complained about the bad facilities, the surly trainers or the ongoing chance of injury, we would repeat a mantra taken from Cassandro: 'It ain't a beauty parlour, honey.'

The shows at Lucha resumed as normal, selling out each month despite the lack of proper lighting or sound. I wrestled two more matches, tagging with Janey and fighting Tigressa and Rosa. This meant that we could get a tag done in eight minutes exactly. Each time, we would try something different, or at least the others would and I would try to remember my moves.

Rana was evolving; I changed the costume slightly so that I didn't wear the leggings, no longer feeling the need to cover up my thighs. Rana wasn't Heather, and she didn't have deeply imprinted memories of being told her thighs were unsightly and that she was fat. She was a frog woman and could do what she wanted. Spraying the crowd with water became a standard part of my entrance, with someone once complaining because it went in his eye. Infuriating men – because it was only ever men who complained about Rana – was another thing that wrestling gave me the freedom to do.

At the occasional corporate gigs we did, for things like staff parties, we would be taken to places in Shoreditch where any old ring had been hired and set up. We would perform the most basic matches we could, noting how the floor below the ring was concrete, or whether the audience were particularly drunk so might get in the ring. I found these shows hard, as I was out of my comfort zone – my comfort zone being the grotty but familiar Resistance Gallery.

One particularly bad show involved the audience being

brought by coach to a mystery location, where they were
treated to burritos and a surprise wrestling match. They had
no idea how to react and were mostly silent, taking pictures
on their phones. I came near one guy who grabbed my arse;
I turned around and grabbed his beer, spraying it in his face.
Then I got into the ring as Rana. I pretended not to care but
I was full of fury. I tried not to react to the sounds of the man
screaming at me that I was a cunt, and I didn't make eye contact with Greg, who I know would disapprove of my reaction.

I remember that show especially, because I messed up every
single thing I had to do. I forgot to get in the ring at one
vital point to do a spot with Greg, which was embarrassing. At
another point, I didn't jump high enough to get over La Diablesa; instead, I knocked her over with my vag. I tried to cover
it but then we both forgot what to do and for some reason
ended up tagging out. The finisher was a satellite DDT with
Mercurio, which I had done perfectly a hundred times, but this
time I landed weirdly, winding Freddie at the same time.

The next match was between our best guys, but just as they
started to do their dropkicks, and just as the crowd began
cheering at the right point, the coach arrived to take them
away. Only five people remained to see the finish, and they
were running the burrito truck. Still, they liked it so much they
gave us all the leftovers.

Both Rosa and I were in tears in the dressing room afterwards. Nobody got paid, and instead all we got were free pairs
of trainers. Even the pros who had been on the circuit for
decades seemed disdainful at the end of these hollow performances. There was no pride in it; you were just a sideshow.
These were the times where I would remember my ego wasn't
my amigo, and that I needed more training. That was the only
way to make these botched matches feel better.

Because there were other times when matches went well,

when I could look into the eyes of every audience member and see them shining with happiness, their mouths open with shocked delight when there was a spectacular move. When I did something that made them boo their lungs out, I would get up and blow them kisses, my heart soaring.

I worked on how to choke people on the ropes in the most horrible way; how to throw punches well; how to slow down. Rosa, on the other hand, was improving faster than anyone I'd ever seen, or indeed, faster than Greg or Vanderhorne had ever seen. She'd taken on several bookings with her unmasked gimmick and was busy every weekend, travelling to places like Slough to get as much experience as she could. She was earning her dues in the traditional sense, while I found other uses for my love of performance.

Because I was no longer the beginner, and because I also encouraged everyone with whom I ever spoke to try wrestling – whether it was in the smoking area at shows or in the pub – I brought in new faces. People like me: queers, feminists and women with confidence issues. Many of them came for one session and then never returned, the macho-ness still too dense to navigate. One woman, called Drastik, was six feet, with green hair and a tiny little beard. She was curvy but confident and very, very into sex. She loved wrestling, and I adopted her quickly as my protégée.

Drastik came into my life with some other recruits who seemed unlikely candidates as wrestlers. There was also Dolly, who trained in her pyjamas and remained consistently jolly, and who was always willing to have a pint with me after training. There were many more, who remain my friends even as I write this book. My circle started to expand away from wrestling and into other people's lives, and I liked it.

As the new year started, Gary had figured out a way to take the ring apart so that it could be stowed away again. It meant that, finally, the Gallery could be a working venue again, not just relying on wrestling.

A drag show called 'Mariah and Friendz' adopted the Gallery for their circus-horror shows. Baby Lame presented the show – a seven-foot, bearded wonder with a simpering voice and dark sense of humour. It was organised by Crystal Beth, an icy blonde who would do trapeze in stilettos and homemade superhero outfits. I started off working the bar for them, but as soon as they saw me wrestle they asked me to start working on acts with other female wrestlers – a kind of violent cabaret, so to speak. I jumped at the chance and recruited Tigressa, and some other new female trainees to start a performance group called the Super Luchadoras in Training – the SLITs. I cared less about wrestling ability, and more about the fact the women were all fittingly unladylike.

I got a job for a spell as a backing dancer in Baby Lame's show, which was a new kind of fun I couldn't handle. Drastik and I wore cartoon animal heads and learnt basic, camp dance routines, while Baby would roar along to Britney Spears and Tina Turner.

I managed to persuade Vanderhorne to come along to one of these shows for his birthday. I felt like he needed a good night, as the fire and the ensuing stress had pulled his life apart. He and his partner had split up, and he only saw his kooky three-year-old daughter at the weekends. He'd ended up moving into a house with Greg. Thankfully, the night seemed to distract him – particularly when Baby pulled him from the audience, strapped him to a chair, put a pig snout on him, and gave a shrill serenade of 'I'm a Good Girl for Daddy'.

Afterwards, Vanderhorne came to our house, and we sat around watching the cult classic *The Abominable Dr Phibes*. I made Vanderhorne a terrible cup of coffee and we talked nonsense, until he casually said, 'By the way, are you free two weeks on Saturday? Because I've booked you on a show in Berlin.'

I couldn't speak – I just smiled – and I walked into my bedroom next door and jumped up and down, sort of screaming as quietly as I could. This was the first of many nonchalant, big deal bookings that I was given with Lucha. No information other than where I needed to be, and that I would need to be a poisonous frog woman.

The Berlin gig turned out to be particularly spectacular; we realised that Vanderhorne didn't know actually what we were being booked for, only that it was well paid. Ten of us met at Stansted Airport at some ungodly hour to catch the cheapest flight available. The ring girls found out two hours before take-off that their plane was leaving from Luton Airport instead (note: Luton is *not* in London, it's two counties away) and Vanderhorne had to drive them there himself, receiving a barrage of swear words the whole way.

An American, about the same age as me, met us at the airport at the other end with a sign that said 'Awesome Wrestlers'. This was very exciting because none of us had ever been greeted with a sign at an airport. We were then bundled into a family-size taxi and driven at illegal capacity to the centre of Kreuzberg. It was eleven in the morning, and Fraser looked out of the window and said, 'It doesn't look very German, it looks more like Lewisham High Street.'

I'd been to Berlin a few times before to stay with friends, so I explained that this was the beauty of Berlin. It was diverse. The Turkish kofta shops on every corner with fresh garlic sauce; the hundreds of bakeries still churning out bread to old grandmas who had quietly survived three decades of Soviet rule. The passengers in the car all listened as I pointed out the occasional bit of the Berlin Wall that was still standing, just another bit of concrete between the other concrete buildings. The driver asked me lots of questions in German, to which I replied that despite being from a German family, my German was shit.

After around forty-five minutes we pulled into the courtyard of a huge building that was all Weimar-era friezes and pillars, with the surrounding walls covered in fresh graffiti. We were taken up marble steps to a ballroom, and out of the windows we could see down to a courtyard where people were hurriedly flash-welding life-size metal tigers to tricycles; around them lay a litter of surreal objects, including carousel horses and burned-out cars.

The ring had been rented from a local wrestling federation. It was the size of those that the WWE used, and a good five feet wider on either side than what we were used to. Immediately, we dumped our bags and coats, and began getting used to the differences. This ring had a plastic sheet instead of canvas, which made most of us lose our footing. The ropes were also looser than what we were used to, with the apron set higher.

A stout man walked in, smoking a joint. He welcomed us: 'It's a party, David-Lynch style; the audience will drift into this room and then there will be you! A spectacular! Until then this is your home – help yourself to beer and Red Bull – but after eleven you need to stay in the dressing room.'

He pointed over to a room accessible through a tiny wooden door. Inside was a red-velvet boudoir with beds everywhere and soft lighting. There was no food or water, just two fridges stacked with beer, Red Bull and bottles of gin. We walked around the rest of the building for an hour or so, exploring the party venue. There was a room full of branches lit like a forest; another was a pure-white bar filled with life-size farm animals painted white. Later, it transpired that the unassuming stout guy was the one who was holding the party, in honour of a friend's birthday. He also happened to be the richest drug dealer in Berlin.

We spent as much time getting used to the ring as we could, and then we went into another part of the building for a sprawling German banquet. I managed to translate everything on the menu. This proved particularly helpful for Cara Noir, the Black Swan, who was a personal trainer with a love of computer games and a fear of heights. More importantly, he only ate meat and raw vegetables. The only thing he could find to eat that met his dietary requirements was schnitzel, without the breadcrumbs, and a salad, no dressing. The waiter looked offended. Meanwhile, the rest of us ordered plates of flat noodles covered in cream; a massive platter of salad made up of cheese, salami and fruit; and we had beer – a lot of beer.

It felt like a cross between a lads-on-tour holiday and a school trip as we sampled 'genuine' German cuisine. The resemblance to any other holiday I'd been on changed when, at eleven, we were whisked into the room we now referred to as the 'luxury sex dungeon', where we waited in our costumes.

The waiting before a show is always the worst bit. You have no choice but to go through your moves and also think about all the things that could possibly go wrong. Rosa had to pee about ninety times, and there was still nothing in the room to drink except the Red Bull, beer and gin. After we'd been kept waiting for two hours, every single person except Cara Noir had given in and had booze. We all agreed we were being unprofessional, but we were also trapped in a carpeted room, waiting to put on a two-match show in front of what we imagined would be a room of people on drugs. We were correct.

The wrestling was given no introduction; we simply followed Freddie Mercurio out to 'I Want to Break Free' and made our way to the ring. The Germans love Queen and this was the best possible way to get everyone on side. I leered in people's faces, touching their shoulders, even licking one girl on the face (this is what gin and Red Bull do to a person). The match itself was a collection of easy moves: all I had to do was give someone a low blow and then take a dropkick off Rosa. I was pleased about this arrangement because as soon as I ran the ropes, I realised drinking and wrestling was a terrible idea.

Thankfully, no one got hurt, though Fraser fell off the ring. There was one point when Cara Noir jumped into the audience and was caught, like a baby, by a seven-foot-tall woman, who just placed him back inside and told him she wanted another fight.

It was all over in twenty minutes, which was our allocated time slot. The audience was then herded through to the white room, while we went back to get changed – to find our dressing room was filling with people who were about to watch an intimate jazz quartet. We ended up stashing our gear behind the bar and joining the party.

There aren't too many memories of that party. They played Madonna, and Cassius went mad, screaming, 'Oh my God, it's like we're in *Skins*!'

I begged the barman for something without Red Bull in it, and all he could muster was warm, neat gin, so that's what I drank. To this day I still don't understand why he insisted on giving it to me without ice or a slice, or anything. My only memory after this point is of riding a white cow through a crowd of topless people. Apparently we all went to a shisha bar afterwards, but I can only remember the alarm going off for our return flight at six in the morning. I was determined to have the continental breakfast, most of which made me feel sick and which included dishes such as ham wrapped around melon. The others, apart from Cara Noir and Freddie, were all still drunk.

We stumbled through security, where I had to remind everyone to remove their sunglasses, and somehow, *somehow*, we all got back to London in one piece – thirty hours later and each a hundred quid better off.

The year passed into summer again. The Gallery ticked along slowly, never quite gaining in popularity, but with the numbers of the school and Lucha tickets staying constant. Every month I performed as Rana, and without fail I would be doing the same match between the same four women. While this did become frustrating, it also meant we could experiment a lot more with the story, such as choking out Rosa with cake on her birthday. At one point Tigressa got injured so we started bringing in random men to each match – 'Rosa's choice'. It was almost always Cassius, so half our matches became dance-offs and twerk-based spots.

We toured music festivals in June, driving in convoy to Bournemouth to a particularly poorly attended festival where the Buzzcocks were headlining. We spent most of the day walking about in our costumes and having our pictures taken with mums who were tipsy on daytime cider with fake flowers in their hair. When it came to our time to wrestle, we drew more of a crowd than the headliner. One of the wrestlers had sunstroke so I pulled 'double duty' and wrestled twice wearing two different masks, which was simultaneously exhausting and exhilarating.

The hard parts, I suppose, were the ways in which Lucha was embroiled with the same tensions that faced a typical extended family. The fact was that, a year after the fire, the Gallery was still struggling to get by each month. The place was still, after all, primarily meant to be a gallery – not a music venue nor a wrestling gym – and this meant that it was hard to attract the right clientele. A few times, we turned up for training and there would be no power because the bill hadn't been paid. We would end up training in the park opposite, or in the worst case scenarios, all go to the cinema or the pub.

Members of the roster argued, and as a result, some left. There was a lot of disdain about Lucha from wrestlers who also worked on 'proper' shows, where no one wore masks, and where the bookings (known as the 'card') were decided months in advance. These wrestlers tried to build up storylines and rivalries that Vanderhorne would often nay-say, so they just started doing them anyway. We gained a new female member to the roster, Dragonita, a quiet but dedicated Spanish wrestler who had moved to the UK to work in Sainsbury's and learn *lucha*. This meant we now had four women again, and we went back to having the same old matches.

The strain was getting to Greg and Vanderhorne, who began lashing out at those closest to them. Santeria, the zombie, left because he was tired of not knowing who he would be fighting until an hour before the doors opened. Necrosis left to be a full-time fetish circus performer with his burlesque star partner. He was replaced by another Necrosis, a consultant for a bug tech firm, who also ended up leaving soon after, due to family commitments.

Tigressa, after months of investigations, was told she could no longer wrestle because she had a weak area at the back of her skull that was giving her migraines whenever she turned upside down. There were others who came and went, and we missed them. We would continue to turn up at training and at shows, and do our jobs, waiting for Vanderhorne to tell us his problems before giving us a roll of sweaty tenners as payment.

Things are never as glamorous from the other side, but I still couldn't explain the rush I would get when I landed a move, and when I glared into the audience, or surprised myself with my own skill. Wrestling had given me a confidence that I wanted to own, and it had also given me a partner. It gave me the confidence to quit my job at the auction house, and surprisingly, after mentioning Lucha in an interview, I managed to get a higher paid job for a leading women's charity. This was a proper job with rights, a contract, central heating, and windows to look out of.

But more than anything, wrestling had stopped London from swallowing me up. It was here that I inhabited a world I never could have imagined when I was growing up in the arse end of nowhere. I wasn't in the rat race, but I was running alongside it, trying to make every show I did bigger and better than the one before. Half the time I would complain about the commute, or the cost of living, or the difficulty of crossing the river after 9pm, but still I loved London. I would find myself walking its streets – the gleaming tourist traps of Chelsea; the cleaning-down of market stalls on early evenings in Whitechapel; the hilly, Victorian terraced streets of New Cross – and I would feel alive in that moment. There was a strange comfort in not being observed, and in no one realising that I could put on a mask and throw a man twice my weight over my head. In London, I became just another person entering an underground station who looked like they knew where they were going.

But that's just it, even with the glory days of wrestling: you are not sure why you are doing it, or where it's going. You are just doing it because wrestling makes you feel alive. It gives you an identity and a skill that is fleeting, and has no purpose other than to bring both you and the audience joy.

All wrestlers know we have a brief window to live this type of life, and I was clutching to it more than anything I had lived through before.

7

The Womb Witch

I sustained numerous injuries during the first few years of my wrestling career. The minor concussions gained when first learning to bump are countless, but one day at training I landed fully on my head and had to take two days off work because I couldn't keep food down or look at lights.

Shortly before I became Rana, I gained something called a 'stringer', a trapped nerve in my neck. I had landed oddly and wrenched the muscle so that sometimes it would go into spasm, and the only way to soothe it was by holding ice on my neck and cranking my head to one side. It took about two weeks for it to go away, during which I couldn't turn my head or look down without wincing.

As a frog, I was expected to learn the 'frog splash' – a dive from the top rope, which involved a flourish in mid-air, then landing neatly on your opponent. Three wrestlers on the roster could do a beautiful frog splash, but despite being the frog, I could never complete the move. I always struggled, mainly because the first time I attempted it without a crash mat I winded myself and landed on both my big toes, breaking them. There is nothing you can do for broken toes except wear comfortable shoes and pray no one steps on your foot. They took about two months to heal, and it didn't help that I kept being told off for doing press-ups on my knees, so probably rebroke them a couple of times during training.

The second time Cassandro came to train with us, I had graduated to wrestling at Lucha, yet I was still inexperienced. I worked hard to impress him, but messed up big time when taking a 'flap jack' – where a wrestler picks you up by your legs and you fall forward as they fall backwards. Rule number one with bumping is to never, ever put your arms out straight when falling forwards, and for some reason I did exactly that. My right arm took all my body weight, popping the elbow in and out of the socket. I was lucky it wasn't broken, but it swelled to the size of a grapefruit and I had to wear a support on it for a year. To add insult to (literal) injury, Cassandro told me to 'toughen the fuck up' again, and I cried.

The dislocated elbow also developed into a gross abscess called bursitis, where the sac which protects the joint fills with fluid and pus, and grows to the size of a small egg. There was no cartilage left at the point, so if I came down too hard on it, the nerves would take a jolt, similar to the sensation of hitting your funny bone – times eighty.

But I came off lightly for injuries. Rosa trapped a nerve in her hip, which meant she had to have physio for about a year, and was told she would never be able to do the splits again. She also lost her voice during one match, when she dislocated her shoulder. She was unable to tell her opponent about her injury, but put the shoulder 'back in' – so her opponent assumed she was selling, and dislocated it again twice before the match was over.

Steakley also had a shoulder that would just pop out sometimes. He would swear a lot until someone, usually Jerry, would pop it back in.

McBitch was unable to wrestle after she was dropped on her leg badly during a night out and messed up the knee forever. She also broke her finger in three places and it had to be pinned.

But no one died.

In my body, beneath the sudden appearance of abdominal muscles that had shocked everyone, including myself, I started to develop an ongoing issue that would define my life, and my wrestling career, forever. I refer to this cacophony of gynaecological problems simply as 'the Womb Witch'. She is my nemesis, my main-event title bout. It's easier for me to see her as an opponent I can beat when the reality is that I couldn't beat her then, and I still can't now.

I am one of those lucky women who started having their periods aged eleven. When it happened my mum bought me a hamster as a present – the hamster of fecundity.

She, of course, didn't tell me that I had genetically 'bad' periods. I was the girl at school with the super tampons in my bag. When Mum left, it fell to my dad to try to talk me out of my monthly fits of suicidal gloom. He used to drive six miles to the nearest 24-hour shop to buy me a Snickers.

At university, I encountered a plethora of birth-control suggestions. I went on the pill aged sixteen to 'sort my skin out'. I asked to come off it in my second term of university, and it says a lot that I felt I needed a doctor's permission. To avoid the risk of pregnancy (and quite rightly because, as previously discussed, my university discoveries, good and bad, were mainly made through my vagina), they suggested giving me an implant – a weird little piece of plastic that I was told would basically play whale sounds to my ovaries to stop pregnancy. Actually, the implant made me have a period for three months, which they then tried to counteract by putting me on the micro-pill to 'calm me down'.

At some point, my friends marched me down to the women's clinic to sort out my messed-up hormonal balance. This is the same hormonal balance that may or may not have contributed to my fun-ass suicide attempt, aged twenty. I had a coil fitted, which meant no worries for the next five years. I kind of imagined my womb during this time as a storage facility watched over by one of those hovering guard-droids you see in sci-fi films. Things seemed okay except for the weird pains that would just appear, for shits and giggles, about a week before my period. But when I asked the GP about this, I was told it was normal.

So I carried on, and then I discovered wrestling, where period pains were just a part of life, along with muscle ache from training, and the occasional busted body part. Wrestling, because it is about contact and toughness, respects people who can withstand pain.

The stories of our heroes are about those who carried on through a match with a broken ankle, or who returned to the ring after several knee surgeries. Wrestlers, in short, don't retire, and in the twenty-first century they have justified the fact that they are professional purveyors of fake violence by having a 'no excuses' attitude to training and performing.

It is hard to explain to people that we find pain – in a masochistic way, I suppose – a point of pride. There is good pain, when you have pushed your muscles to the point that they are bursting for growth, or you have trained so hard that you ache all over. To be injured and in recovery does not mean lying on the sofa; it means doing one-footed push-ups, or avoiding certain moves but still performing. I have one friend who broke her ankle and who lied about her doctor's advice for six months so that she could continue to wrestle.

Wrestlers are dumb, and they are stubborn, and we never, ever, like to give up.

With this attitude in mind, and also the fact that around me my wrestling family was on edge, I ignored the fact that my periods began to hurt even more.

In April 2015, I remember a sudden, sharp period pain that wouldn't go away. I felt that my coil might have moved, so I left work to go to an emergency clinic. They assured me it was exactly where it needed to be, and advised me to see my GP.

The pain continued and then ten days later my period arrived. Throughout this time I trained. I tried to sit out anything particularly risky, but it always seemed to happen on the days where I was the only woman present, and without fail it would be a night when one of the handful of twats who trained there would be around. One wrestler delightedly asked me if I was sitting out because of my period, and when I said my coil might have moved, he went a funny colour.

Burridge told me that I should use the rage to become a better wrestler, so I tried to laugh it off. I was surrounded by people who had injuries and aches, and they all should definitely not have been wrestling. Burridge had a metal pin in his leg but he still trained four nights a week; Vanderhorne had recurring back problems that he ate painkillers for, and he was also lactose intolerant, but, of course, couldn't turn down pizza. It was the life of a wrestler – to carry on regardless, to ignore doctor's orders, and to try not to get addicted to pain pills.

But the Womb Witch wasn't familiar territory for Vanderhorne and Greg; it wasn't like I'd taken a move badly or hadn't rested an injury – it was something they couldn't relate to or understand, even if I had been able to tell them what was causing it. As time dragged on, I found that at the office, on the tube, at home on the sofa, in the ring – it didn't matter – I would get these very intense menstrual cramps, which were unaccompanied by bleeding. I began to be in pain three weeks out of four, and I became tired, irritable and constantly anxious.

My GP told me it was IBS and gave me some tablets, which didn't help. Then she gave me some mefenamic acid, which didn't help either. Eventually, she requested I had an ultrasound; the appointment took two months to come through. In the meantime, she told me I shouldn't wrestle. When I asked her if she thought wrestling and the pain were related, she told me that they didn't seem to be, but that wrestling wasn't good for the body.

I decided that, going forwards, I would just ignore doctors' opinions regarding my wrestling. Ultimately, the pain was something to do with my ovaries or womb, and last time I checked there weren't any moves in wrestling that affected this. But just to be on the safe side, I started a regime of Kegels, pelvic floor exercises, which actually seemed to help. Whenever I was in pain I would lie on my back and stick my vag in the air (a tool that, unsurprisingly, I could not use in the office).

The vaginal ultrasound is exactly what it says on the tin: you are taken to a lovely little room where new parents get to see their small beans wriggling in their stomachs for the first time, while other women get told they have ovarian cancer.

Fraser came with me, making jokes about how this was all a bit soon, but it was okay if it turned out we were having some kind of alien child, which would be a fitting tribute to our love.

I'm not sure he was expecting to be sitting next to me while a nurse casually lubed up the ultrasound wand and whacked it right up me. And announced, 'Oh, it's a cyst. An ovarian cyst; very common, nothing to worry about.'

My first reaction was: 'Can I keep a picture of it?'

'Why?'

'Just to show people—'

'Like a baby,' added Fraser.

'No, sorry, that's not something we offer.'

All the while, the nurse was moving the vag wand about. Then she nudged the cyst and it was like a wave of lightning; the urge to vomit and cramps shot through my body. I screamed.

'Gosh, sorry, it must be... about the size of... a small melon.'

All three of us looked at the screen, where there was no tiny human, like you see on hospital programmes. Instead, there was a blob that shouldn't have been there. I wanted to ask if it was cancer, or a twin that I'd ingested in the womb. Or cancer. Was it cancer?

But it seemed inappropriate to put this question to a woman with a metal wand shoved up my vagina. Once the wand was removed, and having mustered up the courage to ask her, the answer was worse than I'd anticipated.

'Your guess is as good as mine, but it needs to come out.'

I suppose what people are thinking at this point is, well, that sounds awful, but it's totally common. One of Fraser's male relatives even had the gall to tell me, 'It isn't that bad at all, a tiny procedure.' This is indicative of my entire experience since first discovering the Womb Witch, and her campaign to kill me.

Despite an awareness of my painful periods and my ability to grow a beard since my early teens, no one had told me about the joys of Polycystic Ovary Syndrome (PCOS). When I was younger, the sum total of my knowledge of my own ovaries was twofold. Firstly, I was educated in the form of the vivid and pantomime-esque 'sex talk' at my middle school, where aged ten, all the girls in my year were shepherded into a hall and told what periods were. The teachers brought in an external expert, who gave a talk called 'Nits, Tits and Dangly Bits' in attempt to make puberty less ominous to us and our parents.

We were told that a period was something natural and not

something to be scared of. We were then promptly given a large bag of sanitary towels and sent on our merry way. This led to many whispered conversations with friends, never boys, and occasionally with my mum. Periods were not something to be discussed. Mine arrived without much trouble at first, but soon descended into cosmic fits of doom once a month. They were regularly so heavy that I would bleed through a tampon in a morning and spend the rest of the day horribly aware of how much dried blood was there, waiting to become visible, on my school trousers.

The second point I learned about ovaries was in a biology lesson when I was fourteen. The nature of how foetuses are formed and why periods happened was explained to us – three years after the joyful process had begun in earnest for me. The ovaries in my workbook were these passive blobs that produced big, fat, floating eggs that swam down tubes and into the womb, like a middle-aged woman floating in one of those rubber rings at Center Parcs.

Unless we make a point of telling girls otherwise, we don't assume that this placid, natural event in our bodies might go horribly wrong. There was no pamphlet given to us that said: 'What you should do if your periods go to fuck.'

My periods calmed down when I went on the pill, aged sixteen. It would have been useful to have known earlier that I could go to the GP about them, but this would only have happened if I'd have realised that, you know, my periods were particularly bad. Sitting here now, with the gift of hindsight on my shoulder, I know this absence of knowledge and awareness around periods needs to change. (The gift of hindsight is actually a furious goblin, covered in menstrual blood, screaming 'THE PATRIARCHY' at my screen while I type, but I will try to mute that goblin as this is primarily a book about wrestling.)

However, what I need to say is that in no wrestling books to date have female wrestlers spoken about their periods. They do not point out the fact that women train just as hard as men, but have the added bonus of a monthly hydrogen bomb of oestrogen to contend with. In theory it should make us better warriors, but it also makes you go to the toilet and cry if you can't do a shoulder roll correctly.

However, by the time 'Cystelia' (the growth now had a name) arrived in my life, one thing I could rely on to make me feel better was wrestling. Being able to carry on with this... thing... living inside me, while I was scanned or prodded or tested every other week, gave me some medium of control over my own body. I was a size ten who could squat a man twice her size. I could pretend I wasn't the same person who walked into the gynaecologists, weeping about the pain and the waiting time and lying awake at night in fear of my results.

While this was going on, Lucha was starting to spring back into life. Juventud Guerrero, a Mexican ex-WWE *luchador*, trained with us for a month and taught me how to bend over backwards and balance on my head.

I took my violent cabaret troupe, the SLITs, on even more adventures. We performed three times at a festival with an act that was a battle royale between Disney princesses. I was Queen Elizabeth I, bursting in near the end and cutting a promo on those 'fictional bitches'. The finale was me giving Marie Antoinette a backbreaker after she had choked everyone else out with brioche.

The week I got my surgery date and the hypothesis (a borderline tumour that was to be whipped out with keyhole surgery), I finally told Vanderhorne and Greg about the cyst. Greg was angry I hadn't told them. In a typically direct and unarguably truthful way, he said, 'It could have burst.' Whereas Vanderhorne called it 'the potato that must die'.

The cyst was in fact the size of a large sweet potato – one of those weird, long ones. While I was waiting for surgery, I kept one on my bedside table, a bit like a mother expecting a child, measuring the size of the foetus by comparing it with a vegetable. It was there to remind me that the pain had a cause. It was not my imagination, not some age-old genetic misfortune, but a thing inside me – and soon it would be gone and I'd have my life back.

Ten days before surgery, I wrestled my last match at a Day of the Dead festival in East London's Tobacco Docks. It was a corporate gig, and Mexican cultural consumption at its height.

Fraser and I arrived before anyone else. We got through security by putting on our masks and the security guard waved us through as soon as he'd taken a selfie with us. Our ring was set up in a beautiful space surrounded by flowers and sugar skulls. The stalls around us were selling churros and every kind of Frida Kahlo item you could imagine. Hundreds of people were in Day of the Dead make-up, and you could hear the foodies talking about their trips to Mexico last year amidst a backdrop of artworks borrowed from the Saatchi gallery. Cynical as I was, I also felt myself smiling under my gross frog mask as I wandered around, bearing my teeth for the occasional picture.

How had I come to be in this place full of colour and nonsense? I thought to myself. More importantly, why had my body co-operated in being thrown around a ring, but then suddenly decided to come along and screw it all up for me?

Slowly the rest of the Lucha family trickled in – Tigressa, Cassius, Freddie Mercurio – and to my shock, Juventud Guerrero, too. We had two shows during the day, and we began our backstage rituals in a dressing room that was five times the size of the one we were usually crammed into once a month.

Wrestlers all have something they do to get ready for a match. Some will sit in the corner in a hoodie, plugged into music, eyes shut, getting psyched up, and remembering the moves they'd practised recently. Others will pace around, muttering the match moves under their breath. Tigressa would always stretch like a dancer. Fraser would chat away, happily, to whoever was free. Juventud was complaining about the food, or the lack of, which I appreciated because we were at a food festival. My ritual was always to sit to one side, trying to hold on to the moment before the storm so that I could recollect it one day; maybe even write about it.

We walked out through the crowd at noon. There were no introductions that day, and no backstage to hide in. The ring was free standing and a mere five-minute walk from the dressing room. The ring girls strutted either side of Vanderhorne, who was wearing his referee mask. Cassius had the belt, and he waved and beckoned the crowd in to follow us, which many did. The rest of us walked in character. Fraser had recently been re-cast from a bar man to a monkey and he danced about in snug, furry pants and a tail (we were all concerned his balls would fall out, as they had done a few times at Lucha shows). Tigressa prowled ahead, while Rana naturally snarled and blew kisses to the staring crowd, many of them on their second mojito.

My first bout was with Tigressa, who had come out of retirement. By that point I had worked with her so many times that we should, by rights, have been able to have a match without speaking. I went straight in with a bear hug, with kicks and blows to take her off her feet. She wouldn't go down, however. Instead, she took my wrist in a clever reversal from a punch, and went to jump off the ropes into a cross body, but lost her footing and fell into the crowd.

I followed and beat her back into the ring, muttering, 'Give me something then I'll cut you off.'

But she stayed down, slumped, not fighting. I kicked her a

few times and pinned her. She kicked out at the count of two, and I looked up at the crowd hoping she would pull in some encouragement. I found myself thinking of horrid things to do to her fingers and hair and eyes that would make the audience gasp and boo. Eventually she stood up and went for a comeback, which involved dropkicks then a hurricane DDT. I took them all, but then was back on my feet too soon.

What wrestlers fear in a wrestling match is a dead space, where you 'kill the crowd'. If wrestling is a story, killing a crowd is like giving away a plot twist too early on, or brushing over a huge cliffhanger when you begin the next chapter in a book. It means losing the momentum, or the feel, of why you are doing a move, and of why you are even fighting an opponent. Killing the crowd happens when suddenly the audience goes from booing, cheering and paying attention, to just a distracted mutter; a crowd who clearly don't care any more who wins or loses.

In a show that was billed as a spectacular of skill and violence, Tigressa and I had lost our momentum. Luckily, there were two more matches with dropkicks and flips. Fraser even dove off a twenty-foot-high balcony. But both Tigressa and I knew we could have done better. Looking back now, we were both injured and unsure of the strength of our own bodies when they used to be indestructible.

I still remember blaming myself so violently, the 'no excuses' mantra rolling around my head. Vanderhorne said 'well done' in a distracted way as we trooped back to the dressing room, gasping in our masks, and desperate for water. When we had shut the door everyone took off their masks, and Tigressa sat on the floor and cried. I put my arm around her and then quickly reached into my bag to take a codeine for the fire raging up from my pelvic floor. I lay on the floor, in the vag-to-sky position, my hips pushed up towards the air like a table top.

Feeling rejuvenated, I came up to her and asked, 'What happened?'

She sniffed and muttered something about falling off the rope, and then forgetting the rest of the match. Juventud overheard us and spoke directly.

'That's not what happened! Yeah sure, it was bad but you can cover it up... you just had no fight in you; like, you didn't look at the audience. Every time she hit you, you just took it. The audience need to see fight from their hero or they won't care that you're getting beaten up. You need to do that in the next match, okay? You're lucky because you get to do it again and change everyone's minds.'

I leant over and rubbed Tigressa's shoulders in comfort. I totally understood. I mean, I often felt like bursting into tears after matches but somehow I always seemed to forget about it by the next training session. Taking into consideration, though, the fact that she was worried about her migraines, and that I had an alien egg inside me, it seemed like it might have been a good time for a pep talk. Juventud turned to me and said, 'You were good – you were horrible.'

'I aim to please.'

But my body had given up. An hour later the pain was still bad, and I told the others. The next show, I was in a six-person *lucha*-chaos match at the start; all I had to do was give Tigressa a couple of kicks, catch a dive in a crowd of three others, and then do a 'cunt-drop' finish, which I had graduated to being able to do from the top rope. I didn't want to risk a repeat of the disappointment Tigressa had felt, though. My own heart soared when she jumped off the rope and the crowd went wild. But the pain pulsed up my lower back, and I got pinned by Fraser and left the ring, making a solo limp back to the changing rooms.

Three drunk men asked me for a selfie: 'Look, Jeremy Corbyn is over there, and we'd rather have a picture with you than him!' (Naturally I went up to Corbyn afterwards, and somewhere on the internet there is a picture of him looking confused while a sweating frog woman grins at his shoulder.)

As soon as I was back in the dressing room, I bent to a crawl and lay on my back, ignoring the vat of guacamole that had miraculously appeared, along with three plastic bags full of corn chips. I took off my mask, now cold and sopping with the sweat of a day's wrestling, and let my body sink into the floor. It was as if until now I hadn't accepted that I was ill. The reality hit me, now, like a wave. It was as if the parasite in my body had decided, finally, to become a physical entity, and not simply 'the Womb Witch'.

Fraser and I got home at midnight. I lay on the sofa while he made us tea and filled a hot water bottle. The familiar buzz of adrenaline left my body and filled my ears, and my joints were aching, reminding me that I had been thrown to the floor countless times. I had misplaced an elbow drop and was developing a purple, egg-sized bruise.

'I don't know when I'm going to wrestle again,' I thought aloud.

Fraser sat next to me and handed me a mug. 'You probably should have stopped ages ago, but you didn't because you're tough.'

'What if that was the last time I wrestle, though? What if it goes wrong, or they find something, and then... I don't know what.'

'That won't happen, you're a honey badger; you'll be back training again in no time.'

We held each other, neither of us acknowledging that we were both unsure if this was true. Fraser probably thought about the weeks ahead, and his vibrant, loud girlfriend being cut open, the cyst then being identified as cancer. I thought about whether they would talk about wrestling at my funeral, the crowning achievement in my life. I hadn't realised up until that point that not getting back into the ring would be the most heartbreaking thing in the world.

The week before my surgery I was off work, and in that week I didn't get out of bed much. My family called and would regale me in hushed, secretive tones about how both my mother and grandmothers had suffered with periods so bad that they sometimes wouldn't be able to leave the house. I even discovered that my grandmother had a cyst the size of a watermelon removed when she was in her seventies. These women had also just carried on, admittedly not by continuing their wrestling or weightlifting careers, but by pretending it wasn't happening. I was lucky I could be open about it, in comparison to previous generations of people with ovaries that had to deal with this kind of shit as deeply private, and therefore as if it were their own fault.

When I admitted to people I had a cyst and I was going to have surgery, countless women messaged me on social media, or even came up to me at work, and told me their own 'cyst story'. Few of them were positive. The worst one was when a friend came round and told me in detail about how her cyst had burst and given her a liver infection, and that later she ended up having to have more surgery and a blood transfusion. Someone even told me about a woman that she knew who had got a skin-eating disease in hospital and had died in follow up surgery. (Note to all readers – never, ever share these kinds of horror stories with someone who is about to have an operation.)

I was terrified and furious. I had been healthy, covered in muscles and ready to break out of a railway arch in Bethnal Green into the wider world of wrestling. This blob of matter that was causing me so much pain could possibly take this future away from me, and for no reason other than my body messing up the simple process of getting an egg from one place to another.

The surgery itself went well. When I came to, the surgeon was there, smiling. She explained that the cyst had burst inside me, meaning it wasn't cancer, but that they had found a lot of endometriosis, which had been removed. I was flying around on morphine, and wasn't even shocked when I realised that they had gone through my belly button to get the cyst out (like the scene where they implant the bug in *The Matrix*). She didn't tell me what endometriosis was, or perhaps I didn't give her the chance due to my being so high on drugs. I merely thanked her as if she'd just prepared me a lovely dinner.

Endometriosis, like PCOS, is an incurable and common disease. The cells in your body begin to emulate the function of the cells of a womb lining. These cells fill with blood and goodness, expecting to feed a growing foetus, and every month, when they haven't been used, they make a crimson exit. Endometrial cells outside the womb also absorb and thicken, pushing into parts of the body where they are not supposed to be. They form in patches, anywhere from your abdominal muscles, to vital organs, such as the lungs or the bladder.

I think of these patches as if they were black mould that's spreading in the corners of a bathroom. Or like Japanese knotweed, pushing out and strangling everything around it. Inside my body, these patches had been burned off when my cyst was removed. But they would, almost definitely, come back. This information was shared with me, two days later, by a pamphlet that someone had slipped into my discharge papers.

God bless the NHS, and God bless the fact I didn't have to pay for the privilege of this surgery. It was 17 December, just before Christmas. In reality, quite a good time to be off work and to be ferried around between events consisting mainly of eating. My mum visited and I insisted I was fine going to the pub, where I had a pint and ate a burger. Soon after, I turned white as a sheet and had to go sleep for four hours. Fraser and I had our first Christmas together, where we ate a leg of lamb in our underwear, ripping it off the bone with our teeth like Vikings.

By January, I was up and moving around again, and aside from three tiny scars that were like kitten whiskers, and a lot of splodgy bruising around my pubic bone, I was perfectly healed. I passed my post-operative appointment with flying colours and was told to come back in two months. Ten weeks after surgery, I returned to the Gallery and started to train again. But things had changed.

All wrestlers leave a promotion or stop eventually, but it's a lengthy process. Most wrestlers love being in the ring so much that they will wrestle for a show they actively dislike countless times before they move on.

While I had been away, Dragonita had left. She went to Japan where she wrestled in front of huge crowds. The three remaining female wrestlers had performed the same 'ladies match' several times in a row. All three times Tigressa had won. On my first Lucha event since coming back, I could feel that the excitement had started to dwindle in the locker room.

Things were tight, and the Gallery had almost gone bust. Sometimes there wasn't enough money for everyone to get paid. On Juventud's birthday, before he left to go back to Mexico, he had called for an open bar. Somehow the thirty or so people who stayed on after the show managed to drink all the stock, with not a penny going into the till.

A queer club night had ended with the police being called because someone had kicked down a door in the toilets and had to be dragged out by Greg. The police noted not only that the bar was open past its licensed hours, but that there weren't enough fire exits for 200 people.

Vanderhorne, under all this stress, had ruptured a disc in his back. He couldn't work, he couldn't teach, and the bins at the front of the building constantly overfilled, giving him anxiety about another fire. There was a period where training started to become a chore, and you never knew if you would be there with your friends. This was a place that relied on friendships, and that had literally been held together by these bonds, shared sweat and gaffer tape. If you weren't seeing friends, you were doing punishing drills, during which, no matter how hard we pushed ourselves, our teachers wouldn't look up from their phones as they were trying to make ends meet and keep their relationships alive. We came to expect regular 'Burridge Bollockings', when Greg would rip into us for the smallest of things – whether it was leaving empty water bottles around or not doing shoulder rolls perfectly.

Janey was in a faction called 'The Army of Darkness', which was now just her – Santeria and Necrosis having left of their own accord. Without a reason to be a zombie, Janey decided to do a new character, 'Psycho Lolita', a schoolgirl with an obsession with violence. This was shot down, so she stopped coming to training, a huge blow for the few new female recruits that joined over the months I was away. Meanwhile, Tigressa's health didn't improve. Every time she was unwell, she would be told she was making excuses and that if she didn't want to be treated the same as everyone else, she should stop wrestling; she'd end up walking out in tears. Diablesa and I would look at the floor and not know what to say. By May, Rosa and I were the only women left in the show, but at least I was back in the ring again.

My first match back was a singles match against Fraser,

which should have been perfect but which my severe case of 'ring rust' led me to perform terribly.

Yet it wasn't all gloom, and the atmosphere at training changed slightly with an influx of new people. One later became Muñeca de Trapo – an outspoken feminist acrobat and performance artist, who had seen Lucha, and like me, had made the decision to try to get involved in this world she knew nothing about. I realised I could pick her up and base her complicated but impressive moves. I made a huge effort to get back to my former shape, learning a few new moves but mainly letting others tell me what I should do, hoping it would get me back up to the speed of where I'd left off.

There were also a lot of younger trainees, almost all of them male, who had come from a few other schools across London. For the most part they were nice – overly enthusiastic if anything – but it did mean that some of the wrestlers who had been there longer were unnecessarily cynical about them. A kind of hierarchy formed between students, the ones who were 'proper' wrestlers and the rest. I found myself grouped with the 'strawbs' (newbies) because I'd never performed outside Lucha, which I was fine with at training, but backstage at the main shows my imposter syndrome got out of control.

It's never meant to be unkind, yet wrestlers will tease each other relentlessly. The prickliness of a tense and machismo changing room started to make me lose my enjoyment of wrestling. In the ring I would forget my moves and end up standing about like a lemon, much to the admonishment of Burridge.

Three months in a row, though, I would see delighted faces in the crowd as I came out and continued to perform at the Gallery, where everyone knew my character. This crowd would make all the right noises, booing and hissing at me, and probably didn't notice when my foot slipped on a rope or I didn't move out the way of an opponent's move in time. But as soon as I was up the stairs, panting, a trickle of blood coming from… somewhere… I'd receive a nod at most from the other wrestlers. I would still get words of encouragement from a select few who were trying to teach me, like Fraser or Nordico Fuego, or Cassius, who was retaining his championship belt in the face of a similar onslaught of criticism. But for the most part, there would be snickers and snatches of jokes aimed at my half-turned back from the 'proper' wrestlers. These men didn't see a woman trying to improve her wrestling, but an imposter who was yet another example of why Lucha, as a promotion, was going to the dogs.

Maybe I was taking it too personally, but there weren't enough people encouraging me to make the good outweigh the bad.

Little by little, the pain came back. At first, it made itself known in the form of period pain the week before I started to bleed. Soon, it was a daily gripping around my belly button and womb, just as it had been before. Four months after surgery, my GP recommended I stop wrestling for two weeks, take it easy and see what difference that made. She also emailed my gynaecologist. I stopped for two weeks, but the pain didn't go; it was still there, unchanged. I went back to wrestling because it was clearly not the cause.

Just as before, I felt drained. I was in a state of disbelief: how could this weird thing still be happening to my body, even though whatever had been causing it had apparently been removed? I became something of a recluse. I saved my energy for training once or twice a week, and the rest of the time I read and drank wine. I was, I can confirm, depressed.

Then something particularly unpleasant happened at training. I was using the toilet when I overheard a conversation between two 'proper' wrestlers, both having a shit in opposite cubicles. They weren't my friends, but it was unmistakeable who they were talking about.

'She's rotten, but at least she isn't trying to get booked anywhere else.'

'They just need to keep in some token vaginas. Rosa's great, though; I don't understand how she can be so good while the Rana Banana is so rubbish.'

'It's because Rosa gets it. She actually knows wrestling; Heather thinks it's fucking performance art.'

'Yeah, well, that's the bollocks Vanderhorne puts in their heads, isn't it?'

I didn't pee; instead I just sat and waited on the toilet. What's worse, the smell of protein-heavy shit started to engulf the room. I covered my face as they made some more jokes, flushed (unsuccessfully, one remarked) and left. I had a little cry and then went back out to train. Eventually I missed a move and fell weirdly on my own arm and went home, a scattered heap of self-esteem ashes.

Remember the big match at York Hall that I told you about right at the beginning – where I felt like a queen, and then we took the *luchadores* to a sex party afterwards by accident? That took place a week after the toilet incident happened.

To this day, that show is a beautiful and sacred memory. All the while I was dosed up to my eyeballs on co-codamol – not to stop the ache of wrestling injuries, but to make my womb just stop being there. The adrenaline was enough to get me through. Also seeing the joy of the wrestlers around me, who were all amazed to be wrestling in such a legendary venue. (The two men who'd had a shit in opposite cubicles were absent from proceedings. I was clearly not the only one who didn't like them.)

The week after the match, I received the results of an MRI scan that had been conducted to see whether I had more endometriosis: I didn't, which meant seeing a pain specialist rather than a gynaecologist. The appointments were hard to come by, and mine was two months away. I knew I had no choice but to try to carry on, and I did. Until one fateful night at Lucha.

I was wrestling in the schmoz, a brawl-like fight with a group of wrestlers. Diablesa was now having matches higher up the roster with friends like Cassius and the Bakewells. Even though I was early on the roster, Vanderhorne had decided that I was going to win this particular bout. With ten bodies in a match like this one, getting to the winning point involves a lot of people trying to 'get their shit in' so they leave the biggest impression on the crowd. After I'd suggested a lot of ideas, it was decided that my winning move would be a 'low blow' (a punch to the balls) and a roll-up.

Remembering the buzz of York Hall, I swallowed my ego and did what I thought was the best low blow of my career. At the end of the schmoz – when the winner is usually always crowned with the same crown that survived the fire at the Gallery – I stood waiting for my prize. It was a rusted, metal thing, and the ref that night, Darcy, muttered, genuinely disappointed, 'They forgot the crown, sorry.' No one ever forgot the crown.

But I tried not to take it personally.

Later, when I was getting paid, Vanderhorne told me I'd done great.

Someone said, well-intentioned, 'You'll get a shot at the title before you know it.'

Vanderhorne laughed and said, 'Rana will never get the belt. Even she knows that.'

That is not something you need to hear from anyone. Of course I wanted the belt – and I know Vanderhorne. Looking back on it, he was searching for a spark, for me to argue with him, to convince him otherwise, and to offer to make a comeback. Instead, I took my fifty quid, went home and when Fraser asked me why I'd been completely silent all the way back, I told him that I was going to stop wrestling.

I slept on it, woke up, and announced my retirement from the world of unprofessional wrestling to the world. There was dismay, but no shock or surprise. My womb was trying to kill me, and it seemed like as good a reason as any other.

But, aged twenty-seven, I felt like I needed to look around and find something that wasn't wrestling. For about a week, I'd be able to tell people I was a retired wrestler; then a month later I was a former wrestler, and that quickly turned into I was once 'involved' in wrestling. Then I had to stop trying to mention wrestling altogether. Wrestling was almost like a basement staircase that I was trying to force the door closed on, trapping that part of myself somewhere out of sight so that I could try to forget about it.

8

Pain

Immediately after my telling the world I was going to stop, Vanderhorne tried to change my mind. 'Of course I was joking – you could be the champ by Christmas,' he told me. I held my ground, and explained that as it was, at the moment, my body would never allow me to be that good – I just didn't have the energy to get to the standard I had been at before surgery.

Stopping wrestling is like breaking up with a partner. There was a feeling of regret that pitted in my stomach. I hadn't ever been confident enough in my own ability to flourish. I should have been like Dragonita or Janey or Rosa, and pushed for singles matches and a shot at the title. Instead, I had just followed instructions obediently so that I could make everyone else look amazing – the job of the unprofessional wrestler.

The feelings of regret followed me around so I took down all the pictures I had of me wrestling, and hid them away. I removed my Rana mask from the mannequin head that sat on my dressing table and I stowed it away in a bag under the bed, along with my boots, my kneepads and about six variations of Rana's leotard. I missed my monthly excursion to the Gallery for Lucha; it was only the second time I'd not gone in three years. The first time was to recover from surgery, but now it was because the very idea of standing at the sidelines made me want to cry. Fraser went but came home early out of solidarity. By the time he got back I'd already drunk two bottles of wine, so he found me where I'd passed out on the sofa while playing Viva Piñata. I hadn't paused it, and all my piñatas were dead.

Fraser tried constantly to cheer me up, but I was wallowing.

Becca came round to try to put me on an upward spiral too: 'There was always going to be a day when you wouldn't be able to do this any more. You wouldn't be able to keep wrestling until you're, I dunno, sixty.'

'Mae Young, the greatest wrestler ever, wrestled her last match at eighty-seven.'

'Okay, work with me here, you're not Mae Young.'

I opened my mouth to argue but plugged it with a beer. I wasn't Mae Young. But I did remind myself Mae Young also retired before she was thirty and there was a hiatus of four decades before she got back in the ring. During that time she found, and then renounced, evangelical Christianity; and got off a manslaughter charge when she beat up a rapist in the desert. Even though she stopped wrestling, she was still a badass.

Becca continued, 'Look, you can't just cut this thing out your life like it never happened. You just need to channel it into something else; do things that are... I don't know, not quite so high impact. As soon as people ask you about wrestling, your eye does that twitchy thing when you're trying to think what to say.' She had a point.

The next step in my break-up with wrestling involved a sense of hollowness that I needed to fill with something else, like an equivalent of Tinder. In wrestling terms, it meant starting to write my thoughts and feelings down about everything I hated about wrestling. I embraced the fact that I no longer had to worry about having a six pack (which I had never achieved), and that I wouldn't have to negotiate relationships with the toxic men that I would always end up encountering.

I told myself I was 'over' wrestling, but like many a heart-broken person before and after me, all my willpower shattered. Within a month I was back at the Gallery on the third Friday of the month, pulling on my mask and blacking out my teeth, not to wrestle, but just to be 'involved'.

I was stuck on the door with the ticket list and few instruc-tions. My new job was to welcome the audience to the show as Rana. I would screech about the fire exits, the cash only bar, and then draw cocks on people's hands as a stamp. I took no bumps, but I could drink, and I got paid the same as the wrestlers. When I went backstage a few of the wrestlers would full-on ignore me, but they couldn't say anything else about me now, for I was in my element as an out-of-control frog woman, something I excelled at. The crowd loved it: I was breaking down the fourth wall by not being in the ring, I was a walk-about performer, or something like that.

On paper, I had found the perfect solution to my ennui, but I still dreamt, constantly, about getting back in the ring. And usually, the pain would arrive, gently, when I had these thoughts, as if to reassure me that I would be incapable of ever doing such a thing.

I was trying to find ways to be active, to get out the house. Fuck pilates. Fuck swimming. I could only ever love wrestling.

By the spring, I was waiting to see the pain specialist, having tried nearly everything else: the emergency removal of my IUD, every type of swab ever invented, a biopsy of my womb lining (which I understand they got using something that looked like a ham slicer). I had spent so much time at the Lewisham women's health clinic that I could tell you exactly how many ceiling tiles needed replacing in the waiting room

(fourteen – I even put a note in the feedback box, also request-
ing some kitten pictures on the ceiling to make the experience
less daunting).

The process was gruelling. The fact that the appointments
would always run late, the constant requests for time off work.
The worst thing was at the start of every discussion, when they
would repeat the same sentence: 'So, tell me how this started.'

I described the last year of my life, the decline of my health,
the slow death of my wrestling career, and my increasingly
negative relationship with sex and leaving the house. At first
I would cry when I recounted the sequence of events; by the
sixth or seventh time I just felt numb as I did it.

The appointment with a chronic pain specialist was different; a surgeon shook my hand, but a woman was also sitting
there, who told me she was a therapist. This immediately put
me on edge – I remembered someone telling me once that
it could all be in my head, something even more terrifying
than having a cyst the size of a Furby inside you. They were
both kind faced, though, and they were honest from the outset
that they were the last department I would visit before being
referred for a hysterectomy.

The surgeon let me register this, then continued, 'However,
I think that having a hysterectomy is the last possible solution
for what you're going through. If you went to a private doctor,
which many women do, this would be the first thing they
would suggest. Here, I look at things more holistically. I'm not
saying that I am going to be able to cure your pain, or that you
won't need surgery, but I am going to try and do everything I
can to stop you having your womb removed… Now, tell me
how this started.'

I cried more than I had ever done before; he could tell this
was not the best tack, so he asked me what was happening *now*,
and I basically gave them a five-minute rant about how sad

I was. Every day I was in pain, every single day, and everyone had a theory. Most people told me it was wrestling, so I'd stopped. One colleague dared to imply that they had messed up the surgery, or that they might have missed some of the endometriosis. All I wanted was to have a life where I could do something other than cry, at least once, daily. And, then, of course, I added, 'And get back to wrestling.'

I hadn't realised that I was not only living with the indignity of having a pain that wasn't medically categorised or that appeared untreatable; I was also living with the fact that it had stripped me of something that defined me. And once I admitted this, I suppose like a break-up, I cried it out and realised that it was only me who had imposed the ban, because I didn't know what else to do.

The head shrink and the doc let me cry for as long as I needed, and they both reassured me that I had been going through a draining process and after almost two years of this, anyone would be at their wits' end.

The doc then said, 'You know, Ms Bandenburg, because you're a woman, everyone thinks your issue is in your womb, including you, I believe. What I want to look at is your whole pelvic area – by that I mean the bowels, the stomach, the bladder.'

I was clearly going pale because I *did* have an unreasonable fear of someone looking up my arse hole. He was being, in many ways, very feminist about his approach to my health, though, so I listened.

Then he did the kindest thing a gyny doctor had ever done; he said, 'I'm not going to examine you internally, Ms Bandenburg, because it's clear that whatever signs we could detect in your reproductive organs can be ruled out. I do, however, need to press your stomach.'

I lay on the table, and the head shrink asked if I wanted her to leave, but I told her no. Instead, she maintained eye contact with me and asked me to talk about wrestling. How I got into it, why I loved it, what it meant to me. While the doctor prodded my stomach a bit, with his stethoscope out, I waxed lyrical about the empowerment of being in control of not only your own body, but also the audience. To be able to suspend disbelief, all while channelling a character so entirely different from what you have to do every day.

She smiled; the doctor had finished, but she hadn't. 'And, I suppose, you wrestled until recently, and now you have to look at this *real* person that you were trying to use wrestling to escape from. I can understand how that could be very hard.'

I'm not really sure what happened, but I do remember nodding with wonderment because she had pulled aside a veil. I was sad about not being in front of a crowd; about not being able to move as fast as I had before; about not being introduced as 'the wrestler' to strangers. I missed the ability to slide out of Heather's body, and head, and mannerisms, and fears; and to become someone else. It was not a duality, but a form of escape. And now, forced to stop, I felt imprisoned.

The doc asked me to come and sit back by the desk. Then he said, 'So, how long have you been bloated?'

'I mean, I have a bit of a tummy but that's because I haven't been exercising—'

'Ms Bandenburg, are you aware that your stomach is protruding because your intestines are reacting badly to something? I can assure you that your stomach is mostly muscle, but the bloating, that's what we need to find the root cause of.'

Bloating? I thought bloating was something that happened when you ate two pizzas, or after Christmas dinner. I'd barely had cereal and a cup of tea before my appointment, so how could I be bloated? The doctor started tapping into his computer.

'I want you to do the following. Firstly, record every day when you are in pain; write the time down in a diary, or the times, that you get the pain. I also want you to write down what you eat. I want to recommend that you change a few things about your eating – no dairy, no gluten, nothing too rich. I'm also going to give you some tablets called Buscopan...'

I opened my mouth as if to say, 'it's not stomach pain', but was cut off.

'I appreciate the pain you describe is in your pelvic region, but it's all connected. I am not saying that you'll cut out wheat and all your troubles will go away, but until your stomach is no longer bloated, I don't feel I can proceed further.'

The head shrink also slipped a card into my hand. 'I want you to make an appointment to come and see me. We need to understand your relationship with pain. The fact is that you are describing an alienation from your body, from your sense of self, and we need to rectify that as much as we can. I'm not saying this is caused by stress' – again, she anticipated my cynicism – 'but if you are as sad as you described, it can't be helping one iota.'

I left the pelvic pain specialists, and just before I exited the room, the doctor said, 'Ms Bandenburg, I also want to say that you don't need to give up wrestling; in fact it's important you exercise, but you do need to do it at your own pace. Try to make it less impactful – ask your trainers to go easy on you.'

I smiled, pleased to have a green light – but this guy didn't know that there was no such thing as 'non-impact' wrestling.

Wrestling hurts like hell.

On the bus home, I looked out the window, my eyes dry from a cry-fest at the doctors, something I was used to; but for the first time there was some hope. I thought about what the head shrink had said. If I took up wrestling to gain control of my body again because of being overweight, or unconfident, or a rape survivor – no matter what I was trying to heal, it had worked for a time. I'd managed to claw back some self-esteem by becoming fitter and more confident, standing up to people who criticised my sport and my relationships. But I'd done this by pretending to be a different person; ultimately, I still saw my 'non-wrestling self' as the sum of all my failures.

I needed to realise that I was not an empty vessel that wrestling had filled – that the person behind the mask was not an empty skin that I could grow out of and shed – it was the other way around.

This optimism lasted a grand total of forty-eight hours before I ate a chocolate éclair and found myself in agony. It turns out the doc may have had a point. Though it did seem a great injustice that I now not only had half an ovary missing, but I also couldn't eat cream cakes when they were offered to me.

Out of the blue I got a message from Janey.

'Hey, how are you? Are you free on 3 April to come to an all-female training session? The teachers will be Dragonita and myself. All levels are welcome. It'll be in Mitcham.'

This was followed by a quick message: 'I know you've retired but we would really like you to come down and see what you can do. No one will make you push yourself too far; we are trying to start a new project and I really hope you can be involved with it.'

The doc had told me that wrestling was allowed so long as it was low impact. I wasn't quite prepared to return to Lucha, where, though well meaning, everyone expected you to push past a pain barrier in order to improve. Vanderhorne would always proudly tell the story of when he snapped two tendons in his ankle and finished the best match of his life without stopping once – this was the kind of bravado that I'd come to accept as standard in wrestling. I remembered Janey and her safe, reliable move set, and the fact that no matter who her opponent was, she could always do a match that lasted exactly eight minutes. I thought of Dragonita, and the way she could knock you to the floor with one clothesline, but who was also as easy to move as water.

I had nothing to lose. In fact, as I was prepared to do as low impact training as possible, I even invited Becca to come along. She, shockingly, accepted: 'As long as they don't make me do any of that weird side bump shit again; my head hasn't shrunk in two years, y'know.'

On a Saturday morning at ten o'clock, Becca and I met at Mitcham tube station – which is almost the furthest you can go south on the Northern line. Mitcham consists of several motorway junctions, an out-of-town shopping centre, a couple of warehouses and the suburban overflow from Tooting and Croydon. Even though it was 25°C and sunny, the streets were grey, the buses empty, and men could be found drinking special brew on park benches.

We walked for twenty minutes, following Janey's directions: 'Google Maps takes you as far as a Chinese wholesale; then you go down an alley and look for signs for the boxing gym, above a garage.'

Sure enough, we passed a vast Chinese supermarket, and saw a man coming out wheeling a trolley filled with frozen duck carcasses in see-through bin bags. Behind the building was another warehouse, and a white sign told us we had found the Bottleneck Gym.

We pushed open the metal door to a corridor that led upstairs to a large, bright room. To our left was a desk covered in papers and safety deposit boxes (later we found out that there were no lockers, so watches, money and jewellery were kept in boxes in a locked drawer). Behind the desk stood a fish tank filled with green, opaque water and zero signs of life. The ceiling was a mix of broken ceiling tiles, with lengths of black sacks and tarpaulin ominously drooping down from it, held in place by gaffer tape. Windows let in bright light all around the room, a few of them missing the glass. In the centre of the room, emerging from a graveyard of discarded boxing gloves in every size imaginable, stood the ring.

Boxing rings are larger than wrestling rings; they have four ropes instead of three and they are not taut enough to be climbed on. The main difference is that the canvas has no bounce; it's just wooden boards, because you don't hit the floor until you lose in a boxing match. In the ring there was a guy shadow boxing; he was black, wiry and about fifty. He smiled to reveal three gold teeth and welcomed us. At the other end of the room, partly obscured by an assortment of weights and punch bags, I could make out the small figure of Janey and the muscly, domineering figure of Dragonita, both lacing up their boots.

I could tell by the way that Janey kept glancing at the clock that she was deciding if she should wait for more people to turn up. We waited half an hour, and two more women joined us.

Janey, always the optimist, was pleased it was an even number.

One of the girls who turned up was called Hellcat LaVae, and she had the most impressive neck muscles I'd ever seen on a woman. She was wearing all black and had several tattoos, and we later learned she was a trained veterinary surgeon who drove a huge black jeep. She was also five feet one, with hair that fell down past her waist. She had been wrestling for five years, but had taken a break because being a vet meant she had a gruelling schedule. *Animal Hospital* had lied to her as a child.

The other trainee was Daisy, six five with a rockabilly haircut and absolutely no prior experience or knowledge of wrestling. She'd given Janey her email address after meeting at a mutual friend's birthday drinks, on the off-chance that Janey might one day actually start the women-only training school they had been discussing. That was a month earlier, and now here we were.

Dragonita explained that she would lead the warm-up based on what she had learned in Japan. Unlike Lucha, there was no rave music and jumping, although the radio did blast out Magic FM. As Bonnie Tyler played, we stood in a circle and counted together, repeating stretches for ten reps. We did a round of sixty squats, and I could feel the familiar but satisfying rush of blood entering my muscles. Then we paired up to lean on each other as we stretched out our arms and legs.

When Daisy struggled with squats, Dragonita said calmly: 'This is conditioning: now you struggle, but the third time you do this you'll find it easier, and eventually sixty squats will be nothing at all.'

I wanted to say that this was a lie, and sixty squats will always be sixty squats, but I kept quiet.

Dragonita's style of teaching was a lot like her in-ring style, understated but methodical and precise. She never wasted movement or sound, and she would save her flashy and impressive moves for the exact moment when they had the biggest impact – nothing was given for free. We did circuits of weights, all of us lifting the same amount and counting reps together, always going at the speed of the slowest.

There was something important I noticed about Dragonita's training; it made me see how we all had certain strengths. Becca, who was a performer accustomed to moving around a stage all day, could run around without getting out of breath. When it came to lifting weights, Daisy, naturally strong, lifted a 20lb steel rod over her head like it was a broom handle. As we stretched, I bent straight to the floor, when everyone else had to be pushed gently on the back. Janey couldn't even bend enough to put her elbows on the floor. But we laughed, and we supported each other, and I could feel my smile grow the more exercise we did. It was like my body had remembered what endorphins were.

Next, we did an hour of shoot fighting – essentially wrestling to pin each other to the mats for real. The only person who beat me was Dragonita, which was a huge ego boost. By the second hour of training, we hadn't even got in the ring but we all felt like we had learned about our bodies and our strength, and what it actually felt like to fight. What's more, we were sweating so much that both Becca and I were now just in our bras. Dragonita had a small towel that she used to wipe away the sweat, but even that was sopping.

Then I heard a cough, a male cough, signalling the start of an announcement. The whole time, there'd been two men watching us from near the desk, one of whom I recognised immediately as Oswald.

Oswald ran a wrestling promotion that was badly attended, but which he wrote about on social media as if every show were filling Wembley Arena. I had never heard him speak, but knew him by his questionable social-media reputation. He would write long posts about how people didn't respect the wrestling industry; about how badly everyone else was doing, and how he was betrayed at every corner. He would wait outside rival wrestling shows and tell people not to go in.

He had never acknowledged my existence, and I had been fine with this arrangement. Once, when I drank too much at a party and needed to be sick in order to be able to get home without passing out, it was by conjuring his image that I was successfully able to vomit. That is really the best way I could describe him.

He reminded me of the kind of man who had most likely

run the wrestling industry for decades; men not bound by duty or skill, but sociopaths who spent all their savings on buying a wrestling ring, knowing that then they would have a modicum of control without having to be particularly likeable. Men who exploited the idea of 'paying your dues' and who would get workers blacklisted for personal disagreements.

In short, as soon as I saw him I glanced at Janey with an expression that said one thing: 'What the fuck is he doing here?'

Daisy, Hellcat and I exchanged glances.

Janey looked behind her, then said, quietly, 'Look, this is just so we get to use the ring. We're going to be a separate promotion; I'll explain when we've left the building, okay?'

The rest of the session we spent in the ring. There were some rolling drills that were more punishing than they needed to be because the ring was so hard. We agreed that the boxing ring was punishing to learn in, so Janey showed Becca and Daisy the basics on old yoga mats we found underneath it. We had a water break and Janey explained that in the last hour we would wrestle.

'In every session, I want us to do matches. It's all very well me teaching you moves on their own but if you don't understand the way that a match is structured, then if you forget a move, or mess something up, you won't know what to do next. If you know what's coming next in a story, you can improvise.'

Janey took Daisy and Becca to one side to teach them some basic moves, while I planned a match with Hellcat and Dragonita. Janey made it clear we should all change from what we usually did. I was to be the baby-face and Hellcat and Dragonita would be heels, because during most of the shows they had done, they had been the token women, so faces by default.

The ideas came to me thick and fast about what I could do

in the match. As a heel, I'd never had the opportunity to do flashy wristlock rehearsals, or kicks, or even jumping moves off the ropes. Dragonita and Hellcat both found that when they punched me, or knocked me down, it looked brutal. Hellcat even admitted that, as a goth and death metal enthusiast, she'd always found it hard to get the crowd to cheer for her. It all seemed so fake.

The ring was like concrete so I only took one bump from a clothesline by Dragonita, which shook my body and ribs and made my teeth rattle. In eight minutes, I fitted in a double wristlock reversal, three arm drags and a few arm locks; it was pretty basic but it felt good to be wrestling again. I was impressed with how much my body remembered.

Becca and Daisy screamed at the most basic moves, both new to shows, and I realised that I had got so used to trying to make everything flashy enough to impress a seasoned crowd, I had moved away from the basics of telling a story.

We left the gym and agreed to go to the pub – Janey, Dragonita and Hellcat all had orange juices, while Becca, Daisy and I drank pints of cider. We sat in a surprisingly leafy pub garden opposite Mitcham tube, and Janey explained the situation.

'When Dragonita and I first decided we wanted to do a women's training session, and run it ourselves, we literally asked every wrestling promotion in London. None of them responded except Oswald.'

'Wait,' I said, 'not even Lucha?'

'We asked, but they're clear that they don't agree with single-gender training sessions – they didn't really get why women would just want to be with other women, which I understand. But at least they gave us a reason, the rest just ignored us.'

'Please tell me it's not because you're women?' asked Daisy, who had thought that wrestling would be some kind of feminist paradise that happened to have men in close proximity. She had never been to a wrestling show.

'Yes, it's because we're women,' said Dragonita, matter-of-factly.

'Anyway,' continued Janey, 'both Dragonita and I have wrestled for Oswald before, and he said that he was really interested in booking new talent, specifically women. But he doesn't own a venue, so he said he'd put us in touch with a place we could train, and in exchange we could put on two women's matches at his next show. And these would be "our" matches, so we would come up with a promotion name and it would be like a mini-show.'

'Okay,' said Becca, putting down her empty pint glass. 'Well done, Oswald, you're a gender warrior… except I'm assuming he's not going to pay us for our time.'

'I think he heard you were starting a school and wanted to take the credit,' said Janey. 'Sounds like Oswald…'

'But you need to know now that we aren't wrestling for him, or for anyone else. We want this to be a team, something that we're in control of. These training sessions are open for women of any ability to get the opportunity to train and appear in shows. The first show is in a couple of months, and I'm going to open it up as an opportunity to every female wrestler I know and see who says yes. No, we won't get paid, but that's how it works at the moment. We're doing it because we want to, and no other reason.'

'Well,' said Becca, 'I'm in; I had an awesome time today. Sure, I can't do anything other than a wristlock and a forward roll, but I can help.'

'You're funny and good at talking, I really want you to be involved,' smiled Janey.

'I loved today, it was great,' said Daisy. 'Plus I can get a jacket with Daisy Mayhem on the back and that'll be sweet.'

'Daisy Mayhem – that's great!' I said.

'You can't start wrestling without a cool name.'

I asked Janey, 'So what are we called?'

'Burning Hearts – no acronyms, and it sounds like a girl metal band from the '80s.'

We agreed that we would keep the day of the show free, and start to tell people to come. That next week we would train again in that sweaty, weird gym on an industrial estate in Mitcham. Our numbers didn't grow by more than a few each time, but we always left feeling happy, a bit sore from bumping in the horrible ring but sure of what we had learned. The owner with the gold teeth started to know us by name and recommended that a few women he taught should join us.

Janey had been kind enough not to ask if I wanted to wrestle in the show. Ultimately I was still unsure of what I could do. The pain still appeared every day but the changes to my diet had made me feel less sluggish.

I started to train on Mondays at Lucha, in a beginner's class that was always attended by ten or so dedicated trainees of mixed ability, and occasionally by a complete newbie. Fraser would take new trainees to one side and teach them, gently and reassuringly, how to throw themselves backwards on to an unforgiving mat.

One night, Greg and Vanderhorne took me to one side: 'Are you training with Janey and Dragonita? Why aren't they training here any more?'

I kept quiet, remembering what Janey had said, and then thought about the real reason she and Dragonita had turned to Oswald.

'They want to do it on their own.'

I was not angry with Greg and Vanderhorne for asking me about the training. They themselves were still struggling to get new people through the door. They were never ones to besmirch the success of others, and they didn't play dirty like other promoters sometimes would. In fact, I think they felt betrayed by their trainees. But I could tell by the way Vanderhorne talked non-stop at me for ten minutes about gender equality, and Greg silently gazed off into the distance and sipped his coffee, that I was going to be stuck in the middle with this one.

Sure, Lucha was still my wrestling home, and the Monday sessions became more fun once I took the pressure off myself to try to learn new moves. But I knew why Burning Hearts had to exist. Even at Lucha, we were never described as 'wrestlers' alone; we were always 'female wrestlers'. The prefix could be a source of empowerment, of being able to weaponise your feminine body – but for many it denounced us as secondary in every respect to the 'real' wrestlers, who were all men. Vanderhorne and Greg never meant it like that, I knew, but the wider industry instilled the sense that we were 'others'.

The next Burning Hearts training session made the sexism embedded in the industry even more clear. There is this recognition, you see, of mutual respect with other female wrestlers. In every locker room, your eyes will shoot straight to the other woman, the one you are likely to be fighting or whom you will possibly fight in the future. Word spreads fast about new opportunities, and something as open and simple as 'women-only training with a match in a month's time' was enough to bring people in. Our numbers began to double.

We could all take it in turns to wrestle each other because there were no perceived barriers apart from, perhaps, experience. There were women who had seen wrestling matches as kids, yet who had never realised they could actually *learn* wrestling. But more seasoned female wrestlers came to the sessions than newbies, and speaking to them made me appreciate again how I had been trained, treated and welcomed by Lucha.

One woman told me she was groped by a fellow trainee in a wrestling exercise and then told not to come back because she clearly couldn't handle 'the pressure'. She was serious about training so kept her mouth shut, the groper being quite a well-known indie star. Another girl had only done one session, when she was offered the chance to wrestle on a show. She was told that she wouldn't have to do anything except sell, but she ended up bumping badly and breaking her own nose. The match then went viral on the internet and she read comments describing how she was 'proof that women couldn't wrestle' and 'a shame on the sport'.

There was a survivor's humour in the air as women spoke about not being booked because they weren't attractive enough, or being booked only as a 'token girl'. And I would encourage them to come and train more regularly at the Lucha school, where at least they would be respected and welcomed. It never felt like a betrayal to Janey, because she had made it clear she didn't want me ever to feel I had to choose between Burning Hearts and Lucha, but she 'knew how things could be'.

Things were like this: I would turn up at Lucha once a month, and Fraser would wrestle and I would dress up as Rana and work the door. I still looked up to the ring with sadness every now and again, but I was, even if only behind closed doors, back to being a wrestler again.

Another month passed and the day of the Burning Hearts show arrived. We didn't charge the audience to come to our show, and emphasis was put on our being the 'warm up' for the main act, Oswald's event. Despite this, word spread and we knew there would be at least thirty people coming, which was definitely a decent size for an unknown wrestling promotion with three matches on the card.

We arrived at eleven, though no one let us in until twelve,

because the venue was a pub. It had panelled wood fixtures and a huge skylight and balcony overlooking a main space big enough for a ring. It was a beautiful place, and I was suddenly comforted by the fact that we wouldn't be performing in a community centre with a low ceiling and no windows.

I had agreed to be the ring announcer with Chow Mean, who was now also involved. Janey was keen to have two clear teams at Burning Hearts; something that happened at most female shows in Japan. She had told me that I was going to be the 'face announcer' while Chow would side with the bad guys.

Chow greeted me with a huge smile; at some point during my illness she had stopped training because of work commitments. We could already tell that we would be throwing out the idea of being on opposing sides, and fill our commentary with banter about vaginas or something similar.

An hour before the doors were scheduled to open, the van with the ring arrived and, without a fuss, we carried the metal bars inside. There was a look of surprise from passers-by on Tooting High Street as fifteen women carried massive pieces of metal into the building. But we worked together and it only took half an hour. A couple of people had a go in the ring to get a feel for it, and we then walked through their matches before heading backstage to get ready.

The energy was different from the usual atmosphere before a show. For a start, all of us were putting on make-up. Becca happily drew some abs on her stomach with eyeliner, smeared her lipstick and stuffed her bra with tissues. The other wrestlers all started wrapping their feet in strips of canvas to protect their toes and some straightened their hair. The most preparation I ever saw backstage in Lucha was the application of some fake tan, a bit of stretching, and people putting on their trunks and a mask.

The other wrestlers were all new faces to me, but we immediately clicked on the basis we were female wrestlers. There was Mesha East, the East London Strong Girl, her head a mass of blonde braids, with muscles and a pair of amazing velvet shorts. Nye-Oh was a tiny woman with a grey bob wig; she was 'the wrestling engineer' because she had spent her years perfecting submission holds as she could never pick up her opponents. There was also Daisy, who, as promised, had got herself a rockabilly leather jacket with her name on the back, and was busy styling her hair into a quiff. She seemed incredibly undaunted in having her first match.

The final girl, Amarah the Voodoo Queen, much to Becca's delight and mine, was working in Bury St Edmunds. We couldn't understand why anyone would actually choose to live there.

As I wasn't wrestling, I went out and saw the room starting to fill with our friends, mostly women, all at a wrestling show for the first time. I could see Oswald eyeing them all from a corner; he didn't seem to be marketing for his show at all – I think because our crowd was decidedly not one who would go to a 'proper' wrestling show.

By the time we started, I found that I was actually very nervous. I hurriedly tried to write notes on my cue cards that reflected the witty banter of earlier – but nothing came out. I was wearing a dress with a print of bacon rashers on it and hoped this would be enough to win me respect from the crowd.

We entered the ring to 'Rebel Girl' by Bikini Kill, hoping it would become the official anthem for our adoring crowd. The audience cheered us, but also looked like they weren't sure what they were supposed to do.

'Ladies, gentlemen, and everyone in between, welcome to

the first official show of Burning Hearts,' screamed Chow, while the crowd cheered at least two tones quieter.

Janey had given me the simple task of introducing the announcers and then explaining what wrestling is.

'I'm Heather Honeybadger, this is Chow Mean, and we are here to take you through the concept of wrestling. The most extreme fight of good and evil that you can see in a square made of elastic and canvas! Leave pause for laughter.'

I thought saying this would incite a reaction, but there was just a pause.

'Wrestling is a… you win wrestling by pinning your opponent's shoulders to the mat for a count of three, or by getting your opponent to submit. You can be disqualified for cheating, biting, or being counted out of the ring for ten seconds… and just to be clear – there is no oil in this wrestling, no sir; this is proper wrestling with proper wrestlers. We just happen to have vaginas.'

Silence, a single 'whoop' from my good friend Ruth, who was in the audience. I wanted the ground to swallow me up. The vagina banter was not working.

Chow added smilingly, 'Okay, who wants to see some wrestling?' And there was a little cheer again. 'Our first match is a tag match! Which means two teams fight for a winner. Let's bring our first competitors to the ring.'

'Human Fly' by The Cramps played and out came Daisy Mayhem, the psychobilly brawler, unsmiling and in a pair of neon leopard-print shorts. Psycho Lolita, also known as Janey, followed her in a schoolgirl outfit, wielding a frying pan at the audience. I introduced Mesha East and Nye-Oh as 'the really good team of…' Luckily, they were both so experienced at wrestling they knew how to get the crowd on side – by going around and giving them high fives.

The match was basic but though the audience were slow

to start, they got louder as the violence increased. Of course the majority, being radical feminists, wanted to cheer for Daisy because she was over six feet tall and didn't smile. Chow and I found that our main job, apart from announcing the matches, was to boo and cheer loudly at the right places, right next to the ring. By the final pin – a pump handle slam from Daisy to Nye-Oh, made spectacular by their height difference – the audience were out of their seats.

Next, Becca came out, screeching in an American accent: 'So, I'm here for this so-called wrestling show. My name is Susannah Deville Trump – no relation – and I am a bona fide wrestler from **AMERICA**. None of this stupid British empowerment bullshit you lot are all about... Where are the lights? Where is the wind machine? The referee is overweight and frankly you look like the worst audience I've ever seen.'

She went on, getting boos and laughter from the crowd. The plan was that I would roll her up when she challenged someone to a fight. For some reason, I had taken this simple instruction from Janey as: 'Then you stand behind her, take off your dress to reveal a wrestling leotard, slap her and roll her up.'

Becca was nearly halfway through her speech and I was looking as pissed off as possible, when I nonchalantly tried to take off my dress. But of course, the zip got stuck. So I struggled for about a minute with my dress tangled over my head, while in front of me, Becca tried to stall for time by slinging more insults at the audience.

'Everyone knows women can't wrestle – they're too weak. Apart from me, that is, an *actual* wrestler with loads of wrestling experience... moves... Look at my abs!'

Eventually I managed to get out my dress and by that point I could tell Becca had forgotten what she had to do to let me slap her. So I just shouted, 'I'll fight you', then slapped her, for real, around the face. She didn't fall over, so I swung behind her and went to roll her up by putting my arms between her legs. She just sort of sat down, and I put her down for a three-count. There was a reaction from the crowd, but mainly just sniggers on the faces of the ten or so 'proper wrestlers', who had arrived before their show and who were watching from the balcony.

Becca left the ring cursing the audience, who all booed her. Despite my misapprehension, when I looked from the faces of the wrestlers to those of the audience, I could see they were all smiling. In some ways it was a blessing the crowd had no idea what wrestling was, so they probably thought the clusterfuck Becca and I had just performed was to be expected.

Chow introduced the main event; I stood next to her without a microphone, like a melon.

'From parts unknown, welcome to the ring the Voodoo Queen – Amarah!'

Amarah had transformed from a bubbly professional into a terrifying force of nature. She came out screaming, covered in white make-up and all the cultural signifiers of 'crazy voodoo woman'. It would have been weird anywhere other than in wrestling; I could see this on the faces of the audience, not knowing whether to cheer or – or what? But they were also terrified, and that was a powerful reaction to get at a show. I managed to not mess up the next part.

'And her opponent, from Barcelona, my personal girl crush, Dragonita!'

She came out looking stern and tight lipped in her custom-made jacket from Japan and her *luchadora* mask. She meant to take no nonsense. She seemed unbeatable and everyone cheered her. Dragonita circled the ring twice, staring out her opponent. Amarah threw herself against the ropes, hissing, and the atmosphere swelled. When she finally climbed through the ropes, the crowd were chanting Dragonita's name.

The match was a strong one, with both competitors putting

in hard-hitting lariats. Dragonita bent Amarah into strange holds, and at one point wrapped her up like a pretzel and sat on her back. They brawled out of the ring, and Amarah launched Dragonita into the bar with a satisfying crash. A few members of the crowd were at the point of screaming when Dragonita looked beaten, but she came back stronger, running circles around Amarah, and then delivered a huge show of strength as she scooped her up into a Michinoku Driver. The place erupted.

Chow and I climbed back into the ring. We had been given strict instructions to get the crowd out so that the 'real' wrestlers could come downstairs and practise in the ring for an hour before the next show started.

'Thank you for coming! Now please come see us again, follow us on Twitter, take a flyer home, and exit the building as quickly as possible please!'

'Yeah, Heather just let off a rotten one and the place is going to become a toxic zone pretty soon!'

The audience left. A fart joke and it was over. We'd completely forgotten to plug the next show so I blithered into the mike as the building emptied: 'Oh, and come back in an hour to come see another amazing show, which will be much longer, and have men in it, and will only cost a tenner!'

This, it seems, was not the way to persuade a group of women how to spend their Sunday afternoon. We packed up and went next door to another pub, where seventy-five per cent of our audience were now sat drinking and talking about the wrestling.

They were buzzing from having seen a bout for the first time, and surprised at how much they'd enjoyed it. After a couple of hours of being asked by nearly everyone if wrestling was fake, and if anyone had got hurt, and how come there hadn't been more people there, most of the wrestlers who had taken part in our matches now moved back next door to watch the 'proper show'.

There were fewer people in the crowd than there had been for our show. They were quieter, and the only match I watched with all my attention starred the Fabulous Bakewell Boys, who spent most of their fight going to the bar to get bottles of Newkie Brown. There was also a women's match in which two veterans of the circuit had an incredible fight – but I watched with dismay as a third of the audience left to have a slash or a cigarette as soon as it was announced.

Watching the women's match offered me a bit of an optimistic perspective on the show we had done. Yes, it had only been two-and-a-half matches long, lasting less than forty-five minutes, and had made no money. But we had brought wrestling to people who had never seen it before, and we had done it with them in mind; we knew that those who had come did so half out of support for their friends, and half to see what women's wrestling actually looked like, as it still seems so foreign to most people.

And why does it still seem foreign? Precisely because of the barriers we had faced ourselves just to get to this point. What we had done, what we had created, was ours. It had been built up by a small team of women, doing it because of the love of wrestling, despite the fact that it seemed to be an industry that ignored us.

None of us knew exactly how much that was about to change.

9

The F Word

It was 2016. Things were changing in wrestling and all the women around me could feel it. We were persevering by working together.

Even in my weird little corner of underground and independent wrestling – the sweaty glow of the Resistance Gallery and the battered boxing gym of Burning Hearts – I had heard horror stories of how women had been treated when wrestling. We were the latest wave in a century-old struggle for a 'revolution' for women within wrestling.

Women have been wrestling as long as men, even in the days when it was illegal. Women wrestled throughout the twentieth century across Japan, Mexico, America, England and many other places.

Wrestling has grown, in part due to the WWE turning wrestling into a show with high production values that has become an exportable product; but at a grassroots level, this growth is mainly down to independent promotions, like the ones I wrestle for, putting their faith in their own shows.

And within this, women have had to fight for recognition. Like me, women have to train to be wrestlers in an industry that does not see them to be as valid as men in terms of their strength, ability or knowledge. Often, training is more difficult for women due to constant sexism and misogyny, which accompany the expectation that women are a novelty act or there to provide titillation. As early as the 1930s, women were training and fighting to change this. As you can probably glean from some of the encounters I have had within the relatively liberal London wrestling community, many minds have yet to change.

A huge part of this prejudice is down to the fact that the WWF sexualised women from day one, and picked wrestlers for their looks rather than their talent. This came to a head in the 1990s (when I was a child), when women were made to take part in contractual bikini contests. To compete with WWF ratings, every independent wrestling promotion booked wrestlers who fed the same kind of appeal. Men had to be tanned, with rippling muscle and 'tough-guy' gimmicks. Women, in the same vein, had to be chiefly about their appearance. Women also went from being relatively regularly featured in shows, to being an element that could easily be added or removed like an optional extra.

Because there was no longer an influx of workers from Japan and Mexico, and because they didn't have the big tits and blonde hair that the WWF assumed its fans wanted, little girls stopped wanting to grow up to be female wrestlers. Many older female wrestlers also hung up their boots rather than train other women because they couldn't earn an income from it. The final nail in the coffin was when the WWE (having changed its own name in the mid-1990s) renamed all of its women wrestlers 'divas' in 1999, and the championship Red Belt that had been awarded with the American title since the 1950s was replaced by a pink, diamante, butterfly-shaped, Barbie-esque accessory.

By the mid-2000s, British wrestling was struggling as the public's interest in wrestling waned. There were fewer gigs for men, even fewer for women, and those who were good looking were usually favoured. This is how women's matches became referred to as the 'piss break'. Yet there were nevertheless a few women that were determinedly teaching the younger generation to wrestle properly, or who wanted to learn themselves. Women like Klondyke Kate, who had become a wrestling legend despite being eighteen stone and coming from Stoke-on-Trent. There was also Sweet Saraya Knight, who ran a wrestling promotion with her husband during the diva years. Trained by these rebellious, stubborn women, who persevered in the face of institutionalised sexism, some of their students became my contemporaries, and others went on to achieve global stardom.

In 2012, two things happened. First, I got into the wrestling ring for the first time, and second, the only two women's wrestling promotions in the whole of Europe opened their doors. Both, ironically, were within thirty miles of my birthplace of Bury St Edmunds. I never would have guessed that East Anglia was secretly a mecca for female wrestling.

Anyway, these promotions, Bellatrix in Norwich, and Pro Wrestling: EVE in Sudbury, were both run by husband-and-wife couples, and both with the sole purpose of showing that women could wrestle just as well as men – something that the world had seemingly forgotten despite a century of struggle.

The WWE picked up a handful of these women, and when they eventually had their debut matches, the wrestling world was shocked when they saw a woman walk out and, instead of just pulling the opponent down by her hair, put her in a half nelson. The internet exploded with fans who had 'realised' women could wrestle.

By the time I was having my first match, the WWE proclaimed there was a 'revolution' in its women's division. All of a sudden, women's matches became longer, the competitors became better, and the WWE stopped giving their female wrestlers names that were like porn monikers. The 'Four Horsewomen' of wrestling included Paige, a goth from Norwich; Becky Lynch, a red-head from Ireland; Sasha Banks, a petite but hard-hitting heel; and finally, Charlotte Flair, the blonde daughter of a famous wrestler, who could pull a somersault literally out of nowhere. They all had incredible talent, with characters more relatable than the tinsel-and-tits of previous years – and now they had the fans behind them, too.

Sure, I hated the idea that a big, evil corporation had decided to brand something a 'revolution' when it was deciding to whitewash its problematic past. Since 'the revolution', the WWE has started to get its competitors to talk about empowerment. They talk of women's rights and the fight for recognition, but they *never* drop the F-bomb. The word 'feminism' was not used in any of the coverage describing these changes. It was only used by well-meaning outsiders, like myself, who quickly learned that using 'the F word' brings you instant heat.

I watched as my comrades wrestled for EVE and Bellatrix matches alongside mixed gender promotions. But even as Burning Hearts dawned, we never thought that things would change. We could see right through the WWE's revolution: the only thing that could change our circumstances on the ground was, as always, grassroots resistance and teamwork. But we weren't all cynical. From about 2014 onwards, rather than finding women's wrestling down a YouTube hole, I could watch the WWE and see a women's match that I knew would be really good.

However, my attention was always focused on the wrestling I was directly involved with. Burning Hearts was growing based on the success of its first show, bringing some new women into training.

In 2016, WWE's annual WrestleMania event took place – think of it as being wrestling's equivalent of the Super Bowl or the World Cup – which Chow had recommended to me when I first trained. Unlike every other wrestler on the planet (so I'm told), I had not watched WrestleMania that year, having decided to skip it. Why? WrestleMania was usually all about the same big male wrestlers who I could watch (and only partly relate to) all year round – except they would all have new costumes and longer entrances, and the arena was bigger. Plus it would start at midnight in the UK, on a Sunday night, and I wasn't going to use up a day's holiday to deal with the sleep deprivation.

I had been working with the girls' charity for a few years by this point, and my colleagues were mostly unmoved by having a wrestler in their midst – though it must have become annoying for them over the years when I showed up to work with something broken or concussion. Anyway, on the Monday morning following WrestleMania, a colleague emailed me an article that had popped up that morning online. The headline was: 'Wrestling is becoming feminist.' What?

The article informed readers that the WWE, in a move to show that they valued their female competitors, had introduced a women's belt at WrestleMania. It hailed the company as being feminist champions. I was incensed. In fact, I found myself responding to my well-meaning colleague, explaining why this was all grade A bullshit, in the following email:

Dear Susannah,

Thank you for the article, here's my critique:

The belt was not new; in fact they had changed it to the 'Barbie belt' in 2010 several years after all women in the industry were rebranded as 'divas'. They were simply changing the belt back. Therefore this is not a feminist but a revisionist act. Clap, clap – well done, men.

The WWE constantly drop the world 'revolution' into their coverage, but actually they are referring to merely four women. Four exceptionally talented women, but still only four. The writer of this article didn't seem to realise just how much women had been erased from wrestling history, and has hailed these women as protégées. The other women who have made these changes in history have remained unacknowledged by the company for the most part.

The article called this a feminist act – there is no way that the WWE, or wrestling companies in general, will ever use the F word. In fact, those employed by the WWE are likely to be contractually not allowed to say that they are feminists.

This article was written by a man. They could have at least found a woman to write it.

Kind regards,

Heather

Her response was one line long: 'You should write an article on this.'

It was a slow morning at work, so I Googled the *Guardian* and, thinking it would be more difficult, found the email address for freelance submissions. I explained I was a wrestler and that there had been a huge change in the wrestling world, and they needed to be covering this as part of a vested interest in their female readership.

Five minutes later I got a response, asking if I could give them 1,000 words by the next morning. I said I absolutely could. Even though I hadn't written for a public audience before, apart from the zines I had made at university, which I'd photocopied using a librarian's card I found on the floor and sold for a quid. And those had been about whales; this was a bit more of a contentious subject.

But driven by a renewed passion for wrestling, I pulled an almost all-nighter, the merits of sleep deprivation reconsidered. I skipped training, drank three pots of tea, and researched women's wrestling for three hours. I ate an entire packet of dark chocolate digestive biscuits. Becca read through my piece in an hour; she was travelling back from a gig in Glasgow and had intermittent signal on the train. She loved it, but pointed out that even though it had been only a decade since getting an A* in English, my grammar was horrible.

I rewrote it, constantly trying to re-phrase sentences such as 'wrestling for women for the last decade has sucked donkey balls' to, 'long derided by the sport's chauvinists, female bouts are being taken seriously for the first time in decades'. I summarised how wrestling had saved me from my depression, explaining, 'I took up wrestling five years ago after a long hiatus from exercise – I'd been told I was too fat and angry to be good at netball at school.' I urged anyone who felt the same to take up contact sport immediately.

The next day I emailed it off on the way to work, and at 11am my phone went crazy because not only had it been published online without informing me, but a picture accompanied it, showing Rana choking out Diablesa Rosa on the ropes.

I'd broken 'kayfabe' by telling people who I was behind my mask, and what's worse, the editor had taken out my references to Lucha Britannia. Vanderhorne and Greg were both proud and furious that I had missed out on a perfect opportunity to get Lucha some media attention.

By Friday, their feathers had been unruffled, and the *Guardian* had been given a gentle reminder in the importance of free advertising for independent venues. However, just by wading into a debate about wrestling, I had had over fifty strangers leave comments on my article, telling me that not only was I not a 'proper wrestler', but I was a disgrace to the industry. I didn't read the comments, but this is how they were summarised to me.

Other than that, the article was well received and a week later the *Guardian* approached me again because Chyna had died. Chyna, you may remember, was the giant woman in a pink bikini who had appeared in the ring with a flamethrower, blowing my tiny mind when I was eight years old. An hour after I heard the news – a suspected overdose – thousands of heartfelt tweets appeared from wrestlers who, only a week earlier, would have called her a washed-up slut. I was asked to write an obituary, of sorts, from a female wrestler's perspective. I could now boast that I was 'the leading feminist freelance wrestling journalist in the UK'. ('Only' was also implied.)

The article was provisionally titled 'A Love Letter to Joanie Lahrer, aka Chyna', but it was changed. I had poured a lot of energy into getting across her life outside the ring, and how difficult it had been, and that it was precisely due to her perseverance that she had become a feminist icon – there had been no women's 'revolution' for her. Chyna is largely remembered for being on steroids and having a pair of breast implants named after her, but she was a survivor.

Chyna didn't realise she wanted to be a wrestler until she was twenty-eight. Before that, she was a belly dancer and a waitress, and she also sold pagers to drug dealers. She had spent most of her twenties competing in Miss Athletic America as a professional bodybuilder; despite never placing, she entered every year because she wanted to create some diversity from the skinny, blonde gymnasts who did ribbon displays. When she learned to wrestle, she had to pay more to learn because she was a woman, even though she could bench press 300lbs.

Chyna got into the WWE as a valet, later becoming the eighth wonder of the world and winning championships in her own right. She was the first woman to win an international continental belt off Jeff Jarrett who, allegedly, demanded $300,000 to drop the belt to a woman. (He came to Lucha once and I didn't recognise him, and asked him to pay for a ticket – a very embarrassed-looking promoter had to explain who he was. Chyna, I imagine, didn't have that problem.)

After being dumped by her then boyfriend, Triple H, in favour of the boss's daughter, Stephanie McMahon, Chyna ended up in increasingly sexualised storylines. Eventually, she was fired by fax.

Then she started taking a lot of drugs and increasingly turning to alcohol. She began a porn career with another wrestler who had also been let go by the industry. She was not mentioned once throughout the coverage of the women's revolution, despite the fact she was the first of a handful of women to hold a man's belt.

The article finished by saying that she was an example of what wrestling does to women: it makes them work to prove themselves twice as hard as men, just to be told that they need to be sexier, and then dropped because they've become too sexy and not authentic enough. It's important to be honest about her life so that we can learn from it and truly appreciate how important it is to call out misogyny within wrestling.

When it was published, the obituary received less of a reaction than my first article, but I now felt I understood what my place was within the wrestling world. First, I'd thought I wanted to be famous, but that stopped as soon as I saw how little clothing I would have to wear in order to be a 'diva'. Then I worked harder than I ever had before to be on the Lucha show, which I achieved – before my ovaries imploded and I was launched into the 'not wrestling' period. I had since spent my time recovering, but also thinking about wrestling, and feeling that so much potential was building for something *feminist*. I wanted to be part of the movement to get as many action figures of female wrestlers into supermarkets as their male counterparts.

It was with this in mind that, shortly after writing my second article, I eagerly bombarded all my friends with invites to the first women-only show in thirty years. Pro Wrestling: EVE had decided to have their first show in the capital. This was an achievement, for I knew only too well how hard it can be to get out of Suffolk.

To make it better, Janey and Dragonita had persuaded EVE to let them take part in the opening match, and we were given permission to hand out flyers for the Burning Hearts wrestling training. I offered to support them by getting new recruits, and of course, selling t-shirts, in exchange for entry.

On the day of the show I got off the train at Hackney Downs and found my way to the venue through the hipster graffiti and warehouses that had been converted into brunch cafes. As I turned the corner to the Arts Centre, I saw it – the line of men. Just men. Two hours before doors. Almost all of them were there alone, not talking, staring at their phones, and most had a plastic bag by their side. I can't really explain it in more detail than that. The plastic bags. You know the men who get on the bus, in slightly discoloured macs, jeans from the market, plastic bags filled with their belongings. Why not just get a rucksack? Why?

Anyway, these are the men that I'd seen at a number of wrestling shows, but usually their numbers were diluted by screaming nanas and children hyped up on lemonade, or in Lucha's case, drunk punks. I had never seen so many of the plastic-bag men together in such a high number. It was no coincidence that it happened to be a women-only show. For fuck's sake.

It takes three decades for women to have a show at a legitimate venue, with their names on the posters, and not just a nameless picture of a woman in a bikini. The cream of the UK's wrestling crop. And here they are. Men. Men are claiming this when it should be something that women know about. But of course, outside the wrestling world, why would anyone know that this was a huge step towards gender equality? I tried to stop myself from being a bigot, and told myself that it was good that the show had such an eager crowd – that's what mattered.

My phone vibrated with another message from a friend saying they couldn't come to the show. That made a total of five. I'd expected this, but it was more pertinent now. I wished some of them were here with me to see that numbers were so important in order to up the female quota even slightly.

I told a doorman I was there to help, and he looked me up and down, noting that I was probably not a fee-paying audience member as I didn't have a plastic bag. I was let in, and I introduced myself to the owners of EVE – Emily, who had a bright pink bob, and Dann – and they politely shook my hand. Then I helped a group of enthusiastic men put up a light rigging around the ring; they were all very nice and I found out most of them had come from Suffolk. But then there was a dead space for me – not one familiar face, and no one practising in the ring. I found all the wrestlers backstage, talking and putting on their make-up.

I shook hands with the people in the dressing room who didn't look too busy, and I swallowed my star-struck awe when meeting Kay Lee Ray, Nikki Storm and Rhia O'Reilly – all women I'd seen on the few indie shows that had been taped. Kay Lee Ray was well known for doing suicide dives and missile dropkicks off the top rope – she was completely fearless. Rhia, meanwhile, was hard hitting, a tank, but also an outspoken Irish nerd; she was currently sporting a dress with a Zelda print on it. In the ring, Nikki was a short, feisty, terrifyingly technical wrestler, but here she greeted me with a big smile.

In the other corner were my friends. Dragonita was doing squats. Janey took me to one side, and told me that my job was simple.

'So, just try and sell some t-shirts for me, and then give out the flyers to women who look like they might want to train.'

On Psycho Lolita's t-shirts, there was a picture of her mask with the words 'Kawaii Crush' beneath it – a reference that I didn't understand. I did make an obvious point about the flyers, though.

'Janey, I don't think there'll be many women here today. There's a queue of a hundred people outside and they're all men.'

'Well, yeah, it's a women's wrestling show. This is how it is.' I clearly looked agog at her resigned acceptance. She glanced around to make sure that no one else was listening and continued, 'When I started out, I wrestled some of these girls. On one show there was an elimination match. Whenever a girl was eliminated, the ref got to spank them. So, you have to remember, the fact that this is being billed as a proper show is what matters. It isn't who the crowd is, it's important to send them home happy... and even if just five women come to this show and then take up training, it's been worth it.'

Calm, professional Janey, who was never thought 'sexy' enough to get the bookings, or able to afford to wrestle full time, had persevered. Janey was like every other woman in this locker room. I swallowed my misgivings, feeling like I really didn't have any reason to be outraged; it wasn't my outrage to bear. I was determined to try to sell a Kawaii Crush t-shirt to every single member of the crowd, even if I had no idea what it meant (I do now, thanks).

The doors would be opening soon so I went to my little table with a pile of t-shirts, and then my only friend who hadn't flaked on me arrived – Jen, a non-binary Bantasaurus Rex, the hilarious producer of Sh!t Theatre. They came rolling in on the wave of plastic-bag men, who all went straight to the side of the ring to stake their places. No one spoke to anyone else.

Jen's face said everything I thought, their eyes slightly too wide, registering the fact they'd just stood in a line of middle-aged men queuing up for what had been described as a feminist landmark event. They hugged me, scraped in behind our table and said, 'Well, I've already had someone ask me if I'm a boy or girl.'

'Was he holding a plastic bag?'

'Yes.'

'Yeah, that's the reason why no one comes to wrestling shows.'

We quickly began drinking bottles of cider, and by the time the room had filled up, we were playing a game of spotting women in the crowd. By the first bell, I had sold one t-shirt and the head count of women had reached twelve. Jen and I had drunk two bottles of cider each, which meant the whole situation now had a gloss of surrealism. This feeling was enhanced by the nature of the merchandise that was lined up on the tables next to us: signed glamour shots of the wrestlers and little plastic bracelets with their names on them for kids. Jen and I both decided we were going to have a good time even if we felt like observers at a convention.

Emily came to the ring; she looked like she was bricking it and my little heart flew out to her. I had never seen a female ring announcer at a pro wrestling event. She said they were so excited to be back, to be making history, to be holding on to their feminist principles by showcasing the best female wrestlers in Europe at this event. This was the first show after a hiatus of four years.

The crowd chanted her name; being nearly all men, it was a low and guttural chant, but I chanted for her too. It was her passion that made me see directly into the heart of EVE. I forgave the men with their plastic bags and realised that they had been the ones who had stayed and watched the 'piss-break' matches for years, and they were the ones who were outraged on social media and spurred on the changes that were happening. Now it wasn't just their presence I noticed, but their loyalty. Wrestling fans are, after all, if not bitchy, judgemental and often introverted, fiercely loyal.

As the first match of the show, Dragonita and Janey were well received. This was in part down to Emily emphasising who Burning Hearts were, and saying that part of EVE's job was to support sister promotions with the same principles as them. This was the nicest introduction we could have had. Dragonita was a strong professional wrestler, having worked the circuit and spent nearly every weekend (since I'd known her) wrestling around the country; she was an instant crowd favourite. Janey was wrestling as Psycho Lolita, but because her tiny frame and move set were instantly recognisable, she got 'Janey' chants. Here, my friends were famous. Even though Janey pulled on the hair of her opponent, even taking a lollipop from her mouth and choking her opponent with it, the crowd still loved her. Janey choked out Dragonita with her fingers and held on after the match had ended – pure sadism – so she left, triumphantly, to a deafening boo.

The matches after that all seemed to be with fan favourites. As soon as the entrance music of a wrestler began, the crowd would immediately boo or cheer, and chant their name.

'Er–in, Er–in, Er–in.'

'Kay Lee, Kay Lee, Kay Lee Fucking Ray.'

Jen, now on their fourth cider, was shouting as loud as they could, quite often cheering the baddies. The occasional grizzled fan would turn and glare in disapproval, as if shouting were a tradition that could only be adhered to strictly. Jen would smile and wave. After the second match, my friend Drastik appeared with her partner; two queers, one with a stick and the other over six feet with a beard and a green Mohawk. Drastik had a loud voice, and was often so noticeable in a room that not making an entrance was impossible for her. She said, loudly enough for some to hear, 'Bloody hell, this is a sausage party, isn't it?'

It turned out they had been there for a while. They had tried to get ringside so that they could take some pictures, but the men at the ringside told them they absolutely could not 'just squeeze in' and that they should have arrived early.

'Haven't you heard about the girls-to-the-front principle of women's punk shows? Come on, mate, you're like a foot taller than my friend,' Drastik nodded to one man.

'Neither of you look like girls,' was his response, and he turned round and ignored them. Drastik then defiantly came to find us, swiftly bought a cider and stood directly behind the man. The poor fucker would be treated to a whole barrage of loud screaming right in his ear for the rest of the show. Good work, Drastik!

In the interval, Drastik and I handed out leaflets; the twelve other women there were all very excited about coming to train to be a wrestler. A few of the men put out their hands expectantly, to which Drastik would smile and say, 'Sorry, this isn't for you.'

Jen sold four t-shirts and did a much better job of conducting PR for Burning Hearts, and the majority of people we spoke to were very supportive. A few dropped in the words 'revolution' and 'empowerment'; I just nodded the practised nod of a feminist having feminism explained to them by a man. This is a learned act from three years spent at university parties.

Looking back, yes, we had a chip on our shoulder. But we were also new to this, and we had come to the event with fresh eyes. Maybe we were looking around at the space and wanting it to be filled with femme bodies. It didn't help when I stood in the crowd for a bit and could hear the muttering of some of the less savoury fans. I heard a man describe a young-looking wrestler as 'busting out her clothes' with approval, and another agreed that her opponent was also 'budding'. The term 'budding' still makes me retch.

The show made me experience two very strong feelings. Firstly, pride for Lucha Britannia, and its open slate and crowd of weirdos. The fact that it had set out from day one to be 'more than a wrestling show'. Secondly, I was also sad for EVE, and that it had taken me so long to realise how women could control a ring, and how they could feature in every match of a show and hold a crowd. Maybe I was surprised about the level of talent because I had believed that being a female wrestler was so rare – maybe subconsciously I had doubted them as well.

The last match was between Rhia O'Reilly and Nikki Storm. It included about twenty spots where they kicked each other in the head, and it featured countless near falls and ended with Rhia holding on to the championship belt. She stood over her opponent and said, 'Nikki, you know we've fought for this belt six times now, all over the country. And there's one place we've never been together, and that's the bar. Let's have a beer.'

They shook hands and were handed cans of beer and everyone went home happy. I was ecstatic; the show had been completely not what I was expecting. Jen and I walked home together; the only other time Jen had seen wrestling was when I'd performed at York Hall. Being so much closer to the ring, and seeing women beat the crap out of each other had been a spectacle in a whole other way.

But they summarised the problem pretty well: 'I don't get it – how come there isn't a shit ton of women here? This should be for *everyone*, and there's this… disparity. There's only creepy men. I just don't get it.'

I didn't get it either. Something had to change. I sat on the Overground on the journey back across the river, and figured, okay, maybe I couldn't change the world. Maybe I had spent most of my life up to this point trying to find something I was good at, and that had been wrestling. And I had hit a wall.

I was not brave enough to travel to Japan, or Mexico, or even Scotland, to train and follow my fortune. I wasn't about to start performing in front of the plastic-bag men. I wanted to make it easier for women, and queers, and people like me who didn't feel like they belonged at a wrestling show to become valid audience members without constantly being reminded that they are outsiders. Maybe I was brave enough to try to change that?

Somehow I needed to put all my energy into encouraging new audiences to shows. More women who had been told all their life they were too fat, or too weak, or too unfit, to ever become something as tough as a wrestler. To show all the queer kids, who had spent so long trapped inside a lie of themselves, that they too could create a character they could pour themselves into, and find self-love. But not just to watch: to discover how amazing it was to learn to be a wrestler. I wanted them to know the feeling of lifting someone over their head. Of making the audience hold their breath. A real revolution, not on the big screen, but on the mats of every wrestling school around the globe.

Yet how to do it? It was happening, but I didn't know where to catch on to the wave.

A few months passed and I sat on these thoughts. I started to note things down, bits of history I read, my thoughts on matches I saw, and my own experiences. They weren't memoirs, as such, more like scribblings. Since the article had been published, I'd put a few other features online, which had attracted some attention, but I mainly put this new zeal back into the other women at training. I made myself available to help as many new trainees as I could, and I came to know some of the Burning Hearts girls better.

Summer arrived early that year, and in May the Burning Hearts crew were told, via text, that the boxing gym we used was being knocked down to build luxury flats. Janey spent hours finding places we could train but the cheapest we could afford didn't have a ring. One was a warehouse room used for trapeze practice in a squat. It had mirrors, one crash mat and a carpeted floor; we had to take it in turns on the mat.

The other room was a judo studio with a matted floor, but there were no windows or mirrors. We would mark out a ring with rolled-up clothes and practise mat wrestling – the room would get to 30°C and we would have to go sit outside in a line to cool down.

But our spirits were always high after training, and there were never more than ten of us, so everyone got to know each other well. Often there would be other wrestlers there who had worked the indies – girls like Mesha and Nye-Oh. And even Rhia O'Reilly would pop in.

Rhia and I got off to a slightly rocky start when I asked, 'What do we do to fix women's wrestling?'

'It's not broken.' There was a horrible pause. Then she said, though still toneless, 'Wrestling is the problem, not women. If more people get into wrestling then it'll be good for all of us.'

Luckily, Rhia forgave me at some point, probably when I took every pointer she gave me at training to heart and we got drunk together at a barbecue.

At Burning Hearts we were united by the freedom of being able to discuss wrestling in a neutral environment, where no one was going to talk over us or try to change what we were doing. I remember one afternoon when it was boiling hot, and after training the whole group walked through Mile End cemetery to find there was a free arts festival taking place. There were all kinds of trendy, thoughtful areas of entertainment – but we were mainly overjoyed someone had brought the pub *to us*.

We sat under a tree that had been decorated with a hundred papier-mâché breasts, and talked about wrestling. Mesha talked about how she had lost her confidence so many times she couldn't even count. She said that she was now trying to pour her aggression and strength into her character, and it was working. Nye-Oh talked about how she had watched wrestling with her brothers, and from day one knew she would take it up because she would always be better than the stars on TV. Daisy lapped up the names and descriptions of wrestlers she'd never heard of.

I left that afternoon with a renewed sense of wellbeing, which I remember because I went straight from training to the Gallery where a poster had appeared on the wall: 'Pro Wrestling EVE – feminist wrestling'.

Feminist. The word, spelt correctly, even underlined, was on a poster for a wrestling show. At the Resistance Gallery. Even Burning Hearts hadn't got to the point where we put the *actual* word feminist on the posters – even we weren't that brave.

The poster featured a shot of one woman being dropkicked in the face by another, hair and limbs flying everywhere – there were no pin-up shots or pink lettering. I was knocked out by it, like something from a lucid dream.

I casually asked Vanderhorne about EVE coming to the Gallery.

'Yeah,' he said, 'they want to have a more punk venue and obviously Lucha pulls in a non-wrestling crowd, so they want us to bring in more people.'

Who were these people who were running this magical escapade?! This is what I had laid in bed half-dreaming about for five years, and now without ceremony there was going to be an all-female show at the Gallery, with feminism in the title. Then I reminded myself that if it was going to be held any-where, it was going to be here – and I personally thanked the universe for bringing it into fruition.

I immediately found Emily Read on Facebook and asked if I could work the door in exchange for free entry, and she graciously agreed. One Saturday morning a few weeks later, I found myself at Bethnal Green; I realised I had never been to the Gallery on a Saturday morning this side of dawn. As I turned into the alley, the plastic-bag men were already form-ing an orderly queue.

I thumped open the metal door front with my shoulder (it had warped in the fire) and was hit by a cacophony of female voices, shouting, with the ring creaking as they practised their moves. The roster was very much the same as the one I'd seen in March, with a few other women whose names I didn't know.

Janey and Dragonita hadn't come, I assumed, due to it being at the Gallery, and I guessed they were perhaps not on good terms with them since leaving Lucha to start their own show. I looked around for something to do and started to re-stock the bar with Bryan, the barman who worked at the Gallery. Bryan never looked happy to see anyone, so I had made it my mission for the last three years to make him like me and I had won him over with overwhelming optimism in the face of his constant cynicism. And always collecting glasses.

The first thing Bryan said was, 'Why aren't you up there, then?'

'I'm not wrestling at the moment, also I'm not sure this crowd are ready for a poison frog who knocks people out with her vagina.'

As I said this I noticed that Emily had got in the ring with another woman and was trying to put up a banner. The banner was a picture of a female reproductive system, ovaries and womb, on a bed of glittering stars and flowers. Above it were the words 'Pro Wrestling EVE: Fight Like a Girl'.

I ran over to help stick this in pride of place – an emblem I had never, ever, thought would be within the same room as a wrestling ring. I found myself being overly eager: 'I like your banner, can I help you with some gaffer tape?'

This came across like a weird pick-up line used nervously among the staunch feminists I'd found myself surrounded by in the wrestling ring.

'Yep,' Emily said, 'I think it could do with some more sticking behind the fallopian tubes to stop it from drifting – it's just a bed sheet, after all.'

'It's really nice to be given directions based on female reproductive organs.'

Emily and I continued to work our way around the room, putting up banners, avoiding the wrestlers practising dropkicks or posing for headshots – the general hubbub of a pre-show atmosphere. The banners included the words 'fuck shit up' on a series of large crocheted squares. There were also printed copies of a safe space statement, reminding punters that any hate speech, be it deemed sexist, racist or homophobic, would result in immediate rejection. There was a byline: 'We are petty and we will encourage the world's feminist killjoys to troll you on social media.'

The final fitting was a sheet with 'Secret Girl Gang Club House' and an arrow pointing to the door outside the Gallery. I think when they had decided to put on a show, they at least expected there would be a sign for the venue.

The plastic-bag men looked confused as we did this; the majority laughed or smiled, but the others checked their tickets on their phones, possibly confused about how their wrestling match had been co-opted by some angry feminists.

Back inside, I asked Emily, 'Why have you decided to suddenly be balls-to-the-wall feminist?'

'It's not been a sudden decision…'

'Sorry, no of course not, but feminism isn't allowed in wrestling.'

She laughed, which relieved me; I didn't want to be *that twat* again. Emily continued, 'The fact is, we stopped for years because I had a mental breakdown, we've managed to get back up and running but now we need to change things. Before we were so determined to keep everyone happy so we could sell tickets – but now we need to actually use the fact we have the most badass women in wrestling to make things different. No more time wasting. That's why.'

I planned to take tickets on the door, fully geared up in a *luchadora* mask and a pair of dungarees to add to the riot-grrrl aesthetic. But as soon as the doors opened the crowd came in, flashing their printouts at me, then rushing inside to get a place. I felt like warning them that there was no danger of them missing anything at the Gallery; the wrestlers flew out the ring. In fact, the only people I knew were some trainees, men and women who had come down to support the show in any way they could – that filled me with happiness.

Like the last show, there were about ten women in the audience, who were all decidedly punk and conspicuous. They were all thrilled to be there and all said something along the lines of: 'Are there always so many men here? It's weird.'

To which I had come up with the stock response: 'Well, you can be any gender to be a feminist.'

Of course I just wanted to say, 'I know, right!' But I figured that they needed to see the show to understand why they should come back, and not be put off by the plastic-bag men.

Riot grrrl music played, and Emily climbed into the ring in ripped hot pants and a black t-shirt. She looked different from how I'd first seen her. I realised she was tall and angular, and that she was masking any fear she had with a strut that seemed to have come from nowhere. Emily delivered a speech, a manifesto; about how this was the real revolution and it had been here for years, just underground. She talked about how the women on the roster had been wrestling for a combined sixty-eight years and had to persevere through a tidal wave of shit just to do something they loved. Then she said that, as a riot grrrl organisation, they had a 'girls to the front rule', and that if there was a woman behind you, or someone shorter, you had to let them to the front.

Half of us screamed with applause, the others sat in stunned silence. I made eye contact with a few women who had been standing behind the people who had staked their place earlier at the ringside. I noticed, coincidentally, that one of them had been the guy who Drastik had been infuriated by at the last show. He didn't meet my gaze so I tapped on his shoulder and smiled. He begrudgingly gave up his place and I was in my favourite spot at the gallery – ringside, in the centre – meaning that I would have to move out of the way as bodies were hurled towards me. I started to bang the ring with excitement and others joined me, as a chant started for EVE.

Like the last show, the wrestlers turned it out. It was more basic wrestling than what the ring at the Gallery was used to – and I noticed the women did a lot of mat wrestling like headlocks and leg scissors, which half the crowd wouldn't be able to see because of the low ceiling. The few high-fliers were in their element – jumping off the ropes, flinging themselves into the crowd as if they were doing stage dives. By the end of the show, the crowd, who had probably never experienced wrestling this up close and personal, were stunned, sweating and astonished.

Emily thanked everyone for coming, and at the end she announced loudly, 'And women – come back! Tell your friends! Come to wrestling training here at the Resistance Gallery! We don't just need wrestlers; we need a whole army to change the industry! I mean, for God's sake, we haven't even got a female ref! Can some women please become referees?' That was the light bulb moment I needed.

The building emptied quickly, unusual for a show at the Gallery where usually everyone would hang around and have a drink. The wrestlers left as well with their wheelie suitcases, off to catch trains back to their hometowns of Colchester, Norwich and Southampton. I helped to clear up the glasses, and when I could I spoke to Dann, Emily's husband, a nerd with a beard and the heart of a cynical golden retriever. He said he was really pleased with the Gallery and that they'd be back.

'It's like we're at the right place – we want to change the mould of what women's wrestling is, and we're going to lose some fans over it, but for the right reasons.'

He told me afterwards that he'd had to eject about ten men for 'hate speech'. Another fifteen or so had left because the venue wasn't up to standard – meaning, the toilets were dark and only two of them locked. EVE was embracing the chaos and freedom of suddenly giving no fucks about what 'normal' wrestling fans expected. And I wanted in.

Before I left, I found Greg, who said he'd really enjoyed the show. There'd been a bit of tension between us since Burning Hearts started, but after some discussion, he admitted that he wasn't so much worried about the competition, he was just hurt. He hated the idea that women would leave Lucha 'because of feminism'.

'If they'd stuck around, they could be on this show, do you see? It's gonna get massive with the women's revolution stuff.'

'I agree that we should work together, yes.'

'And what about you, you're still here, you could be on that show soon – you're better than most of the girls out there. But well, you know… your health and stuff.'

There was the usual sad moment of silence between us that happened whenever my Womb Witch came up. Greg knew how to handle wrestlers with bust knees, or back problems; but seemingly, ovaries left him flummoxed. And because there was no solution from him, the wrestler who essentially taught me everything, it made me remember that I was probably never going to be as good as I once was. But I also knew Greg didn't want me to give up altogether.

'Greg, I want to be a ref.'

'What, instead of a wrestler?'

'Well, I figure at least for the moment, seeing as I can't be back in the ring for… I don't know how long, to be honest. But there're *no* female referees, are there?'

Greg thought for a second, and then came up with, 'There was one, once, but she's retired now.' He nodded in the way that I love about Greg; he visibly takes a second to think about things, then he nods if you've won him over with an idea. With understated enthusiasm, he said, 'Yeah, all right then, we'll train you up for the next student show. Let's get you in that EVE ring. Let's help you reach your goal.'

My goals changed in that moment. If I couldn't be a wrestler (and being a wrestling writer was proving to be hard), then my next achievable goal was to be a referee. Because then, at least, I would be doing something that women didn't usually get to do, and there was no reason why I couldn't do it. You don't need to be a man to hit the floor and count to three; you don't need to be a man to command the rules of a show that ran itself.

But seemingly, wrestling had just not noticed this – it needed to change and I could be the one to do something about it.

10

Girl Gangs

A matter of weeks after EVE did their first event at the Gallery, a show was released about women's wrestling. *GLOW* was the dramatisation of a real-life TV show from the 1980s, *The Gorgeous Ladies of Wrestling*. Unlike the original *GLOW*, which was a mix of blatant titillation and a level of humour palatable to a child, this series promised to pass the Bechdel test with flying colours and bring a new feminist audience to wrestling.

I had seen a talking-heads documentary about *GLOW*, reuniting the women from the original cast. They were almost all actresses at the bottom of the pile in terms of accessing new acting opportunities, and they talked about being given characters; and about how they were put together in a hotel complex and given two weeks to learn how to wrestle. Friendships were formed that continued for decades afterwards. Two of them had even gone on to have careers as wrestlers; meanwhile, the others ranged from being pensioners to psychics to stay-at-home moms.

But what I had loved about the documentary was how the

women could talk candidly about the problems with wrestling. They spoke of how their characters, watched now, are offensive in their portrayal of stereotypes, and how they'd be directed to do everything from burning the American flag to riding into the ring on a horse to get their characters over. They were open about how hard wrestling was and how they weren't well-trained: one woman's elbow had been wrenched so badly in a match that you could see the bones move under the skin. Like the wrestlers I knew, they told these stories with the demeanour of those who would never change any of it for a second. They gave the impression that being wrestlers was something unexpected, but which gave them an indescribable energy. I was hopeful that *GLOW*, the Netflix series, would reproduce these important qualities.

Ruth, a good friend and attentive tweeter, scored two tickets for the premiere of the series in London from a lesbian lifestyle magazine. The premiere was at a hotel in Mayfair. I wore a gold lamé jumpsuit and had styled my hair into a mini green Mohawk. I'd put on so much glittery eye shadow that everything was a hazy reflection of lights in my peripheral vision. I felt like a rock star until we walked down the stairs of a hotel with marble everywhere, and were greeted by reception staff looking disbelievingly at my get-up. Every single other person at the premiere was wearing something smart-casual; it was a sea of beige and white summer blouses. I felt very, very conspicuous.

This feeling dissipated following my second glass of free Prosecco. We had moved tables three times to ensure we had sampled all of the vol-au-vents on offer, and we had mingled with approximately nobody. We were able to watch two episodes of *GLOW*, and were impressed to see they'd already hit on miscarriage, routine body-shaming, and drugs. That being said, the show didn't portray even one fully-fledged bout; even the training scenes barely suggested what wrestling actually entails.

In the smoking area after the premiere, word had got around that the woman in the gold jumpsuit was a wrestler. And about twenty people, all women, came up to talk to me. They all complained to me about how there hadn't been enough wrestling in the show. I agreed with them, wholeheartedly.

The *Guardian* printed my review, which I tried to make as glowing (ha) as possible, even though the show didn't go far enough to prove what tough motherfuckers female wrestlers actually are. And I wasn't the only one who wanted to explain the fact behind the fiction – female wrestling suddenly exploded into mainstream consciousness.

At work, colleagues who had barely spoken to me would come up and say, 'I saw *GLOW*, I love it – I can't believe you're a wrestler!' The look and feel of wrestling had the potential to change and become something empowering, something that pulled in new members of the public simply because it was being marketed at a non-white-male audience for the first time. And there was a joyful, smug feeling that it had been women, not men, who had caused this sudden surge of interest to happen.

At training, new recruits took to learning with the same reckless glee that Becca and I had experienced all those years ago, when we learned our first forward rolls. Except now there were just as many women as men, so for the first time in Lucha history, Greg and Vanderhorne had to start training an extra night a week to take in the influx of newbies. Many of these knew nothing about wrestling; they were women who were queer, punk, fat positive and anti-establishment. There were some weeks where I would see some toxic 'proper wrestler' return to training hoping for a booking, expecting a hero's welcome, and who would then end up sat timidly in a corner.

These girls, even though they couldn't jump higher than about twenty centimetres, and despite all their wrestling references coming from a feminist Netflix show, would walk into the ring with a confidence that shone out of them. Their characters were different and funny, and were clearly already giving them a way of releasing their alter egos:

'I'm Goldy, Queen of Trash – I take my opponents, beat them, visit their mothers, sort through their treasured possessions and sell them for a profit *after* I've fucked their mum.'

'I AM CUNTZILLA, THE PSYCHODYKE OF BRIGHTON, AND YOU WILL FEAR ME.'

'I'm Tracy Bachelor's mum, and I know what you said to her about her weight and I'm here to teach you a lesson.'

There was never a confused silence, but rapturous applause and laughter. The new blood meant the Gallery felt like a completely different place to what it had been for months. There was nothing I loved more than looking over to see Greg and Vanderhorne's faces, a mix of amazement, confusion and pride. Before, Lucha had always been the school that would take anyone, and even though it was never said to their faces, other schools looked down on us for that very reason. Lucha was considered to be performance art, not 'proper wrestling', even though we were still more memorable than most other schools and could sell out a show every month.

The Resistance Gallery, cult-like and shambolic as it was, had now become the new spiritual home for a huge number of women, just as it had become mine years before.

Even in Burning Hearts, we were affected by *GLOW*. We had come up against so many barriers just to get somewhere to practise, and out of nowhere Daisy's flatmate saw *GLOW* and then got us a gig at a beautiful venue called The Old Library. It had high ceilings, wide wooden doors and a capacity of about 200 people. In short, it was the perfect place to put on a wrestling show. All we had to do was sell £200 of booze to the crowd, which was never going to be an issue if you fill a room with people and feed them joyous violence.

Despite the sudden influx of new recruits, it seemed that becoming a ref was the one thing that the other women around me weren't considering. I'd been in the ring, and I wanted something that could give me more credibility, more respect, and which would reduce the number of concussions I was likely to have in the future.

Being a ref was something that you got pulled in to do last minute, or worse, something you do when you admit that you'll never be a professional wrestler. But like every other gender disparity I had encountered within wrestling, I was determined to challenge this. No, I wasn't giving up on wrestling. I just wanted to give this a go. I wanted to get on the EVE roster and be listed as the only female referee in the country, which bizarrely I was able to claim as soon as I had made the decision to start.

Neither Lucha nor Burning Hearts had ever trained referees but they had matches booked within the next month, so agreed that I could make my debut as the 'ring official'. Vanderhorne and Greg had both reffed matches, with Vanderhorne donning a mask when we did big corporate gigs to get his moment in the spotlight. It turned out that most of it was about staying out of the way, which is harder than it sounds. I was trained to know the choreography of the ring, so I would be able to second-guess which moves were coming up, and make sure I was just far enough out of the way to dodge a flying body. But I also had to tell wrestlers to stop cheating without breaking the energy of the match – and that was harder.

Vanderhorne told me that the main thing was to be present,

and that if I ever looked bored it would appear to the audience that I wasn't intimidated by the wrestlers because I knew they weren't really hurting each other.

'You'll be all right,' Greg assured me. The preparation from their side ended there.

Just to be on the safe side, I asked the ref at Lucha, Rob Darcy, for some tips.

He told me: 'Vanderhorne asks me to be purposefully bad for Lucha so that the wrestlers can cheat more, but it's a crowd that doesn't care about rules so it doesn't matter. Just don't do what I do at Lucha, okay?'

I had been planning on copying Darcy in his entirety, from his awkward stance to his easily distracted manner, and now, in a horrible moment, it occurred to me that I was only half sure of the rules of wrestling. Why? Because in the ring I was a heel; I was supposed to show complete disregard for what the ref was saying. For example, I knew that you only choked your opponent in the corner for five counts – or when the ref wasn't watching. I knew that you had to be up on your feet after a count of ten or back in the ring on a count of ten if you left it; but again, I had used these as ways of telling a story. It had never occurred to me that someone would have ended the match because of me.

Both stumped and encouraged by my years in the ring, I knew that there was no way to learn to be a referee aside from being thrown in the deep end and getting into the ring at a show. That's why fate decided to book my first two reffing gigs on the same weekend – because apparently even taking on the nice relaxing role of referee had to be a pain in the arse.

The Burning Hearts show was on the Saturday night in Camberwell, helpfully only a bus ride away from my house. When I arrived at midday, everyone was there; but there was no ring yet. While waiting, we decided to do some warm-ups by having piggyback races and playing tag. After five years in wrestling I had never encountered a ring with an enormous spring in the middle until one was wheeled into the centre of the hall. There was less padding and less give than the Lucha ring, and the ropes weren't nearly as tight. Even if I had wanted to wrestle, there was no way I could have done any springboard moves, and even rolling hurt because the boards were so stiff. I forgave the ring for its weaknesses, though, when I found it was almost seventy years old and on its third owner.

I wondered if the original owners of the ring would be spinning in their graves at the idea that a company made entirely of women would be using it. My brain – hyped up on pre-performance anxiety and a lot of coffee – started to wonder if it might be haunted or cursed. To quiet my whirring imagination, I focused on listening in on the other wrestlers planning their matches, in part so that I would have an idea of what was going on.

Burning Hearts was still operating on the idea of two opposing teams battling it out across the night. In an ideal world, we would have had matching hoodies and separate dressing rooms; instead, we just made it simple by making one team face, and one team heel.

'Then we literally can't make it any clearer to the crowd when to boo or cheer.'

The matches were all fairly straightforward – two opponents, simple structures, with an emphasis on skill rather than high-flying moves. The biggest draw was Rhia O'Reilly, who would be the heel announcer. She practised all her insults on us in person: 'And what are you anyway? A female referee? You don't even look like you can count to ten! I know that we're in South London but couldn't we get an actual referee...? Great, female misogyny and North London snobbery – that's gonna get some realllll heat.'

Becca turned up late; she was the face announcer. She borrowed one of my gold dresses and admitted to me that she didn't really know what she was supposed to do, but had just agreed because she liked Janey a lot. I had to remind her again what a 'face' was, which confused her more.

'Look, you just need to get everyone to love the Wildheart Rebels!'

'Who are they?'

'They're the team you're representing.'

'Who are the other team?'

'Hellfire Furies.'

'Oh, what! Can I change? I'm a recovering Catholic, I've loads of jokes about hell.'

'Ask Janey.'

'Janey told me before that I had to do this because I'm funny and I have a nice face.'

'Nawww.'

'Yeah, but I make subversive feminist performance art, often involving drinking Stella and publicly displaying my body parts – the whole smiling thing is hard for me.'

'See it as a challenge.'

I was having the opposite issue. For me, it wasn't about being a face or a heel; it was about being impartial, and about how to make myself a 'proper ref'. I had decided I didn't want to wear the referee uniform of a black-and-white striped polo shirt and black trousers – it reminded me of school uniform. I ordered some stripy Beetlejuice leggings off the internet. I put them on with a blazer with the arms ripped off, and my training boots, and thought I looked cool, if not a bit pedestrian. Janey's review was, 'Umm, you look like a wrestler...' Shit.

There wasn't much for it, as there was only an hour to go and there wasn't time for me to go out and buy a horrible ref top. I changed out of my training boots; at least that way I just looked like a goth.

Becca was also panicking about her role, which was a bit more complex than counting to three: 'I just feel that I can't be funny in describing wrestling – which is something I know nothing about – and when introducing people with very specific tag lines.'

Becca was right: wrestlers are very, very particular about their introductions. Psycho Lolita *had* to be sweet and sadistic. Daisy Mayhem was the psychobilly brawler. Dragonita was from Barcelona, Spain. Amber had to be the amazing Amber Bree. Becca's job was being done for her, meaning she wasn't sure where she was supposed to insert her likeability. Eventually we decided that the best way to get the audience to like Becca was to enter to 'I Touch Myself', riding on the shoulders of Fraser. Fraser would be wearing my gold lamé jumpsuit, and a latex deer head we'd found in the props cupboard.

The show, like the previous Burning Hearts shows, drew a mostly non-wrestling crowd, consisting of friends of the cast and, predominantly, members of the theatre-going public, who had never seen anything like us before. However, as I walked through the audience before we started, I could see there were only about ten plastic-bag men, poised to broadcast their opinions on Twitter.

Backstage, we huddled and encouraged each other, and finished off our make-up. We then took a group picture that I still have stuck to my fridge. I stood behind the stage and heard the crowd scream for Becca, and then boo for Rhia – who explained without batting an eyelid what the rules of wrestling were.

Becca introduced me: 'To keep order in the ring it's the Burning Hearts referee, Heather Honeybadger!'

I came out to 'Hollaback Girl', checking the ropes in the

same way that I had seen other refs do, for a purpose that was unknown to me. I then entertained the crowd with some C-class twerking. About ten of my friends had come along to watch, one of whom had made a sign that said, 'Heather is the best referee ever'. I didn't have the heart to tell them that by cheering the ref they were breaking a lot of rules in wrestling etiquette – not that I'd paid much attention to this up to that point.

The first match was between Dragonita and Nye-Oh. They made their entrances: Dragonita, now wrestling as a heel, in a floor-length black jacket, staring moodily at the crowd, while Nye-Oh ran in and began high fiving everyone. I stood at the back, arms behind me, trying to remain completely neutral – when inside I was shitting myself in case I counted a near fall instead of a finish, which really is the biggest way that a ref can mess up.

Realising a second too late, I shouted to ring the bell so the match could start. I kept out of the way, but as soon as Dragonita was in her first wristlock I experienced an awkwardness I hadn't anticipated as ref – asking a wrestler if they can submit to something when they obviously won't.

'Dragonita, do you submit?'

'Of course I don't! Is this your first day or something?'

The audience booed her, with my little crowd shouting at her to leave me alone. I loved Dragonita for a second, and even more so when Nye-Oh took this as a cue to pull Dragonita to the floor by her wrist, causing her to writhe with pain. After that I followed the match across every submission and near fall, and it was much more tiring than I had expected.

Eventually Dragonita, with a roar, picked up Nye-Oh in a fireman's lift and threw her to the floor, pinning her where she landed. The crowd booed Dragonita and she got out of the ring before I could hold up her arm. She then arrogantly sauntered through the crowd. I leant next to Nye-Oh, who squeezed my hand – the 'iggy', the international wrestling sign of 'I'm fine'.

I had about a minute to realise that I'd managed to figure out how to ref before the next match started. Keeping constantly alert and upholding the rules in a bout of fake violence was proving to be incredibly exhausting. I had never thought that those fifteen minutes of madness as a ref would be just as draining as most of my wrestling matches.

The interval was announced, and Becca instructed everyone to help us meet our bar tab. Meanwhile, I went backstage to the other wrestlers.

This wasn't like the feeling when you return, gasping, from wrestling in the ring; where your opponent, usually, gives you a sweaty hug and thanks you for the match, and others tell you what they liked, or didn't, about your performance. I just wandered over and sat down; I had no gimmick to take off, I was Heather out there and I was Heather back here.

Dragonita came over and thanked me for reffing her match. But she also said, 'It's good you have a character. It makes it easier to work with you because I'll always get in your face.'

'I was worried the crowd were paying too much attention to me...'

'When you're taller than both competitors, have rainbow hair and stripy leggings, it's hard not to notice you. But that's who you are... own it.'

That made me feel more confident. Sure, I wasn't going to blend in like the refs on TV who aren't introduced, or even acknowledged. At most, they get knocked down by accident or pulled out of the ring. On a few occasions, I've seen a big wrestler lose it in the ring and relentlessly hit their knocked-out opponent – at which point an army of men in stripy shirts appear from nowhere and pull them apart.

No, I wanted to be the ref who kept up the rules, but that also said: 'Hi, come join our girl gang.'

The start of the next half was a squash match. Rhia invited a member of the audience to come and try out against Daisy Mayhem, who stood looking sardonic in one corner, purposefully next to Becca who was shorter and clearly intimidated by her. The member of the audience was, of course, a plant. She was a trainee, and we had put her in a sling and a hair band to make her look like Tiny Tim.

As she got in the ring, Rhia said in my ear, 'Be very visible in this match – squash matches are about the winner annihilating the opponent, so there's no room to cheat. Be on Daisy the whole time.'

I understood exactly what Rhia had said, because as soon as the bell rang Daisy roared and threw her opponent into a corner, running in and choking her. I was on her immediately, counting in her face, one arm on her to pull her off, and letting her turn to me and smile.

'I know the rules,' she said, before proceeding to grab the try-out's hair and drag her across the ropes, face first. The crowd squealed and she let go just as I reached the four count. Daisy basically mopped the ring with her opponent twice, before throwing her to the floor and choking her in the middle of the ring. I made a big deal about raising and dropping the try-out's limp arm as she pretended to be unconscious. Daisy then got to nudge me aggressively until I raised her arm in victory, to a wave of hatred that Daisy ate up with a twinkle in her eyes.

There were two further matches after that, where I found myself on referee auto-pilot – maybe I was too tired to think, or just understood my role better. After the show, my legs shook with adrenaline, and I could barely put together sentences because I had been concentrating so hard for two hours.

Janey said she was really happy with how I'd done. Darcy, who'd been photographing the show, said the same, though pointed out some of the basic things that I'd been doing wrong. These included moving too much, not talking loudly enough and being almost apologetic when I had to break things up: the take-home advice was that I had to be both more powerful and less conspicuous. To my horror, Dann from EVE was there too, but he was happy as well and said it was really promising that I was training to be a referee.

My first show was over as a ref, and I almost missed my stop on the bus because I fell asleep against the window.

Burning Hearts made £15 each from ticket sales once we'd covered the costs. The theatre wanted us to book another date with them almost immediately, and the feeling of our little group being a team, and not just another promotion, grew even stronger.

After twelve hours' sleep, I woke up with my soles sore, my fingers bruised on my right hand, and my knees clicking. Also to my horror, I had slept past eleven, the strict arrival time for all wrestlers who wanted to appear on a student show. I was late to a wrestling gig for the first time in my life.

Fraser and I got in the car, eating toast as we drove to Bethnal Green. I wrapped my hand in a support, hoping no one would notice, and bought two padded knee supports from Boots on the way. I arrived at the Gallery two hours after everyone else, but two hours before doors.

Burridge gave me a right talking to. 'Just because you're not a wrestler doesn't mean you're suddenly Jimmy Big Bollocks. You need to show up on time, like you would with any match. Especially you, you should know better and set a good example to the newbies.'

I mumbled sorry and waited for him to tell me I couldn't ref. I'd seen him do this at a show before. The trainee was supposed to be making his debut and had all his family coming, but Greg told him he couldn't do anything because he wasn't showing proper respect. I waited, but, with a last look of exasperation, he walked off.

Second lesson learned about being a ref: be there on time, because apparently despite not being in the grand roster you will still need to show the same humbleness. Wrestling is, at its heart, about being humble.

I avoided Greg but walked around asking for the card. There was no card; people knew their matches but they hadn't decided on the running order. It wasn't written down and there were ten different bouts. I grabbed some paper and went around every single wrestler; all of them talked me through their matches, most of them at double-speed due to excitement. Greg came around looking for the card, and there was a small feeling of triumph when I handed it to him so he could decide the order.

He copied it down and read it out to everyone in a moment of calm when we crowded around the ring before the doors opened. I remember how he'd done this for my first few shows, where there had been half as many people. He would drum into us the importance of having fun and trying something new because most of us were already in shows elsewhere. This time, many of the wrestlers had never wrestled anywhere else and he had taught them everything that they knew – the pressure was more intense than usual, particularly as Vanderhorne wouldn't be there until later.

He looked around the room, and asked, 'Can you just put up your hands a second if you've worked in a superkick?'

A superkick is a karate kick to the head, a basic move but hard to do well. Half the wrestlers put up their hands, slightly embarrassed.

Burridge nodded. 'I want you all to think of something else.

I'm not having a show of people doing wafty kicks at each other's heads and slapping their thighs. Just because you've seen it on TV doesn't mean that it's going to look good.' I sat at the back, feeling nervous.

Greg paused for a second, then continued, 'Look, you think I'm being hard on you and I know that for a lot of you this is a fun, silly show. But you have to realise that the world's eyes are on us at the moment – we have a school that's busting at the seams; we have reporters in here every other weekend. This isn't a town hall with twenty people in it, even though it might feel like one.

'The reason I've been doing this for twenty years is because every time I get in a ring, whether it's for a match or for train-ing or just to roll about on my own, I give it everything I have. I want you to do the same – if this is your first match, show me your potential. If this isn't your first match, make it the best match you've ever done.' Then he added, 'I'm really, really proud of all of you. I never thought I'd have my own wrestling school, let alone one with so many awesome people. So let's show them we're the best, okay?' We cheered.

'Oh, and Heather is reffing today. It's her first – no, sorry – second time doing it so make sure she knows your matches. And also, well done her because there's no other female refs working in the UK at the moment and she's got a lot riding on this.'

I got a cheer as well, then suddenly remembering how exhausting yesterday had been, I looked down at my crumpled piece of paper on which the names were scribbled in the wrong order. I was going to make this the best event I'd ever reffed.

Sure, I only had one to beat, but it was still possible I might forget to count to three and disappoint everyone.

The first match, it turned out, was going to be a six-man tag, already complicated, particularly as they had planned it around my being pushed out of the way to miss a spear from a 24-stone man. A spear essentially means flying through the air and rugby tackling someone – not something you want to get in the way of. Then, there would be another point where I would be pulled out of the ring by my feet and eventually miss a disqualification finish which would then be turned into a victory. In other words, it was a completely different match to anything I'd done previously.

So I counted to three, stuck to the rules, and tried to stay out of the way. I guess this was a sign that I had done a good job as they'd forgotten I was there. Not that I had more than twenty seconds to consider this before the next lot of wrestlers got in the ring and started cutting promos. I looked at my notes but eventually ignored them, and instead I just followed the rules.

In the third match, Mauro Chaves, the Vegan Warrior, pulled a promo about how disgusting the audience was, then dragged me over to cover his ears with my hands so he couldn't hear their boos. Halfway through the match he pulled kale from his pants to choke out his opponent. When I went to stop him, he said, 'It's a no DQ match! Okay? I do what I want!'

Apparently no one had told the ref this was a no disqualification match – there are no rules. I'd spent the last five minutes counting their choking and telling them to get off the ropes. Luckily the audience of grandmas and children didn't mind; they too weren't a 'proper' crowd.

The next match was between two wrestlers who brawled to the outside and didn't make it back by the ten count. So I had no choice but to shake my head and wave my arms about, and Greg rang the bell as a disqualification. The crowd booed and I thought it was for me, so I just started repeating the rules of wrestling, but I noticed they were booing the wrestlers because they were still fighting and throwing each other against the toilet walls. I jumped out of the ring and separated them, doing my best 'girl in a bar' angry face, until one of them left.

There were two other matches where the wrestlers accidentally pushed me off them to get more heat, but it made me look like I didn't know what I was doing. Afterwards, I was mostly thanked by the wrestlers for reffing their match, but not by all of them. It was just all a bit too intense – it made yesterday look like nothing.

Darcy told me I was moving and reacting too much, and that I didn't look impartial. 'Try and only get excited by the end – it'll help pace the matches better. Right now I'm drawn to you a lot, which is probably because you're still walking around the ring like a wrestler; you need to be the ref, not a wrestler.'

The next matches were better; I toned it down a bit in terms of my character and my movement. I felt less dynamic but by the end of the matches the crowd were roaring for the wrestlers just the same. And these were simple matches; in one of them, Diablesa Rosa came out and took a girl through her paces, playing the heel and giving me something to work with. The final match was a complicated three-way, and no one had told me that the finishing move was supposed to appear twice in it, so of course I counted the wrong pin and the match finished early. I was worried that they would be furious, but the humbleness of the wrestlers about their own craft had been drilled into them by Burridge, and from the moment they exited the ring they too grovelled for my forgiveness.

The show ended, and as ever, all the students climbed in the ring for a group photo. Many of them wandered about, still in their gimmicks, being congratulated by friends and family. I got a beer from Bryan and had a cigarette, waiting for my brain to stop running at a thousand miles an hour. I remembered that even though I was pulling myself apart about refereeing, it was worse for the wrestlers when they forgot something basic, like getting back in the ring on a ten count, or bridging up to break a pin. I could pick up on these now I was watching from the other side.

But I wasn't sure I liked this other side, where I thought I would command respect but instead was blatantly ignored on a number of occasions. I was trying to break the mould by being a woman, and an individual, but if I reacted or drew attention to myself then I wasn't doing my job. But everyone encouraged me and said that I was a natural.

Vanderhorne clasped my shoulder and said, 'But don't get too good; remember you're a wrestler, okay?'

But I had been in a ring for almost four hours and had not drunk nearly enough caffeine. I hadn't realised what he meant so just grinned and nodded.

Dann and Emily came up to me. Emily said, 'I can't get over your ring positioning. You were really good – I can't believe you've only been doing it for what, two days?'

I remained bashful, then managed to murmur, 'Well, I'm only doing it because I want to ref for EVE.'

Dann beamed at me. 'Well look, She-1 is in two weeks and we can start you then. You can ref the easy matches. It's two days and it would be unfair to expect our normal ref to do all of it on his own.'

I really hadn't been prepared for how quickly I could get in the ring as a ref, and it pulled me out of my post-show fug immediately. I accepted enthusiastically, then babbled at them both for twenty minutes until I realised my tongue felt heavy from shouting and I needed to go home. Fraser, lovingly, drove me back and we spent most of the ride singing along to Britney Spears because I couldn't form sentences.

The rain thundered down that night, and I lay awake thinking about reffing. Why had it been easier than I expected to reach this next goal, and why was my imposter syndrome worse than ever? I knew the rules of wrestling, and reffing was so, so hard – but where was the respect that I thought would come with the stripes? To step into the ring as a female body, even if it does not register as an act of rebellion, was worth it just to make women more visible in wrestling. Maybe it wasn't even about my gender – people just didn't care about the ref.

Maybe it wasn't for me, but I would only find out if I persevered.

I considered my dilemma over the next few days. The problem was that I still thought that getting into the ring meant I was a wrestler. At training, I had wanted to ref practice matches, but usually there was no time so instead I would just practise moves that I would not be using. Slowly my wrestling skill had returned, along with an acceptance that I wouldn't learn to do something right the first time round. But I now had enough experience to show other people where they were going wrong. People would ask me when I intended to fight again, and I'd proudly say I was the only female referee in the UK now, although not with as much pride as I thought I would be able to muster.

Heather Honeybadger, the referee, was me. She had my face, and my clothes, she walked like me and had my smile. The freedom of entering a wrestling ring was to forget about the things you don't like about yourself, and project them elsewhere – be it into your opponent's face, or into the crowd sitting in the cheap seats; it liberates you.

Who was Heather Honeybadger the referee? She seemed too emotional, too spirited, to be the 'normal type' of referee. Heather the former wrestler, in a potentially semi-permanent state of retirement. Heather who *previously* wore masks and had wrestled in York Hall. Heather who had survived, in chronological order, family breakdown, rape, depression, endometriosis, a laparoscopy and chronic pain. The same Heather who wrote passionately – and with questionable fact-checking – about women in wrestling. I realised that being a ref was hard because that person was just me, not someone else.

But I couldn't give up, not now, not with all the attention that women's wrestling was getting. I calmed my nerves by saying I was still learning; this was just another mountain to climb. And because EVE was getting so much publicity, and had been so kind as to give me the opportunity, I had no choice but to be ready to ref four shows in two days for She-1.

Since *GLOW* came out, EVE was constantly on the TV, in magazines, splattered across Instagram. Dann and Emily had decided to capitalise on its success by holding an inaugural tournament to see who was the strongest member of the EVE roster – their 'ace'. There would be twenty matches, and the winner would get a trophy in the shape of an apple core, and there would be ribbon streamers. Dann had shipped in wrestlers from Japan to compete, and every time the line-up was announced, my pelvic floor would flip. I would immediately start Googling the wrestlers, in case I was reffing their match. This wasn't the best idea as it resulted in me getting tongue-tied when I met them. There was Emi Sakura, who owned her own wrestling school. And Meiko Satomura, a woman who looked like she'd stepped directly out of some kind of role-playing game as a noble warrior, and who was widely considered to be the best wrestler (her gender disregarded) in the world.

I got to the Gallery *on time* as Greg had reminded me to, chidingly, when I had been training. I spent a happy three hours with Emily, and we talked about a lot of important subjects as we rolled up the She-1 t-shirts for the merch stand. These included conversations on sweets, Suffolk buses, the Spice Girls and Mooncup debacles.

As the wrestlers arrived and the card was decided, I tried to go round and greet all the wrestlers, but I still was unable to get my words out. These people weren't as cuddly as they were in the cabaret scene or at Lucha – they were hardened by years of touring across the world. I didn't know what I'd expected, so I just helped Bryan stock the bar with beers and made sure lots of snacks were ready for the show. It was just like last time, except I was now part of the show, albeit seemingly not an important part.

Diablesa came up to me. 'I got you a present.'

Diablesa had been a dancer for ten years so was the queen of finding leotards online. She presented me with a black-and-white striped leotard, with a 1950s cut. I'd packed some black shorts and tights, and with this new addition the leggings were gone, meaning I now looked more like a referee. She smiled, like it was nothing, and went off to plan her matches against five other women.

About an hour before doors, the other ref arrived. He had worked across the world and had even refereed for the WWE. He told me not to worry and that he'd help me as much as he could. The audience for the first show came in, mainly Lucha trainees and a spattering of plastic-bag men, but also a healthy dose of women whose faces I didn't know. The coverage of *GLOW* had done its job and I was thrilled.

Just to stop me from worrying, Emily decided I was going to ref the first match, and even now I can't tell you who it involved. I practised being invisible, quiet and keeping out the way; all the while my heart was pumping fast in my chest. At one point I raced across the ring to try to count out a choke on the ropes and a crowd member went, 'Come on ref!'

What? It got me for a second – I was now part of the show? The faceless, nameless, ref? The acceptance was nice; the fact they thought I wasn't doing a good-enough job, less so. I counted the winning pin fall of the match, then sat down next to Emily at the ring side, while the other ref gave me a smile and a nod, and then took his turn to ref a match that was about four times as fast and complicated.

The other ref made it look fluid, easy; his voiced boomed with every count or instruction – and no one called him out, he clearly had more authority than me. I realised that was because he was known by the audience as a 'proper' ref. This audience was probably, then, the first 'proper' audience I had ever been in front of. And I didn't know what they wanted. Even though I was the one who was supposed to be keeping everything under control.

I remember the next match well because it featured Bea Priestley. She'd given me a clear rundown of all her moves backstage to help me out, but I got in the way about three times. This was a problem because Bea runs fast and hits hard. In the match, I slowed her pace each time, and because in character she's a merciless zombie warrior, she berated me cuttingly.

The show carried on until six in the evening. I was given a few more basic matches that I stumbled through. I felt like I had to be more subdued here, even though I was wearing a black-and-white leotard and velvet shorts. The last thing I wanted was to draw attention to myself, to get 'come on ref' from any more people. Eventually the show ended to rapturous applause, but there was only an hour until the doors would open again for the next set of bouts.

Dann was standing next to me, talking to someone, and I heard him say, 'Well, yes, there's a few people. *Time Out*, a few people from the WWE, and Regal said he might pop in…'

Regal. William Regal was on the WWE in the 1980s and 1990s, and now he'd aged gracefully into a managerial role in the company. But he was a big reason why more British stars were being picked up by the WWE and was widely respected as being honest and very kind. However, this was the worst thing Dann could have told me.

As Dann went to move away, I grabbed him and said, 'Please don't tell me you're expecting me to ref in front of William fucking Regal.'

'Yes, and you'll be reffing a match with Meiko Satomura.'

'Shit the bed.'

'Stop worrying, you're doing great. You need to be nicer to yourself. Look, can you count how many *shows*, not matches, you've reffed on one hand?'

'Yes...'

'Then you're learning, and everyone here knows that.'

Then the doors opened and the plastic-bag men filed in. I didn't pity them or hate them like I used to, until I overheard them expressly complain that the feminist angle was politicising wrestling. They would complain after every show; not all of them, but enough to make you feel they expected female wrestlers to be glorified show ponies. Chomping at the bit until they're so worn out they can be put out to pasture, and replaced by younger models.

The second show was harder. The matches went at the same kind of pace but I counted either too slowly or too quickly. Meiko Satomura's match, thankfully, was a squash match, and being the baby-face that she was, I didn't even have time to tell her to get off the ropes or even to stop choking. She destroyed her opponent in a mere thirty-eight seconds.

Before the final match, they made an announcement. On 5 May, Pro Wrestling: EVE would be holding the largest ever women's show in Europe at York Hall. The room erupted so hard that the ring rattled. I stood in it, waiting for the final match to start. I knew that on 5 May I would be in New York on holiday, and even though I loved Emily and Dann, and everyone who had helped me become a ref, I realised then that the opportunity was meant to be for someone else. It wasn't my time to do this.

The next day was just as much of a whirlwind but now I had accepted that I didn't need to be a ground-breaking referee if my heart wasn't in it. I refereed six more matches, and then I actually began to enjoy myself.

The time in the ring was still nerve-wracking, but my favourite memories of that weekend were the moments spent with Rhia, there again as a ringside commentator due to a busted ankle. Throughout the show she feuded with the current champion, who had broken Rhia's ankle with a chair during a match; the champion was introduced as 'hailing from the shattered remains of Rhia O'Reilly's career'. And then there was Emily, who would announce every wrestler and who was both delighted and terrified by the fact EVE had sold out all four shows of the weekend.

The final match of the night saw Charlie Morgan become 'the ace' of EVE. She jumped off a balcony on to five people; the other ref was knocked out by this, so I counted the final pin. I had done the same move a few years earlier, and felt a pang in my stomach for the fearlessness that she embodied. All sixteen women in the show had performed spectacularly, and we had a few drinks afterwards to celebrate. About half of the wrestlers thanked me for their matches, including Meiko and Emi, for whom I made a cup of tea to say thank you in turn.

I kept my thoughts to myself and replied with bashful smiles and thank-yous when people said it would be amazing to have a female referee at York Hall *finally*. For the most part, the EVE fans were mainly a mix of nerdy but friendly men and badass women; I smiled at how this niche had been filled, and I was glad I had been a part of it.

Perhaps I might have considered continuing being a referee,

and even seriously thought about changing my flight from New York to be at York Hall. However, this changed as soon as I went out for a cigarette, and a man approached me in the smoking area where he spent ten minutes telling me how I could be a better ref. Another took hold of my arm when I was on my way to the dressing room and said he knew it was my first show, and that the next one would be even better because I'd learn from my mistakes. He then told me he knew *all* the wrestlers and could reassure me. I asked him if he'd been to Lucha Britannia; he snorted and said, 'Not *that* one.'

I wasn't brave enough to tell these men to fuck off, or strong enough to ignore them, so I simply smiled and nodded. Luckily, I turned away from them straight into a crowd of smoking women who wanted to know about how I became a ref, and who ate up my stories about the training school and Lucha. Then the question came: 'So, when are you getting back in the ring?'

And for the first time in months, I said, 'Soon.'

I realised I couldn't fit in, I could only fit out. I couldn't be the rules – my role would always be to bend them wide enough for more people to 'get it'. Being a ref wasn't me, and that was fine because I was something else just as good. I found Vanderhorne and said, 'I think I'm done being a ref now, when can I get back in the ring?'

And he smiled and said, 'You never left, frog-face.'

A month later it was the run up to Christmas. After just one show back as Rana I was given the usual short notice for a massive gig. We had all received a message on a Wednesday afternoon, informing us we were booked to wrestle in ten days' time at a winter festival in Clapham. We were wrestling at The Underbelly. For me, this represented hallowed ground where, on my first solo trip to a cabaret show, I had been told to come back when I had an act – which I'd never had, until now.

Approaching the gig I knew I was a bit rusty, but I was more confident than I had been before. Diablesa Rosa was still in the shows, as well as Muñeca de Trapo, the Rag Doll, who had lost all of her jitters since wrestling at York Hall two years earlier.

On the night of the show, I finished work and I didn't have to rush in the rain because I only had to go two stops instead of across London. On arriving at the station, I realised I only had one contact lens, so I ran into an opticians as it was closing and bought a single one for forty-three pence. As I crossed Clapham Common, a car beeped its horn and slowed down. I turned around, with my water bottle poised as a weapon, only to find Fraser at my side, ready to drive me the rest of the way.

Lucha were performing as a sideshow act in a winter fair ground. One night there was a drag show, another night there was a circus, and then us. The ring was bigger and brighter than any I'd seen before. I couldn't help but walk around the stalls, look up at the tented ceiling, and admire the 1920s mirrors all around the outside. The Underbelly was definitely the most beautiful venue I'd been in, and it had a modest capacity of 350 people.

Bryan was there, and played 'All I Want for Christmas is You' until it seemed the whole Lucha cast was dancing in the ring. We got ready in a Portakabin, with the ring girls doing their make-up in a cupboard, while Snake got ready to swallow swords for the general public. We crammed around as everyone tied up their injuries, topped up their fake tans, and talked through their matches.

I was on in the first match – and it was chaos. We waited outside in the freezing cold, frost on the grass around the plastic walkway. I entered to the spitting guitars, showering the crowd's faces with water and sauntering round the ring to a chorus of booing. Occasionally, I would get back in the ring only to be pulled out by another wrestler, with whom I'd brawl into the crowd.

There was a moment of clarity, as I climbed to the top turn-buckle to treat Burridge to a 'flying cunt drop' from across the ring. I remember my eyes being hungry, all those years ago at Glastonbury, desperate at the mere sight of this spectacle of violence and fabulousness.

I stood and looked around me, balancing twenty feet from the floor, a white haze in my peripheral from the stage lights. The crowd screamed for more, and I knew finally it was Heather, and not Rana, who they were cheering for.

I jumped as high as I could into thin air, and I could hear them hold their breath in anticipation.

11

The Importance of Being Unladylike

It would be great to finish there – to launch myself into the future, unrestricted, a bastion of strength with unstoppable wrestling prowess. In many ways that's what I felt I was doing when I sent off the first submission of this book. Jumping into the unknown, hoping that my comrades, or at least my own resilience, would catch me from a fall.

I learned, however, that we don't ever really, completely fall. A decline is never that neat or simple.

In February 2018, shortly after I had secured the deal to write this book with Unbound and a few months after Winterville, I was on my way to Lucha. As usual, I was eating as I went, running across London during rush hour, my bag full of wrestling gear, including the green glittering marvel that was Rana's costume (version four). The mask was in my handbag, for it was as precious as my wallet, phone and Holy Water drinking bottle. I would check it was still there at every interchange. Rana had had several face-lifts since her birth in 2014, but the base fabric was still the same tired, smelly, warped Lycra that had been with me every step of the way. No one else's face fitted inside that mask.

My phone buzzed with about twenty messages as soon as I came out of the Underground. The card had been announced with an hour to go until the doors opened. I saw I was in the multi-person chaos, and I was happy to see that there were about ten of us and most of them were new wrestlers I hadn't fought before. Lucha had had an influx of new gimmicks: Trif-fidos, the Plant God; Symbol, a head nod to the late Prince; Bukunawa, a Filipino Dragon God; Anansie, King of Spiders. The newbies were young, respectful and straight edge, and always a pleasure to train with. They had started to train during the revolution years; they didn't remember a time when women were relegated to the piss-break match.

Vanderhorne decided that, for a change, I should win the chaos – he'd found that the crowd had decided they liked me after I'd spent a year checking their tickets and drawing cocks on their hands for entry. Even when I spat water at them, at the Gallery, I would get a Rana chant, and I secretly loved the fact I was finally a face.

I'd invited the guy who I'd just signed a book deal with and a couple of other friends, along with my favourite photographer, Damien Frost. He was going to be doing portraits of us and I felt fearless.

The match began without me in the ring. I ran in, ducked a clothesline from Jerry and dropkicked him out the ring. I stayed in the centre as I made a show of throwing three other male wrestlers to the outside, and then did a huge suicide dive into the crowd. As I landed I felt myself be winded by a knee or an elbow from someone that I'd been dropped on, so I stayed at the side of the ring. But rather than ebb away, the pain made it hard to breathe.

Eventually my breath came back and I got back in the ring

to take down the 'tower of doom'. As all the other competitors were positioned in one corner, I wriggled my way to the centre and body slammed the entire group of them. Jerry got up first, gave me a kick to the stomach and threw me to the side. Jerry was bigger than me, and about twenty stone, but he also was the softest worker I knew – and just a tap to the stomach set off the churning and breathless pain again.

Then, I saw the finishers start, and for the second and final time that match I pulled everything out of my guts and climbed the top turnbuckle. I landed a flying cunt drop on to the arrogant, angry Hombre del Rocka – pinning him for the three-count. I remember hanging my head back and taking in the sensation of the crowd screaming for me; then the ref raised my hand and passed me the chaos crown. Behind my mask, there were a few tears of happiness that I was glad nobody else could see.

I limped up the stairs, hugged my opponents, took some ibuprofen and drank about a pint of water. Jerry asked if I was all right as I had gone pale, apparently. Thinking I'd just knocked myself slightly, I shrugged off any concern and went outside to see my friends, who were waiting in the smoking area. They whisked me off my feet, and as I rolled a cigarette, I realised I'd forgotten I had to give Fraser my knee pads before his match. (Being a consummate professional, he'd forgotten his.) I asked my friend to hold the cigarette while I went inside. I never came back for it.

I stopped at the top of the stairs in the changing room, the pain surging up from my womb, through my stomach, into my lungs. I couldn't breathe. I lowered myself on top of the sea of dust cloths and old costumes that makes up one half of the Gallery changing rooms. Whenever I breathed, the pain grew worse. I spoke to no one but I caught the eye of Maz, a ring girl, who was kind, feisty, French – and seasoned at looking after wrestlers when they hospitalised themselves. She quickly got Greg and then sat next to me, holding my hand.

Every person in that locker room had turned their faces, concerned, silent – trying to figure out at what point in the match I could have given myself internal bleeding. Later when I spoke to Greg about it, he said it was one of the most horrible moments of his career; because he'd seen me deal with so much, but this was the first time he'd seen real fear in my eyes.

Fraser and Vanderhorne were there in a flash; Vanderhorne agreed it was a hospital job. The music started for the second half but Anansie tore down the stairs to tell Benjamin Louche to stall – the next match was supposed to have both Greg and Fraser in it. I tried to explain it hurt all over, and I started to cry. Vanderhorne said, 'She's ruptured something, call an ambulance.'

Fraser replied, 'No, it's okay, I'll take her in the car – sorry, Greg, but some things are more important.'

Greg just nodded and patted my head, then turned to the other wrestlers to make a few quick changes, and in a matter of seconds they were going to the ring. With the crowd distracted, Fraser and Rhonda, a new trainee who was possibly the only calm person I could see in my peripheral vision, bundled me off to Whitechapel hospital.

Looking back now, it must have been a funny sight in the waiting room. A woman in a green, sparkling leotard with a half-green face, wheeled in by a woman dressed head to toe in purple like a Prince backing dancer, and a man in a PE kit with a monkey tail hanging out the back. But this was Whitechapel A&E on a Friday night – none of the staff batted an eyelid. However, for the same reason, we waited until 3.30am before being seen by anyone. During the three hours that I lay on the hospital floor, I realised that perhaps I wasn't going to die after all.

I self-discharged and we had a few hours' sleep before going to a different A&E in Lewisham. Here, we were seen in forty minutes and they told me I had a bladder infection that had spread to my kidneys, and that, just to be on the safe side, they would do some other tests. They took blood and urine samples, which they put into vials and labelled in mysterious writing. They explained that my immune system was probably down because of the whole bone marrow thing.

(Oh, I forgot to mention that the month previously, I'd donated bone marrow to a stranger in a simple procedure that won me a lot of karma, but apparently not enough to avoid whatever was happening to my lady parts. Again.)

I went back to training six days later, where people looked at me like a dead man walking. When I explained what had happened, Greg seemed cautious, and asked me, for the first time ever, to take it easy. But maybe he could sense something else, or he didn't want to notice the fact that my stomach was still so bloated I looked about three months' pregnant.

The following day I received an urgent call from my doctor, telling me that I needed to make an appointment that evening, and that any time would be fine. I took the phone call at work, casually returning to my desk and pretending I wasn't shitting my teeth out.

Most women have a blood oestrogen level of 35 when they menstruate; mine was 267. And what's more, I had been on my period since the match – something was not right.

A month later, the day before Fraser and I were due to leave on a road trip across America, I was informed that I had a much larger cyst, which had burst and was leaking. It was about the size of a football, and there was only one way it could come out. By this point I was starting to look so pregnant that people were giving up their seats for me on the tube. Throughout our holiday in America, I was congratulated on my incoming baby and told I wasn't allowed to go on rollercoasters – I soon learned that most people become speechless when told a foetus is actually a giant cyst.

When we came back, coincidentally on my twenty-ninth birthday, the surgeon called us in. He told me that they suspected the cyst was stage one cancer, and that the surgery would be a lot more intrusive than last time. I took this news in, numbly, and Fraser then drove me to Hastings and I cried silently all the way there, and over the course of the day ate four ice creams. Once the C-word was out of the bag I started to feel like an ill person; it slowed me down in everything I did, I was back on the sofa, and I even stopped being Rana at Lucha shows for a while.

The most terrifying experience of my life to date had been when I'd visited the Paris Catacombs aged twenty-one, walking through a tiny underground tunnel flanked by millions of skulls. There was also the time when Fraser and I took the wrong turn at night in California and travelled along a twenty-mile, single-lane route through the mountains, at night, with no map. But sitting in the waiting room in King's College Cancer Centre trumped these, big time.

The surgeon drew me a terrible, though well-meaning, diagram on the back of my consent form, which detailed how they would remove the cyst, the ovary, the affected tube, my appendix, and a big blob of fat. I was told the scar would run from under my tits, around my belly button, down to the top of my pubic line. After being told this, I called my dad, drank three ciders, cried for two hours, and then went to a drag show.

The surgery date arrived quickly, the same day as the World Cup Final and Gay Pride. I remember coming round on morphine to the sounds of a thumping crowd outside, and football quietly playing in the recovery room.

The strangest feeling was when I was finally left to sleep in my hospital bed, which looked out of the window directly on to the Houses of Parliament. I felt a sudden lightness in my entire body: I had normalised the fact I was carrying something, like a child or alien egg, and I felt suddenly, miraculously free. The cyst, when removed, weighed almost seven pounds, more than my birth weight – so this lightness could have been something to do with that. Or it could have been the morphine.

But even now, what I felt was self-validation. This was something I'd sought since being a teenager through the approval of people who didn't like me; or through the affections of boys; then at the bottom of a wine bottle; or eventually in a wrestling ring. It took major surgery and a form of cancer for me to value my very specific and weird set of gifts.

It's strange that the four days after my surgery, lying in my bed, with my own thoughts, were some of the happiest of my life. I felt at peace, but not passive, as if by the time I made it back on my feet I would have no reason to doubt myself any longer.

Meanwhile, I was not the only one who felt their 'very specific' gifts were flourishing. I found myself surrounded by the very people that I've tried to put into these pages, and I marvelled at how – despite society trying to devalue the importance of being weird as much as possible – we were still all holding on.

In the wider world of wrestling, things were changing.

Wrestling had stagnated for the last two decades, and it was due a revival, spurred on by new promotions, new talent, and by, finally, equality for women. Independent promotions around the world showcased female talent rather than hiding it, much in the same way Lucha had been doing for over a decade. I know several promotions that once flat-out refused to book women, which now have female title belts.

The WWE have continued to insist that they invented and lead this 'revolution'; they have not only hired a significant number of women in the last two years, but have had women wrestle in increasingly long and dangerous matches, which is a sign of respect in the world of ripply-muscled America. In 2016, they launched the 'Mae Young Classic', a tournament with huge ambitions to showcase 'all' the talent in the world, though it had some glaring omissions.

In 2018 WWE had its first all-female arena show, *Evolution*. I loved all of it, but like everyone else, could see through the PR glaze. The WWE continue to have massive ties to the Trump administration, and they have also had two shows in Saudi Arabia, where women have not been allowed to attend, let alone wrestle.

I can still not trust the WWE, but now I no longer try to put it in the same category as the weird and wonderful independent wrestling scene that exists around the world – they are completely different creatures. We know just how many 'not famous' wrestlers there are out there, and although the WWE is expanding, so is the belief that they don't represent the only way to be validated as a wrestler. I wanted to write this book for those people – the wrestlers who will not have action figures made in their images, but who have just as much prowess, and can get a whole room of people out of their seats with a single movement.

At the centre of this storm of British independent talent, below the radar of American oligarchs, bursting with energy, is the Resistance Gallery.

I know. What are the chances?

The Resistance Gallery is still hard to find, particularly because many of the landmarks such as York Hall are becoming obscured by new developments of luxury flats. Next door, the sari warehouse has been replaced with a sourdough pizza restaurant. Opposite, on the wall where we once stacked the burned-out wreckage of sofas and Vanderhorne's belongings, there is now graffiti, covered in recognisable masked faces, reading, 'THIS IS LUCHA TOWN.'

Inside the Gallery, there is still a musk of metal and old sweat; the smell of the fire has faded, finally, after three years – though there are still unmarked boxes hidden around, which contain scorched action figures. The ring is still going, Bryan is still working behind the bar, and the toilets are still condemnable. But now there is a wrestling show, sometimes two, every weekend.

Last time I counted, there were ten wrestling promotions that use the Gallery as a venue – the ring is one of the nicest to bump in, and few fans have ever experienced wrestling so 'close'. Many of the plastic-bag men stopped coming to watch EVE, or any of the other shows, because they hated the Gallery. They would constantly complain how it wasn't hygienic, how it wasn't safe, how the bar staff were unprofessional – they shouted into the internet but no one would listen.

The two most popular shows to pull in a healthy crowd of angry women and wrestling fans from across the country are EVE and Lucha Britannia. Both promotions sell out every month and they have an increasingly whacky array of characters. In fact, these shows were both completely instrumental to this book getting published – they let me sneak into the ring with a microphone at intervals and ask for pledges, and I would always leave to chants of my name and a feeling of fuzzy warmth.

As well as the shows, the London School of Lucha Libre runs four nights a week, with a new crowd of trainees. There is now a 'beginners' night twice a week that pulls in thirty people. We have to split up to train because there is so little space. Reliably, half these people are women or fabulously non-binary – my heart sings when I enter the room and see new people. There is no implied sexism anywhere; it's been washed out.

Greg now finds himself more proud of women than he's ever been, and he leads a female training session with Rhia on Sundays. Rhia is an amazing teacher, talking to everyone with honesty and enthusiasm, no matter what their ability. Greg Burridge is known as 'the surprise feminist'. His job is now teaching wrestling full time. He never got to the WWE, but he's said that this is a better dream than he could have had when he lifted weights as a teenager in his grandad's shed. To date, he has trained a growing number of wrestlers who have been signed to the biggest promotions in America and Japan, even to Mr McMahon's.

Vanderhorne has married a Toronto feminist artist called Miss Meatface; they bonded over a love of kitsch, toys and fetish nights. They regularly hang out with Vanderhorne's daughter, as well as his ex and her partner – all four of them were present on his little girl's first day of school. There are fewer club nights at the Gallery that run until 5am, and the ring barely gets taken down because it's used so often, but nothing brings me more pleasure than to stand at the back with Vanderhorne during shows, and watch his face fill with pride as his trainees make the crowd gasp with their skill.

Janey, Dragonita and Daisy are still running Burning Hearts. The number of trainees is constantly growing, and we continue to sell out shows at the Old Library. There is a glorious crossover between the female trainees from Lucha and those at Burning Hearts; any animosity has disappeared. Having been an announcer, referee and commentator for Burning Hearts, I finally got in the ring as a wrestler three months after my surgery. My new gimmick is 'Babe Cthulhu' – I wear a gold tentacle mask and a red swimsuit, and delight the audience by doing very little wrestling, and always leaving victorious. It suits me just fine.

Diablesa Rosa was signed to the WWE during the writing of this book – we watched her on TV and I cried. Steakley lost a loser-leaves-town match, and he disappeared; Jerry has enhanced his solo wrestling career by doing observational comedy in a pair of trunks, and has learned to play the ukulele – he continues to thrive. Muñeca de Trapo is having a baby with another wrestler, and was still able to do handstands in her second trimester. Freddie Mercurio lives in Toronto and wrestles every weekend. Cassius is about to wrestle stateside for the first time with a group of queer and drag wrestlers in New York – I am endlessly jealous. Cassandro has just had a documentary about his life air in Cannes and is planning to come to the Gallery to train Lucha students soon; he is now in his thirtieth year of wrestling.

Becca has toured the world with Sh!t Theatre. They recently came back from Australia where they were delighted to discover that pigeons are called 'bin chickens' and turkeys live on the beaches. She has a dog and lives on a boat, next to Ruth, who also has a boat but no dog.

While I was ill with the cyst, we decided to run a club night about how great Cher is, called 'I Need to Cher', at the Gallery. To date we have sold out five times and Cher tweeted us once – it has become my second passion, next to wrestling.

Fraser is a carpenter and dreams of having a shed. He is still wrestling as a monkey; last month he ran up a wall and jumped off a balcony. Though he did complain that the younger recruits are all too lean and healthy, so landing on them hurts. We also got married in May 2017; the first dance of our wedding was to 'Don't You Want Me Baby' and included four lifts.

I wore my gold cat suit.

The feeling of self-validation that I had after surgery comes and goes, but it is still there, and I think for the first time in my life I am happy. Infertile, broke, a bit overweight – but happy.

As I write this, I have been back training for just over a month. Now when I mess up a move I laugh it off, no tears. This year Rana is aiming to get the Lucha championship belt; she might even get herself a new mask...

But these stories won't end as this book finishes; the people I have written about are all living, breathing. You could walk past them in the street and never know that most weeknights they throw themselves around a wrestling ring with speed and precision. You wouldn't expect the guy from IT to embody a howling werewolf character on the odd Saturday; or that the slightly rotund woman who is running on a treadmill can do a Canadian destroyer. That's what I want you to understand from this book: we can all have our own personal revolution, just by taking a chance on something unexpected for no other person's happiness except our own.

The fight against the mundane is a vital and important one; we cannot let ourselves become beige automatons. We must claim the joy of doing something because we enjoy it and we want to be good at it. Not caring about being rich, or famous – doing something just for boos and cheers and an indescribable rush.

I used to worry I would stop wrestling one day and that would be the end of me; the end of what defined Heather. But now I don't worry, I know that I will keep finding things if I look for them; things that make my life more full of colour and entertainment and community. If ten years ago you'd told me I would be a wrestler, and what's more I would be part of the women who shake the rafters of a hallowed hall of masculinity, I would have laughed in your face, and probably told you it wasn't worth even trying.

But once we take that chance on becoming ourselves, of

finding that thing that makes us untouchable by the taxman, or by health problems, or by disapproving looks, we can think of how to change things permanently so that it benefits everyone. It is not selfishness; it is self-investment. It is the realisation that if you are invested in becoming happier in your own skin then you're more likely to bring happiness to others.

Though we are convoluted creatures, wrestlers have one thing in common. At some point, and hopefully for the duration of our careers, we realise that humbleness is the key to wrestling. That helping each other makes a show incredible, that it is not as simple as keeping secrets about not hurting your opponent, but it is also about supporting wrestling so that it is a better version of itself. This is done by accepting that wrestling is a spectacle that draws on the world around us; this big, diverse, good, evil world. It can break both stereotypes and the monotony of reality, even for a second, through the suspension of disbelief. We are humble because we work together as tools to tell this non-reality, and we are privileged in that way.

When I decided to write a book about wrestling, I knew it was a risk to try to explain wrestling to a world that either doesn't care or doesn't think I'm qualified for the task. Not just because I have had to learn everything from Google instead of a built-in nostalgia for the wrestling of my childhood. And not because I'm unfamous, with a career spanning seven years and 250 matches (which is fewer than some people do in a year). Or even because I'm a woman.

No, the disdain comes from the fact that I want to open the door and bring people here, into the fleeting, temporal, difficult reality of doing something because you want to. Wrestlers are people; we are not superheroes. We must recognise and appreciate the barriers as well as the achievements of wrestlers, of dancers, of musicians – the great underpaid, underappreciated, unfamous majority of the world's creators. Because without us there would be no joy.

It is the little snatches of memory that are among the most marvellous, most precious things about being a human, and wrestling has brought me so many of these that I could never fit them into the pages of a book. But these are the memories that I cherish most.

The barbecues I've had in Bethnal Green, where we all drink too much and talk about nothing but wrestling. The familiarity shared between wrestlers, of using wrestling moves as a form of greeting – a gentle forearm, picking someone up – expressions of our skill that others would just find violent and too intimate.

There are the many car journeys to places where there are still wrestling shows – Tamworth, Hastings, Bexley, Borehamwood, Sheppey, Rainham, Colchester – idling away hours on the motorway with perfect strangers who will soon become, if not friends, at least acquaintances. You will be happy to see each other years later in a dressing room.

There are the constant, expected, stock questions everyone asks you about wrestling: *But it's all fake, isn't it? Does it hurt? Do you wrestle men?* Perfecting the art of constructing answers into responses that last anywhere between four seconds and forty minutes.

The impressiveness of bruises, as they appear within hours of a training session. After a match, when you wake up the next day and a rib, or an ankle, or a wrist is hurting more than it should, but you can't remember why because you were so high from the buzz of the match.

Working with someone to perfect a move where they lift you, or twist you, or throw you to the ground. And only ever finishing it when you have been thrown to the ground with the care of a skilled worker, but to an observer you are having your head drilled into the floor.

The thousands of sleepless nights where you think about your ring gear, dream of a new character, or of a match you want in the future. The huge proportion of those hours spent worrying about things you need to improve on.

The disbelief when you watch a friend on the TV; the same face and body you've thrown about, now strolling down a hundred-metre catwalk to a pristine ring.

The feeling of leaving the outside world, turning and being blinded momentarily by stage lights, seeking, or sometimes not seeking, the faces of the crowd. Letting your character take over your body, as your normal self, the face behind the mask, slips from you.

Perfectly executing a roll. Jumping between two ropes into the arms of another, falling to the floor protected, the people around you gasping for breath because they're so full of adrenaline. The rise of your legs at the right moment as you fly through the air. The slow release as you lay back and take the final pin, and you welcome the three-count, your eyes closed, pleased you took the hit that you were supposed to take. The wrenching of another's body as you pull their shoulders to the ground, gritting your teeth and counting along with the ref as you finally, finally finish the match.

Then the crowd erupts. That is when it has all been for something.

Appendix 1: A Brief Herstory of Wrestling

Let's get this straight now – I am not what wrestling fans call 'a mark'. In wrestling, it isn't unusual for fans to have a terrifyingly encyclopaedic knowledge of wrestling. There are endless almanacs of who defeated whom in which tournament that I've gazed at, begrudgingly, across my huge pile of wrestling research. I simply don't know all the wrestlers of all time, so what this brief herstory aims to do instead is to give you a bit of insight into the historically accepted version of wrestling history, and the place of women within it. But it's a large and complex history to tell, understandably fraught with rumours, due to the fact that wrestling is a sport based on storytelling.

History still remembers the winners favourably, but with the internet and through vox pop, we can – happily – see that there are nuances to every tale. Wrestlers in general live a life less ordinary, but the greats of women's wrestling have been rarely remembered or talked about; or when they are, they tend to be labelled as 'mad, sad or bad' women.

'Something deep in my core had been tapped awake. Immediately I began to fantasise myself in the ring, applying those grips, holds and throws. A desire and drive to fill in those fantasies with flesh and blood came surging to life.' – Mildred Burke

The story of women wrestlers mirrors the story of wrestling as a whole. At first, wrestlers were the bare-knuckle fighters who realised they could earn more money if they weren't physically knocked out every night. When women began to wrestle in the early part of the twentieth century, they featured in sideshows – right alongside the women with the beards, the women who were clinically obese and the woman who could tie herself in knots. Like male wrestlers, women wrestlers would challenge members of the audience to fight them for money, building a performance from the crowd and their assailant's reaction. Of course it was a dirty life, one with little money and with exclusion from polite society. But the performers lived for the thrill of putting on a spectacle for the audience – they do it for the love. This is how I see wrestling now, and how many of the women featured in this book would describe their reasons for being involved. And in this dingy, pre-depression, sideshow world we meet our first heroine of the wrestling scene, the First Lady of wrestling, Mildred Burke.

Born in 1915, Mildred Bliss alias Burke was the youngest of six children. She excelled at sports in school, but left at fourteen, when the Great Depression hit, to support her single mother. In a drive to get away, she met and married a man twice her age, at seventeen. One of their first dates was to a wrestling show in Kansas City; she fell in love, but shortly after getting her pregnant, husbo number one left her. Already things were looking pretty grim for Mildred: she ended up working in her mum's cafe on a reservation, and met, while working and heavily pregnant, Billy Wolfe.

Billy Wolfe is going to crop up a few times in the stories of many female wrestlers, because even then he was considered to be 'the man' for women's wrestling. He was also a gross human being. Billy already had a younger wife, also a wrestler, but left her for Burke who, shortly after giving birth to her son in 1935, approached him, asking him to make her a star. He tried her out at a gym – paying a younger guy a quarter to 'give it to her so good she'll never come back around'. But Mildred knocked the kid out and Billy saw dollar signs. He left his wife and married Mildred, becoming her agent.

So let's smash a first debate right up. In the old, gritty days of wrestling, only five feet two tall and not even twenty-five years old, Mildred Burke wrestled some 200 men during the '30s alone, and she only lost to one of them. I want to say that it was choreographed this way, but in the early days of wrestling there wasn't a huge distinction between real and fiction, apart from the loser *actually* being knocked unconscious. Whenever women are belittled as competitors due to their biology or size, remember that even eighty years ago there was living proof that this was a myth.

But there is also no way to sugar-coat the underlying story: she was a phenomenon but also in an abusive relationship, both with her cheating husband, and the low wages and unreliability of wrestling. Two weeks into marriage, she found Billy having sex with another woman; and then shortly afterwards she found out that he'd beat her infant son because he interrupted a liaison with a different woman. Once Billy punched Mildred in the face because she wanted to leave training and care for her son who had a fever. Though she was the best in the country, Wolfe would be paid on her behalf by other promoters, and this meant she never saw her wages.

In 1937, Wolfe started a wrestling school, in Ohio, with Burke his star attraction, meaning he could monopolise all her bookings and interviews. In 1938 Mildred was featured in *Life* magazine, even though women's wrestling was still banned in a lot of states, with the women nationally labelled as harlots. World War II brought the rise of women competing in public sports, and wrestling became a viable option for a lot of girls. By the end of the war, 200 active female wrestlers were living on their performances alone in America (last time I counted, there are fewer than fifty female wrestlers who are able to be full-time wrestlers in the UK). But it was against great personal odds that they achieved this, and even then women were not seen as 'proper' wrestlers, but a substitute for the real thing.

Burke had managed to garner her own earnings by the early 1940s, so began to tour internationally to stages in places like Mexico City, though with Wolfe in tow while he groomed other rising stars. All protégées had to be under twenty-five, thin and photogenic – and I can't think of a time since then when this hasn't been regarded as the ideal body type for a female wrestler, which says a lot about how much Wolfe, slimeball that he was, influenced wrestling for years to come.

In 1951, after a car accident, Burke told Wolfe she needed to recover, but he told her she would drop the belt to another wrestler if she couldn't work. She refused, and Wolfe and his son beat her senseless outside a liquor store in front of her own child. It meant she missed a wrestling event, but Wolfe told everyone she had cancer. (Everyone – imagine his face now. And punch it.)

One other trainee-cum-prop for Wolfe was Mary Lillian Ellison, better known as The Fabulous Moolah. Like Mildred, her life is long, complicated and full of scandal. She had a career that spanned over sixty years. She was the head of a school, a world champion. The first woman to wrestle on national TV and the longest reigning WWF women's champion in history, she was part of a campaign that made women's wrestling legal in the state of New York in 1972. You might *want* to remember her as some kind of suffragette starlet, but she isn't remembered this way by many. The stories that survive her are those of manipulation, of greed and corruption, and ultimately led to the talented women being shunted off rosters in favour of pretty, skinny girls, with Moolah in the wings watching like a hawk.

Born in 1923, Moolah was the only girl and youngest of five siblings. When she was eight years old, her mother died and her father took her to wrestling shows in the back counties in her native South Carolina. She remembered seeing Mildred Burke at a show, and suddenly wanting to be her. So, because her father didn't want her to wrestle, she eloped and had a baby (a girl who later grew up to be a wrestler too), and then her relationship broke down. Raising the baby with the help of a friend, she started wrestling at age fifteen.

Her first trainings sessions were brutal; she described going in with a man twice her size and her collar bone snapping and bursting through her skin. After six years' valeting as 'Moolah the Slave Girl' (yep), she approached Billy Wolfe, already known as a notable scumbag. Moolah never slept with Wolfe – and he never let her forget this. He didn't let her go see her father two days before he died, and he also did not forward her a pay cheque to cover the funeral costs. That's when she decided to try her luck elsewhere.

After a string of relationships and stints on other promotions, Moolah married a promoter and started a wrestling school. The women were paid upfront and taught how to flip bumps on mattresses in the Moolah's kitchen. But the world of wrestling from the '50s to '70s was shady; drug pushing was common, exploitation standard. Moolah trained some stars, but she also led countless others down the track to ruination, and many never made it back – but this is common. Other stories have come out of the brickwork from those murky times. If they signed with Moolah, the wrestlers' families received very little each a month while they were on the road, sent by the company, the wrestlers being forbidden from having their own bank accounts. The newspapers described lives of luxury, yet it was all a charade – and Moolah, true to her name, did everything to keep up this image.

Moolah's direct competition, and 'frenemy', was a protégée called Johnnie Mae Young who, in my opinion, was the greatest wrestler ever. Mae Young famously wrestled Moolah for over five decades, but never won a match. This was because Mae was always the bad one, the heel, in these matches; so rather than Moolah retaining her undefeated streak through skill, instead her longevity is in large part down to Mae's legitimacy as a performer. Like a good heel, she was there to carry her opponents, and to make the stars look good.

In interviews, Mae Young humbly recounts almost unbelievable stories, often with a wicked sense of humour. For example, she was the first woman to wrestle in Japan in 1954, and when she lost the title to Burke, her boss, she claimed till her death that if it was a 'real fight' she could have beaten her; she even hit Mildred backstage once to prove she was tough enough.

Born in 1923, Mae was raised in Depression-era Oklahoma. Her mum died when she was a child, and she was youngest of eight. A tomboy who was always in scraps, she had natural ability and was encouraged by her brothers to wrestle on her high school wrestling team, one of the only girls in the whole country. In 1937, when she was aged fourteen, Billy Wolfe exclaimed that her ability to wrestle was natural, after watching her take down two other female competitors. Mae had an advantage over many of the girls, because she already had wrestling training, which meant she didn't need to get trained up and earn her 'dues' as much. With Billy Wolfe and his cronies, 'paying your dues' was usually done with your vagina.

But Mae was no wallflower; like most female wrestlers of the time, she took to wrestling to get out of a nowhere town, but she was more of a delinquent than most (another reason why I love her so much). Even in her early days of 'respectable lady wrestling', her feats included wrestling a bear, an alligator and over 2,000 men and women. In fact, my favourite stories from Mae are from when she used to go out and get drunk and get into fights – *always* with men.

Mae liked a drink, and would often attract unsolicited attention. (I can imagine this was the same as it is now: a drunk creep hears you're a wrestler and tries to grab you, then challenges you to a fight.) The headlines would appear almost weekly about 'out of control lady wrestlers', but Mae would always get off by claiming self-defence, even if the bloody pulp of whatever was left of her attackers claimed it was an unprovoked attack – or they couldn't admit that wrestling was 'actually' real, and a woman could 'actually' beat them.

Mae, Mildred and Moolah kept working shows throughout and after World War II. By the early 1950s, these women had gained the reputation of being bad and dangerous, but they were widely respected wrestlers. Many at the time saw these early days as a 'golden age' in wrestling – it was new, exciting and the audience didn't realise any of it was choreographed. In the early days of wrestling, there were female-only shows, mixed shows, shows that sold out arenas. But wrestling, with

281

the advent of TV, went from being a spectator sport in America, to something completely exportable. See also:

- *Gorgeous George:* a wrestler who was notoriously hated because of his arrogantly feminine stage entrances, wearing furs and a lot of hair pomade.

- *Penny Banner:* a girl wrestler who was considered one of the best.

- *Lipstick and Dynamite (directed by Ruth Leitman, 2005):* literally my favourite film of all time, in which Leitman interviews female wrestlers from this period about their experiences: they are all, essentially, badass OAPs.

1950s–1980s: Wrestling Becomes a Global Phenomenon

In the mid '50s, women's wrestling grew in popularity and public coverage alongside men's wrestling. It was driven by the impetus of women to continue to lead the independent lives they had experienced during the war, and celebrated a certain kind of femininity despite it being 'low culture'.

In 1952, Mildred Burke served Billy Wolfe with divorce papers, and in 1954, in a display of her own prowess and influence, she led a contingent of women wrestlers to Japan. The shows sold out in the largest sumo arena in Tokyo three nights running, with the faces of female wrestlers plastered over walls. She later remembered the long arena walkway lined with thousands of fans as the biggest moment of her life. She was such a hit she didn't adjust back to life in America. She wrestled her last match in 1956 before taking retirement. At one point she said she was writing a book. It never happened, or it was never published, and for about ten years she ran a chilli restaurant with another retired female wrestler.

However, in 1966, Mildred Burke started working directly with promoters in Japan again. She came out of retirement to re-ignite her old belt and start her own promotion. In 1970, she gave her belt to All Japan Wrestling (AJW), and the 'Red Belt' was retained thereafter as the highest rank a female wrestler could hold.

Burke and Mae's match in Japan, 1954, led to renewed demand for rising stars, with the eyes of promoters seeing dollar signs at the hundreds of young protégées who turned up to try-outs. However, as had been the case in America, these wrestling troupes led a vaudeville life, where matches were just as likely to take place in a strip joint as in an arena, and were sold for titillation. The shows had mainly a male audience, but even in the early years, when going to a wrestling show was seen as 'unladylike', forty per cent of fans were female, defying gender norms in order to become consumers of *joshi puroresu*.

The rise of women's wrestling in Japan led to an underground queer movement based on pulp fiction, and a lot of male-presenting 'sister-brothers' would go to shows. Women would open up bars with 'brother-sisters' and perform wrestling bouts as sideshows and comedy acts. There were songs and drag. And the women provided their own security; one sister-brother bar was best known for its owner, an ex-wrestler of 200lbs who once threw a man into a pond for being badly behaved.

Back in America, wrestling was now a huge industry, run by different promoters across different territories. Many parts of this network were run as rackets by their exploitative owners, including Moolah and her spouse, Buddy Lee. Huge as wrestling was, it suffered from the same racial apartheid as the rest of 1950s America, with specific leagues for Afro-American women. The titles, however unfavourable, were won several times by Susie Mae McCoy, wrestling as Sweet Georgia Brown. Despite her success her life was not a happy one.

Susie Mae was the oldest of eleven children, and she already had a child of her own when she was picked up by Moolah and Buddy Lee as a teenager. They toured states for months at a time, during which she was smuggled into hotels and shows in areas where the KKK were active. Although she was voted fourth best female wrestler in the world in 1964, Susie competed in 'negro women' fights, and was not permitted to take on the white women. Allegedly, there were whole years when her family would only get to see Susie a few hours every other month, meetings at which Moolah and Lee were always present.

Along the road, she had four illegitimate children who were raised by family. Her daughter remembers her coming to visit them in a white Cadillac with Moolah and Lee, and being forcibly dragged back to the car because she didn't want to leave. The family received $30 to $50 dollars a month; as Susie Mae confided years later, 'You just expected it, you were a black woman in the '50s.' Apparently she was raped, drugged, pimped, then abandoned, with Moolah denying it all. In a final insult, or show of respect, another woman wrestler debuted in 1988 under Susie's wrestling name. All that remained of the original character was a box of polyester cloaks and leotards, marked 'whore stuff', which her brothers burned in the garden after her death.

There are happier tales from this time for women of colour. Around the mid 1950s, though wrestling remained segregated in most states, there were four outstanding women wrestlers: Ethel Johnson, Babs Wingo, Kathleen Wimbley and Marva Scott.

All four travelled with the promotions that employed

women, many of these managed by Wolfe but, despite set-backs, they fought regularly in four-way bouts, always proving to be the match of the night. By 1956, they were selling out auditoriums of 9,000 people and Marva Scott was listed as the number three female wrestler in the world. They were amongst the highest paid African-American athletes in the entire country.

In 1958, the face of wrestling changed forever with the establishment of the World Wrestling Federation (later WWE), which televised its bouts. Such was the popularity of the WWF, it began to take over 'territories' at a faster rate than any other wrestling promotion in the world. The WWF did not feature black female wrestlers, and black male wrestlers were rare and were always depicted as 'savages'. They also had a view that it was more important for women wrestlers to be attractive than skilled.

The Fabulous Moolah signed with the WWF, and though she trained other women, she ensured that the supply to the promotion was her protégées, none of whom she trained well enough to take her championship belt away from her. Even Mae Young and Mildred Burke weren't selected to work with the WWF, and as a result women in the independent circuit who weren't under Moolah's tutelage started to struggle to get bookings.

The '60s were good for Mae: she became the first National Wrestling Association female champion. She toured various shows with Moolah, and also with other promotions. Even she remembers these as 'wild times'. She took on younger opponents, passing on her skills, although admittedly 'old school'. As a heel, Mae was notoriously hated, describing 'boos like kisses' at her matches. Although Moolah was a heel too, no one hated her as much as they hated Mae Young, who was even *nastier* in the ring than Moolah. People would throw bottles at her at matches, so they had to put up chicken-wire fences.

In 1965 Billy Wolfe died, survived by countless illegitimate children, but was buried alone, not with any of the five women he married. By the start of the 1970s, women's wrestling was no longer growing in America. However, across the world, wrestling promotions had at last begun to employ women on their shows. And over the next few decades, wrestling shows on television turned the sport into an even bigger global industry.

1970s–1990s: WrestleMania

In the UK, where there was no Mildred Burke or network TV, wrestling initially only remained popular in town halls. Then, after World War II, wrestling slowly grew popular enough to merit its own televised show in 1955 – *World of Sport Wrestling* – which dominated British wrestling until 1985. During this time women's wrestling was still illegal in London – to the extent that women had to wrestle in clubs or at private parties to compete in the capital, which of course gained them the unwanted reputation of being a very different type of wrestler. The situation was not unlike it had been in America decades before.

Mitzi Mueller became the first named female competitor in the UK. She would later describe the crowds as disapproving, but receptive to something new. Wrestling shows began to attract what she refers to as 'the mac crowd' (precursors to plastic-bag men) who came to shows for the wrong reasons.

Despite this, women continued to wrestle across the UK. In the early 1970s in Stoke-on-Trent, a girl called Jane Hansford went to watch wrestling in the local village hall with her grandma, who lived for Saturdays and *World of Sport*. Aged sixteen, she went to see a *World of Sport* show, where one of the wrestlers bled all over her dress. Eventually, she persuaded a promoter to teach her to wrestle, alongside greats such as Adrian Street, a Welsh miner's son whose gimmick was as androgynous and glam as Ziggy Stardust.

She moved to Blackpool, then Manchester, to become a wrestler. She was thrown around until she was black and blue; she broke her ankle on her second training session. She became very skilled, but only after she was routinely shamed, once being stripped to her underwear by the male wrestlers and thrown into a chip shop. Despite this, she travelled alone to Nigeria to wrestle when she was just sixteen. Aged nineteen, she wrestled around Japan. She had the determination and credentials of the great, and what's more, she was best known for wrestling men.

She was eventually given the name Klondyke Kate, with a backstory about her father being a giant mountain man. Klondyke was part of a movement, led by other female wrestlers, which demanded that women's wrestling should be decriminalised in London. The mayor Ken Livingstone opposed in particular, saying, 'Women's wrestling always has a sexual innuendo.' I don't understand how Klondyke Kate could even be compared to the erotica that the British public clearly thought happened in a wrestling ring. But still, there was a surge in popularity, accompanied by protesting led by Sue Brittain, known as the 'Emmeline Pankhurst of wrestling'. Sue started her campaign in 1979, and it lasted until 1987, when finally Kate and Mitzi Mueller fought at the Royal Albert Hall, in the first ever women's match to be shown on British TV.

Around the same time, women's wrestling was growing in popularity in Japan, its fan base now being a mix of titillated middle-aged men and teenage girls. Most wrestling in Japan until the late '80s was based on a *joshi* face taking on a big, bad American woman. However, around the mid-1980s, a whole new generation of female wrestlers was emerging in Japan, engaged with the strong femininity of women's wrestling.

One of these was girls was Chigusa Nagayo, born in 1964 in Nagasaki. Chigusa is considered to have been as big in Japan as Hulk Hogan was in America. She started wrestling at age fourteen, and her first ever show was at age fifteen. Chigusa wrestled across Japan for a number of years, winning junior belts and paying her dues to more experienced wrestlers. This whole time is a grey area in terms of what happened behind the scenes; rather than an enforced culture of sexual harassment, you want to think that the *joshi* wrestlers enjoyed a kinship and sisterhood fitting for their teenage fan base. Whatever happened behind the scenes, though, Chigusa was an enthusiastic pioneer in a time when women's wrestling was changing from an import to an export commodity for the country.

By 1983, *joshi puroresu* had climbed to even greater popularity with Japanese schoolgirls. To some, in hindsight, this might seem surprising, but I find there to be a wealth of similarities between male adult wrestling fans and teenage schoolgirls, including a love of overblown drama, intense attachments and hatred for certain characters, enjoyment of bright and revealing costumes, spending all of their disposable cash on merchandise and following every storyline obsessively.

The front runners were the Beauty Pair, refreshingly big boned, strong and androgynous; they sold millions of lunchboxes and wrestling tickets.

However, in 1985, their popularity was dwarfed when Chigusa and Lioness Asuka, her friend since their training days, joined up to form The Crush Gals. The Crush Gals were known for being tough and athletic, and pioneered the style that most *joshi puroresu* use today: a lot of throwing themselves off the top rope, dropkicking their opponents straight in the face and drawing blood. The Crush Gals could do these moves better than anyone else and in jaw-dropping synchronisation, always stopping at the end to pose and smile at the audience.

The Crush Gals took women's wrestling to a level of popularity not seen before or since. In 1985, one of their matches drew 13,000 fans and they were media sweethearts appearing on TV and in magazines. They were even among the first (and then last, for several years) female Japanese wrestlers to cross over to America and star in the WWF shows for a short period. They won the Red Belt from heavyweights Dump Matsumoto and Bull Nakano a year after forming their partnership, defending it on and off until 1989, when they split and began to feud between themselves for dominion. Chigusa retired in 1989, having reached the mandatory maximum age for AJW wrestlers: twenty-six.

In Mexico, from the 1950s onwards wrestling had achieved immense popularity, especially its own national version of the sport, *lucha libre*. *Lucha libre* has a rich and complicated history, and a back catalogue of pop references taken from ethnographies to technicolour wonders of 1960s film such as *Blue Demon vs. the Satanic Power* (the poster alone made me stop everything I was doing and watch it). I have my own relationship with *lucha libre* and its self-awareness in the UK as an important subject to cultural appropriation (see Chapter 5, 'We Need to Talk about Stereotypes'). Many active *luchadores* have explained to me that rather than it being about them choosing to be a star, for them *lucha* is more of a way to avoid getting involved with gangs and drugs. This isn't to say that wrestlers don't also come from difficult and humble backgrounds in Japan, England, America, but Mexico has maintained a rich wrestling dynasty despite crippling poverty for most of the twentieth century.

Lucha libre means free fighting. It's about aerial moves, flashy costumes and posturing – more so than in American wrestling. Moreover, *lucha* is not an American import: not only does *lucha* have its own style, but it also upholds the tradition of wearing masks, which have held a lot of value in Mexican folklore since the time of the Aztecs. Masks were also brought in so that the *luchadores* could hold down day jobs without being surrounded by legions of fans. *El Santo*, possibly the most famous *luchador* of all time, was buried in his mask. The unmasking of a *luchador* is often a way of shaming or retiring a wrestling gimmick: there are mask vs. hair matches, or hair vs. hair matches – just to add a bit more drama to the proceedings. The loser has their identity revealed, or their head shaved – as if watching someone do a double somersault combined with a kick to the face isn't enough.

Lucha libre is also much more family orientated than other forms of wrestling: kids fill audiences, babes in arms are present, old ladies sit at the front and hurl abuse at the *rudos* (baddies). This also extends to the fact that in Mexico, again, more so than elsewhere in the world, there are third- and fourth-generation wrestling families.

This does not mean that, traditionally, it has been thought as acceptable for women to fight as it is for men. Since the 1950s, women's wrestling was banned in Mexico City in order to defend 'the morals' of the citizens. Women still fought on the underground circuit – but their illegality meant they were more susceptible to underpayment, to firings, to last-minute cancellations, and to physical and mental abuse.

In 1974, sixteen-year-old Lola González met some female

wrestlers and was instantly inspired to travel to Chihuahua to try her luck. In 1975, she found the school of the legendary Gory Guerrero, and began training alongside his sons, a difficult feat for a woman, even though *lucha libre* was considered a national pastime. By her second year she had already been to Japan to fight at AJW, and in her third year she met Fishman, a famous *luchador*. He already had two children, for whom she agreed to quit wrestling and care. However, she continued to wrestle as Fishman was always on tour and she missed the ring.

Around this time, there was a growing movement to decriminalise women's wrestling – and after various protests and legal fees, it turned out the 'law' against female wrestling had not actually been written down anyway. It was just the industry and moral panic that made the very idea of female *luchadoras* an offence, despite their featuring in shows for decades. To cover this up, local promoters claimed they 'hadn't realised' women wanted to train or become wrestlers. The *luchadoras* met with a surge in popularity. Lola González was at the crest of this, fighting matches and holding belts across twenty-two different countries.

And what did the huge American wrestling industry glean from this female-forward, female-led movement in Japan, Britain and Mexico? Not a great deal, it seems... The WWF was beginning to dictate what was popular in wrestling, with the result that women became less visible. Mae Young retired to go and live with her mother, and was an evangelical Christian for most of the 1970s and '80s. Mildred Burke was instrumental in raising the *joshi* movement in Japan, before returning to America in the mid 1970s around the same time that girls across the USA were legally allowed to learn wrestling in all schools. She worked as a choreographer, directed adult films, and died in 1989.

But Moolah continued to thrive as the WWF grew in popularity in the 1980s, with the advent of televised matches. The gimmicks became overblown, and the open secret that wrestling was not 'real' had been accepted, to the extent it became more like a pantomime. There was a huge following for stars such as Hulk Hogan, a blond, orange, massive man who could boast '18-inch pythons' on his arms and who would tear his yellow t-shirt off when he entered the ring. There was also 'Macho Man' Randy Savage, similarly ripped but with an underdog quality due to his sparkling suits, sunglasses and openly fragile ego. And then there was the Ultimate Warrior, who shouted at his opponents, had a mullet, wore make-up and had tassels all over him like a child's bike.

The wrestling that the WWF showed had high production values, which meant that the main wrestling shows in Europe were replaced with tapings of their matches. Among the casualties were the 'old school' wrestlers like Mick McManus, a grumpy man with black trunks who old women vehemently hated, and Giant Haystacks and Big Daddy, both huge wrestlers who would essentially sit on their opponents, and who ended up having the same match every single night. The UK scene could not compete with the American imports, and the WWF hindered the popularity of British wrestling massively. Eventually *World of Sport*, the main British TV show, was cancelled.

By 1984, the WWF put on the largest wrestling event ever recorded – WrestleMania, held at the Trump Plaza (*ahem*). Moolah, as the women's champion, was right in the middle of it, already in her forties. But at the same time, the ruthless, matron heel which Moolah became associated with can be typified by an incident known as the 'Original Screwjob'.

While Hulk Hogan was pulling in the TV deals, another person enjoyed a similar rise to fame: Wendi Richter, a tough athlete with a model face and Farah Fawcett hair. She was described as '100lbs of raw steel and sex appeal'. On the fated night of 23 July 1984, Richter was accompanied to the ring in a red swimsuit with Cyndi Lauper at her side. But Moolah, refusing to give up the belt to another competitor, tried to cheat to win. You watch the match back, and it's nasty. The fists that Moolah throws are closed; she tosses Richter across the ring by her hair, which even makes *my* toes curl. But the crowd are entranced, uncontrollable, the women spilling out the ring and throwing each other on to metal barriers. It was televised on MTV, the only wrestling match that ever has been, and at the time was rated as gaining its highest ever viewing numbers. Richter was victorious.

Although Richter's popularity continued to grow, the company screwed her over later in the same year. Vince McMahon put Moolah in a costume as 'the spider lady' to fight once more with Richter. However, on McMahon's orders, the referee counted a three-count on a pin that Wendi had clearly kicked out from. She dropped the title and left soon after; she hadn't been told she was losing the belt – in wrestling terms, this is a 'screwjob'.

Women worked hard wherever they wrestled, but in the WWF there were not the same opportunities as elsewhere. To give you an example, the Crush Gals were on TV in America the same time as *GLOW* – the 'Gorgeous Ladies of Wrestling' – which was talent light and gimmick heavy. It was the only other televised form of women's wrestling in what was essentially a soft porn sketch show. Audiences were just as happy to watch a terrorist called 'Palestinia' pull the hair off a naked woman on a horse called 'Godiva' without a wrestling move in sight.

But as women's prowess grew around the world, the WWF had no choice but to open up to include more female wrestlers. See also:

- *AJW*: All Japan Wrestling took women's wrestling to its heights in the 1970s to 1980s; there are countless matches on YouTube that will knock your socks off.

- *Elsie Wright*: the first female ref in the USA, who started her career wrestling bears, and became a manager for one of the most popular wrestlers of 'Hulkomania', Dusty Rhodes.

1990s–2010s: The Wrong Attitude

In about 1994, Chigusa Nagayo came out of retirement. She shaved her head and muscled out into a more androgynous and tough gimmick, as if to mark that she had passed the age of 'ideal' *joshi* wrestlers. In 1996, she also went to WCW (*World Champion Wrestling*, the WWF's TV rivals) – where truly astonishing female competitors were sidelined alongside women in bikinis and storylines about white power. She fought Medusa, aka Alundra Blayze, who had been let go by the WWF and famously put the women's title in a bin on a WCW show (she was then banned from being on the WWF for twenty years). Alongside this return to the ring, Chigusa created her longer-lasting legacy – GAEA, the first women-owned promotion in Japan. Not only did Chigusa star as the main roster wrestler for the promotion, she also trained new recruits and established performers, providing opportunities for her counterparts.

Chigusa though, unlike Moolah, was not about making her mark and her money. She is shown as a tough-loving matron, determined not to tolerate any weakness in the art of *puroresu*.

In the early 1990s, as wrestling grew more bombastic,

women's wrestling was becoming an even larger industry in Japan and the WWF began to import female wrestlers to face its increasing number of female stars. Particularly of note is Bull Nakano, who had wrestled under Nagayo's tutelage, and who was featured by the WWF a number of times. In fact, Bull Nakano was completely different to the blonde, all-American opponent that the WWF had as their women's champion – Alundra Blayze. Bull was curvaceous, she came to the ring with cracks drawn on her face, and sported nunchucks and a two-foot-high green Mohawk.

In Mexico, *luchadoras* also experienced a resurgence in the 1990s. Lola González divorced Fishman after twelve years of marriage, now a bigger star than him. In 1992, the CMLL launched a twelve-woman bid for their first-ever women's title belt. Lola was amongst those women, though she lost the title to Bull Nakano, with whom she then feuded for several years. She started a relationship with a man in the Netherlands, travelling back and forth, and decided to retire a second time a few years later, again choosing love over wrestling, a decision few of the women featured here seem to make. Her retirement match was against a male wrestler and in front of an audience of 18,000.

These *luchadoras* inspired Luna Vachon. Born in Atlanta in 1962, the adopted daughter of wrestler Paul Vachon and the niece of wrestlers Mad Dog and Vivian Vachon, Luna was bred for the business. But still, machismo in the Mexican wrestling community meant that encouraging a daughter to wrestle wasn't part of the plan. She watched wrestling as a child, seeing local matches that featured her family members. She had been to sixteen schools by eighth grade, due to her family's need to travel to wrestle. Virtually everyone, including her godfather, André the Giant, tried to persuade her not to wrestle. But she persevered and started training under her aunt,

Vivian Vachon, and Moolah at the age of sixteen. Her parents were so angry that she was not allowed to use the Vachon name, wrestling as just 'Luna'.

Luna married at eighteen, but like many before her, she had to choose between family commitments and the road. Aged twenty-three, already divorced and a mother of two, she took up wrestling full time and travelled all over the world. Her father tour-managed her, and she valeted for a number of 'Satanist' tag teams, which is where she shaved half her head and embraced a punk look. She also competed at numerous women's shows in Japan and Mexico. But, by the late '80s, she was making a name for herself, and was working alongside wrestlers like the Crush Gals by 1992, before she was even thirty.

Luna was brought to the WWE alongside Bull Nakano, in 1993, in a stable of other legitimate wrestlers to bulk up their thinning roster. She also appeared as a valet and in mixed gender matches. She formed one with her second husband, but then left him, marrying another wrestler in 1994. Once she was put in the ring against Doink and Dink, a clown and a midget. Ultimately, she was not getting the push she deserved. Spots for women's wrestlers were limited, and with Bull Nakano on the scene, WWE didn't need two snarling heels. As Nakano was the number one contender, Luna quietly left.

After some years working the independent circuit, Luna returned to the WWE in 1996, when Nakano was unceremoniously fired after being in possession of cocaine (although male wrestlers caught with cocaine had been kept on before and since then). Luna was brought back as the manager of Goldust – who was a gold-and-black, Lycra-clad, sex-pest gimmick; imagine Frankenfurter from *The Rocky Horror Show* but then have the character designed by Vince McMahon. Luna became embroiled in storylines involving valets such as

Sable, who was bought in as a manager because of her looks. Nothing else. She ended up wrestling Luna in 1998 in an 'evening gown match' – in which the first to strip the other wins (*puts head in hands*) – though Luna was told she would be fired if Sable, who couldn't wrestle, was hurt *at all*. Luna was committed to the business, and would play the part even in a degrading fashion like this.

Luna had the sympathy of the crowd; they knew she could wrestle but she never had the title, it wasn't given to her. She was remembered for staying behind to sign autographs, and for being the most active wrestler involved with the Make a Wish Foundation – her love for the fans was appreciated. Despite this, in 2000, Luna refused to take part in a bikini competition in the ring with all other female contenders. Sable won for having painted handprints on her tits, but this was then revoked by Vince McMahon as she wasn't wearing an actual bikini. This is where things had progressed to.

Years of wrestling also meant that Luna had started to take prescription painkillers and pep pills. The habit was a norm for many wrestlers like Luna at the time – leaving, and continuing to leave, retired wrestlers across America addicted and crippled by their wrestling careers. She was released from her contract in 2000, because she apparently had 'another' outburst backstage, but it was allegedly really due to the fact she had been diagnosed with bipolar disorder.

Now termed 'the Attitude Era', the period allowed more women to get back in the ring, despite the double-standard of this often being in the form of titillating acts. Ultimately, the women did what was asked of them to do something they loved.

For example, in 1998, both Mae Young and The Fabulous Moolah came out of retirement, both in their late seventies by this point. The gimmick of their being old women meant they fought in inter-gender matches, with bizarre storylines. Mae Young in particular was remembered not only for giving birth to a hand during a match; she also dropped her top at one of the 'bikini contests', baring her seventy-seven-year-old breasts for all to see. (I have debated with Emily Read for many hours about whether she got her actual breasts out, because so many men we know insist they were fake, possibly to avoid traumatic memories from when they were children.)

With all this in mind, Mae was not signed to the WWE until 1999, sixty years after she started, mainly because she retired before the WWE began. Mae wrestled at WWE for the last fifteen years of her life, during which she continued to not give a shit. Between 1998 and 2005 she wrestled numerous male wrestlers less than half her age. Pat Patterson, one of the only openly gay WWE veterans, recalls her at the age of seventy-six, turning up at his hotel room one night at 1am, wearing only her bra and panties, a cocktail in hand, with the excuse, 'Don't worry, Pat. I just want to talk bullshit with you.'

To be honest, hats off to her, she probably thought it was all funny. She had her last match, aged eighty-seven, with Beth Phoenix; it wasn't great, because Phoenix was trying to protect her from doing high impact moves, so she was not able to do what she wanted to do.

There were other women at this time whose talent shone out, even though they agreed to go along with storylines that were risqué (see the story of Chyna in Chapter 9: The F Word).

Two who pop up together time and again are Trish Stratus and Lita, their rise and fall intertwined throughout their wrestling careers. Lita had a G-string appearing over the top of her jeans; Trish had a cleavage vaster than the San Andreas Fault. They were both pushed throughout their careers into on-screen and off-screen love triangles with male wrestlers, but are remembered – in the short and patchy collective psyche of wrestling – as strong women, and good role models for girls. Girls saw past the hair extensions and panties and fake boobs – and remembered clearly the moments when these women were strong and made them want to grow up and be wrestlers themselves.

Lita was born Amy Dumas in 1975. Her parents threw a lot of cocktail parties, and her childhood would have been ideal if she hadn't moved over seven times before she was ten. Far from dreaming of wrestling since girlhood, between roadie and bar jobs, she saw Rey Mysterio on TV when she was twenty-three. At first, she thought that he was a 'fake' Mexican, and that *luchadores* were just a gimmick they used for small guys. When she found out that *lucha libre* was 'a thing', she moved to Mexico to train to be a wrestler. She worked with CMLL – the WWE of Mexico – who liked her and let her hang around in exchange for working as a ring girl. By 1999, she was wrestling alongside *luchadores* like Eddie Guerrero and wrestlers like Luna Vachon and Chyna. She rocketed to popularity when the Attitude Era of tits, innuendo and bizarre activities was approaching its peak. She settled into her role in the Hardy Boyz, who were brothers renowned for their cyberdog outfits and high-flying jumping moves.

Trish Stratus was born Patricia Anne Stratigeas, also in 1975, but in Canada. Unlike Dumas, she was obsessed with wrestling as a child, and got to college to study sports science. She ended up working in a gym, then as a fitness model, then as a wrestling radio talk show host, then got signed to the WWE off the back of her modelling shoots. Again, this was 2000 and women were increasingly in the ring and involved with men's matches, but as a result the women's division was losing kudos. Trish was brought in on this wave of titillation: if Lita was 'girl next door' then Trish was the 'school bike', with cleavage up to the eyes, rhinestone cowboy hat, and representing a tag team called 'T & A'.

When the WWE renamed all their female wrestlers as 'divas', Lita famously disliked it: 'I didn't become a wrestler to be a diva... Before, we all had our own personalities; then we all became one group, "divas". I don't get it – we worked as hard as the men, I wrestled as much as the men, but I was now a "diva", not a wrestler.'

WWE tried to put a spin on it, claiming they revered strong women and calling the women 'divas' showed this. In hindsight talking about empowerment over pictures of women smouldering at each other in lip-gloss is hilarious, but it is also disheartening – to have your cause put back twenty steps for a marketing angle.

At the time, Lita and Trish paid lip service to the idea that it was a 'unique opportunity' for women to express themselves in new ways. But ultimately it was Trish and Lita, no one else, who were pulling out mixed gender matches with double moonsaults.

Trish decided to change her image: 'I decided to put my butt away; they should be here to watch me wrestle.'

Between 2001 and 2006 Lita and Trish swung between feuding and friendship, though they spent most of that time in a tag team and a lifelong friendship came about as a result. They both sustained serious injuries – necks, herniated disks, torn knees. They also both continued to interact with male wrestlers in on-screen relationships – and Trish also had a bizarre storyline in which another female wrestler became her obsessed stalker. Lita's affair with another wrestler became public knowledge and she found herself caught up in a public witch hunt. Despite this, they continued to play out with gusto the bizarre ideas of Vince McMahon, and also took the time to teach newer girls. By 2006, they had a 'loser leaves town' match, which Trish won, but she retired shortly after; they ended their ring careers together. They didn't want to be divas.

It seems that although Lita and Trish stood outside the 'divas' era in **WWE**, they are remembered as part of it. It was a period that made the blatant sexualisation of women acceptable, and lowered the standard to the extent that it took a decade for wrestling to recover.

See also:

- *Gaea Girls (2010):* a documentary about Chigusa Nagayo's school.

- *Ivory:* a counterpart of Chyna, Trish and Lita who was also an original cast member of *GLOW.*

- *Rey Mysterio:* considered by many to be 'the' *luchador,* he brought a huge change of pace and style in the **WWE** (I've met him, he's also really nice).

2010s–Present: Revolution

With the rise of divas came a lull in women's wrestling. Firstly, the struggle to gain new trainees and opportunities meant that there were fewer wrestling schools generally, and fewer opportunities to wrestle in independent shows. Wrestling became an even tougher career. From about 2010 onwards, wrestlers either faded to obscurity or became Z-list celebrities. The stresses of living a lifestyle of excess and injury started to take a visible toll on retired wrestlers; many had addiction and lifestyle problems from spending years in the spotlight.

Luna Vachon struggled with drug addiction for many years and died in 2010, as did Chyna, who also died of a drug overdose in 2016. Lola González went to work in an office. Alundra Blayze had a varied career as a stunt woman and competitive monster truck driver; she also owns a pet salon and does commentary for boat races. Mae Young retired in 2010 and died four years later; although she did get a *New York Times* obituary, she was described as 'an unladylike wrestler who loved to be hated'. Bull Nakano took up professional golf.

As we continue to creep towards the present, hopefully it's clear how recently these wrestlers, and hundreds of others, endured hardships and tribulations at the hands of wrestling. Wrestlers know from their very first bump that they need to be tougher and better than they can imagine, but even for the strongest, wrestling is a hard industry. Female wrestlers are not dumb or desperate; far from it, they often have a good idea what kind of crap they are getting into. The answer is to change wrestling from the inside, and become the person inspiring others.

Kia Stevens was a woman who wanted to change things that way, but who always just missed out on stardom as a result. Born in 1977 in California, Kia grew up watching wrestling. She was working as a social worker, having trained for several years to be an actress, when she entered a reality TV show in 2002 that followed her weight loss to become a professional wrestler. She then trained at a school aptly named School of Hard Knocks, inspired to become a wrestler by watching Lita and Trish perform – but she knew she wanted to be different.

Kia immediately appealed more to a Japanese audience than to an American one as the Japanese market is more open to diverse wrestlers. At the same time, black female wrestlers were generally in short demand, and a large woman was seen as an 'attraction'. But, as I said, female wrestlers aren't stupid, and Kia Stevens became a fixture in AJW. She wrestled for Chigusa's GAEA promotion in 2004, and formed a tag team with legendary Aja Kong, adopting her name to wrestle as Amazing

Kong. They went on to beat the Crush Gals only two years after Kia's debut.

In 2006, the same year that Lita and Stratus retired, Kia came back to the US to wrestle under the name Awesome Kong on a number of promotions, including Shimmer – a promotion opened exclusively for female wrestlers, which exists as another feminist stronghold within wrestling.

Kia was signed to TNA (which stands for Total Non-stop Action, not tits and ass by the way), WWE's rival promotion. She very soon became a fan favourite, particularly as she was the 'anti diva' – a big black girl in a sea of Barbies. TNA had a six-sided ring and brought over wrestlers from Japan, the UK and Mexico – an antidote to the increasingly dull line-up of the WWE. However, this was an era in wrestling when women's matches were still considered part of 'the piss break'. Yet Kia was determined to bring the credibility she had learned in Japan to Western women's wrestling.

In 2010, TNA gave creative control to Hulk Hogan, Eric Bischoff and their mate Bubba the Love Sponge. This turned out to be a terrible decision, not least because Hogan was looking less and less like the all-American hero who had launched him to fame, and was now coming across as an ageing steroid bag with far-right leanings. Only a few months into this change of command there were reports that Kia had hit Bubba the Love Sponge backstage after he repeatedly made offensive comments about relief work in Haiti following the earthquake, a cause for which Kia had done charity fundraising.

Kia requested to be released from her contract, but rather than let her go, she was told she had to remain in the company. She refused to go on a UK tour, then launched a court case against Bubba the Love Sponge over repeatedly threatening her and harassing her by phone. She was let go from TNA and stripped of her tag-team belt for 'not defending for thirty days' even though her last match had only taken place twenty-one days earlier.

Kia signed with WWE at the end of 2010, who gave her a 'slow build' for her entrance, showing her with her face in darkness, pulling dolls to shreds – but in 2011, when her time to debut came, she ended up in tears, unable to wrestle, announcing she was pregnant. Though this meant she took time out, and it was announced by the WWE that she had given birth on New Year's Eve of that year, Kia later admitted publicly that she had had a miscarriage. Despite this, in 2012 she took part in a King of the Ring match, which is a thirty-man mega-elimination event, and though she didn't win, she was only one of three women ever to be entered. This was her only match as Kharma, her WWE gimmick, before she was let go because she'd put on weight.

Despite these setbacks, Kia returned to Japan and the independent circuit, where she was once again topping the bill. She returned to TNA for a year in 2015, back on form. However, Kia decided to change tack and take some time off, eventually to act in the TV series *GLOW*. She became one of the more memorable characters and announced that she had given up wrestling, as acting was what she'd always wanted to do, but the race issues within the industry had been difficult to deal with.

In fact, Kia is an example of a wrestler who had begun to plug in to the new movement in women's wrestling. The 'anti diva' wrestler was growing in popularity, with the divas being given three-minute matches and rarely being remembered afterwards for their talent. The divas' matches had been so bad that wrestling fans started to believe no women could wrestle.

Which was about the time the events described in this book

began to unfold (and can be picked up at the start of Chapter 9 – 'The F Word').

Since the beginning of women's relationship with wrestling, we have been the victims of a collective loss of memory. Women's wrestling has experienced resurgence and revolution a number of times: in the '30s, women wrestled to crowds of astonishing numbers; in the '60s, women's wrestling launched across the world and women formed alliances; public appetite for it became insatiable in the '80s; then it almost died a death in the late '90s owing to a level of eroticism never seen before or since. But thankfully another couple of decades have passed and women's wrestling has a new bunch of extraordinary athletes again – and hopefully more people will pay attention and support their local girl gangs this time.

Appendix 2: Wrestling Moves

This is a list of every wrestling move described in this book; it is also a list of phrases that are some of the best collections of words in the human language (in my opinion). With thanks to Jules Scheele for her illustrations.

SUBMISSIONS

Holds or locks designed to make the opponent 'tap out' with pain.

BACK BREAKER

Back Breaker: an opponent is brought down on a knee, and their lower back takes the impact.

BOSTON CRAB

Boston Crab: the aggressor takes the legs of their opponent, then sits on their back, wrenching their legs uncomfortably.

CAMEL CLUTCH

Camel Clutch: an aggressor wrenches the neck of their opponent from behind, while trapping their arms.

Chicken Wing: the opponent's arms are held behind their back in a way that traps their neck uncomfortably.

CHICKEN WING

THE CLAW

The Claw: the opponent is choked out by the aggressor sticking a hand down their throat.

Figure Four: the opponent has their legs locked at the knee by the legs of the aggressor, who then places their body weight on the opponent's legs.

FIGURE FOUR

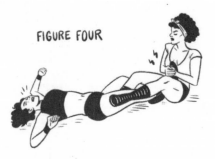

FULL NELSON

Full Nelson: a hold from behind in which the aggressor holds their hands on the back of the opponent's neck, trapping their arms and wrenching their head forwards.

GORY SPECIAL

Gory Special: the opponent is lifted up in a reverse piggy back, their whole body stretched while they are off the ground.

STEPOVER TOEHOLD FACELOCK

Stepover Toehold Facelock (STF): a combination of a leg lock in which the aggressor then bridges backwards to pull their opponent's neck upwards.

Surfboard: using locks on both arms and legs, the opponent is raised in the air on the arms and legs of the aggressor, causing back pain.

SURFBOARD

TORTURE RACK

Torture Rack: the opponent is picked up and slung over the shoulders of the aggressor, and stretched backwards in mid-air.

WRIST LOCK

Wristlock: the wrist is gripped in a way that manipulates the tendons painfully.

OFFENCE

Moves used to disable an opponent or as a form of defence.

ARM DRAG

Arm Drag: the opponent is thrown over using their own arm and momentum.

ATOMIC DROP

Atomic Drop: the opponent is picked up and then brought down on their genitals on an outstretched knee.

BACK ELBOW

Back Elbow: a reverse strike in which the elbow hits the opponent.

BODY SLAM

Body Slam: the opponent is picked up and then slammed down on their back.

CLOTHESLINE

Clothesline: a strike using the whole arm, while running, to knock the opponent down across the chest.

CROSS BODY

Cross Body: the aggressor throws their whole body in the air sideways to knock down their opponent, which can be done from the ground or from great height.

CRUCIFIX

Crucifix: the aggressor swings their body around the opponent, trapping their arms with their body, and pulling them backwards using their body weight.

DROPKICK

Dropkick: a jump into a double-footed kick to the chest.

ELBOW DROP

Elbow Drop: a jump landing in an elbow on the opponent's chest.

EYE RAKE

Eye Rake: scraping the eyes of the opponent and blinding them temporarily.

FOREARM

Forearm: a basic strike using the bottom of the forearm.

Low Blow: a kick or punch to the genitals.

LOW BLOW

317

SHOTGUN KNEES

Shotgun Knees: running up to the opponent, jumping, and landing both knees in their chest or back.

SHOULDER TACKLE

Shoulder Tackle: knocking down your opponent using your shoulder.

SNAP MARE

Snap Mare: holding the opponent's head, then flipping them forward in a somersault to the floor.

SUPERKICK

Superkick: a standing karate kick in which the opponent performs a standing side kick to the jaw of the opponent; also known as 'Sweet Chin Music'.

WHEELBARROW

Wheelbarrow: the aggressor runs up, puts both legs around the waist of their opponent, then, swinging their body upwards, throws them to the floor by their arm or head.

FINISHERS

Moves that aim to knock out the opponent completely so
that they can be pinned.

CANADIAN DESTROYER

Canadian Destroyer:
with the opponent's head
trapped between the
aggressor's legs, the
aggressor does a front
flip while still holding
their opponent, driving
them over and into the
floor. (Fraser calls it 'the
most wrestle-y move'.)

Fisherman's Suplex: the aggressor takes hold of their opponent, links their own right arm and leg, and then throws them over their head backwards, forming a bridge.

Frog Splash: a 'splash' is when the opponent jumps into the air and comes down with their belly on the opponent. The frog splash is a version of this where the aggressor flies across the ring from the top turnbuckle.

German Suplex: the aggressor holds the opponent around the waist from behind, then throws them backwards over their head, forming a bridge.

GERMAN SUPLEX

HURRACARRANA

Hurracarrana: leaping to the opponent's shoulders facing forwards, the aggressor then bends over backwards through the opponent's legs, flipping them on to their back and into a pin position.

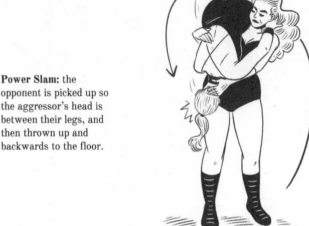

POWER SLAM

Power Slam: the opponent is picked up so the aggressor's head is between their legs, and then thrown up and backwards to the floor.

SEATED SENTON

Seated Senton: the aggressor jumps off the top rope, landing with their legs either side of their opponent's head, knocking them backwards to the floor. (I use this move and call it 'a flying cunt drop'.)

Sunset Flip: while the opponent is bent over forwards, the aggressor leaps over them, holding on to their waist and flipping them over into a pin position.

Suplex: the aggressor puts their arms around the head and shoulders of the opponent, then flips them backwards over their head.

Tombstone: a variation of a piledriver in which the opponent is belly to belly with the aggressor, who falls to their knees.

(**Piledriver:** the opponent's head is placed between the aggressor's legs, and the aggressor picks them up by the waist, while upside down, before 'driving' their head into the floor by sitting.)

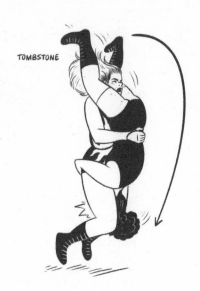

TOMBSTONE

TORNADO DDT

Tornado DDT: the aggressor spins around the opponent until they are in a DDT position, then lands on their back, driving the opponent's face into the floor.

(**DDT:** named after the notoriously destructive pesticide – the opponent is caught in a front face lock and then the aggressor falls backwards, driving their face into the floor.)

Tower of Doom: a combination of several wrestlers forming a kind of human pyramid of super-plexes (a suplex from the top rope), suplexes and power slams in the corner of the ring – eventually they fall down together through the execution of several moves at once.

TOWER OF DOOM

VADER BOMB

Vader Bomb: bouncing off the bottom rope in a corner, the aggressor flies backwards through the air and lands in a 'splash' position on their opponent.

VICTORY ROLL

Victory Roll: the aggressor ducks between the legs of an opponent (from a wheelbarrow position) and rolls them up into a pin.

Glossary of Wrestling Terms

See also Appendix 2 for descriptions of wrestling moves.

Announcers and Commentators: a person, or persons, who introduces the wrestlers and the rules of each bout. They may also talk over the match, naming moves, and help to tell the story of a match; this is 'play-by-play' commentary. 'Colour' commentators are faces or heels (see below), who – much like wrestlers – have a particular style of announcing within a gimmick (see below).

Card: the 'cast' of wrestlers taking part in a wrestling show.

Counted Out for Ten: if a wrestler is absent from the ring, loses consciousness or is knocked to the floor for a count of ten, that wrestler loses the match. If this happens to both wrestlers, the match is forfeited and no one wins.

Face (or 'Baby Blue Eye'): this is the goodie in a match, who always plays by the rules and who will get the audience behind them. They are often good looking, strong, technically skilled, determined, and are championed as an underdog.

Foreign Object: anything that is not part of the wrestler's body that is used as a weapon. If the referee catches a wrestler using a foreign object, the wrestler is disqualified. A foreign object can be anything from a baseball bat, an inflatable, even a pair of tights – most famously, a metal folding chair. Sometimes wrestlers will have 'no disqualification' (no DQ) matches in which the use of foreign objects is allowed. In 'death matches', wrestlers will use foreign objects and weapons to make their opponent bleed or knock them completely out.

Gimmicks: a persona that the wrestler creates or is given to portray in the ring; most wrestlers will go through a number of gimmicks before they find one that sticks. A gimmick is defined principally as being either a 'face' or 'heel'; and then becomes a fully realised character through the choice of name, costume, entrance music, presence and move set. If a wrestler performs on more than one promotion, it is not unusual for them to have another name, or another character altogether, which they can use so they can be both a face and heel, as required.

There are some particularly popular gimmicks:

- **Tank:** can be face or heel, a big wrestler who is hard to move and usually a lot larger than their opponent, e.g. Santeria, Aja Kong, Daisy Mayhem.

- **Exótico:** male wrestlers who are flamboyant and queer, akin to drag queens, e.g. Cassandro El Exótico, Cassius the Neon Explosion.

- **High-fliers:** usually smaller wrestlers who will put a lot of fast and acrobatic movements in their move set e.g. Rey Mysterio, Will Ospreay.

Heel: the baddie who will not play by the rules and who is consequently booed by the audience. Typically, heels are scary, mean, vain, rude to the audience, sadistic or just darn weird.

Kayfabe: the act of protecting the fixed and choreographed element of wrestling by portraying staged events as 'true'.

Managers: supporting characters who accompany wrestlers to the ring, act as their spokesperson and sometimes interfere with matches, or act as another character in the story. They provide a lot of hype but do not 'manage' the wrestler outside the ring in terms of finances, etc.

Match: a fight between wrestlers; there can be a number of matches during the course of a show.

Move Set: a number of moves that a wrestler develops in line with their character; for example, Zombie Janey's move set reflected the fact she was an undead, deranged monster, so she used biting, a lot of eye rakes and her finisher was 'The Claw'.

Outside Interference: when a person who is not a wrestler gets involved in the match by entering the ring, or by attacking or distracting a wrestler.

Pinned for One, Two, Three: the opponent's shoulders are pinned to the mat for a number of counts, and if a wrestler pins an opponent for three counts they win the match.

Promo: when a wrestler calls out or threatens another wrestler, usually as a way of building tension before a match. They can be quite silly, like a monologue but directed at an enemy.

Promotion: a little like music labels in the music industry, promotions organise wrestling matches, hire the wrestlers, decide the card (see above) and often determine the storylines of the matches.

Referee: an official who is in the ring with the wrestlers to remind them of the rules and proclaim a winner. Refs usually wear black-and-white striped polo shirts, black trousers and sensible, formal shoes.

Ring: a raised surface, measuring from 12 to 24ft across. Wrestling rings are usually engineered, using springs or rope tension, to have some bounce in them so they can take the impact of wrestlers being knocked down. A ring has three ropes around its sides, with a metal post at each corner. Though wrestlers are not supposed to step on the ropes or turnbuckles during fights, these are often used to execute high-flying moves or to cheat. The floor of a wrestling ring is traditionally made from wood, covered with foam mats, and then a square of canvas, tied to the ring with lengths of rope or elastic. Wrestling rings are usually square, like a boxing ring, but six-sided rings have been introduced in some companies.

Rumble: a type of match where there are several stand-alone competitors, each entering the ring in quick succession one after another. Opponents are disqualified by going over the top rope and both their feet hitting the outside floor. The winner of the rumble is the last person not to be disqualified.

Show: a number of matches presented on one evening.

Storylines: in matches, wrestlers are portrayed as being opposing sides; usually one is a heel and one is a face (see above). Often, certain wrestlers will have friendships or rivalries around which storylines are built. The character the wrestler portrays will change over time, depending on who they win against or lose to, and often wrestlers will form alliances or 'stables' that war with each other. Storylines are designed to bring an audience back to see how rivalries play out in the future – not unlike a soap opera.

Submission: rather than pin an opponent, a wrestler can get them in a hold in which they choke or hurt them until they can go on no longer. The referee asks wrestlers whenever they are put in a submission hold if they submit, which they can do by 'tapping out' on the canvas or the opponent's body.

Tapping Out: when an opponent submits to a move they must tap their own body, their opponent, or the floor, to show they concede defeat in the match.

Title Belts: akin to a leather weightlifting belt with ornamental brass studs. They are owned by promotions and 'won' by wrestlers as a sign of prestige; wrestlers then fight to defend their belts. Due to the nature of victories being pre-decided, belts are also given to wrestlers to improve their standing if they are considered crowd favourites or particularly exciting. Belts change hands according to storylines.

Turnbuckle: a rod and hook device that holds the ropes in place to form a square. The corners of a ring are referred to as 'turnbuckles' rather than corner-posts and they are padded with foam to prevent the wrestlers cutting their heads open on metal.

Valet: like a manager, but seen as a team member supporting the wrestler. Quite often, they can do as little as hold the costume of a wrestler or give them encouragement when they're in the fight, but they also have their own characters that interfere with the action or who are part of the stories. Women in wrestling were only ever seen in this role on TV for years, never being wrestlers themselves but sometimes becoming involved in the fight.

Wrestling: uses a combination of entertainment, martial arts and Greco-Roman grappling techniques to 'perform' a fight between two or more competitors. Wrestling is typified by the fact that the winners of matches are secretly pre-decided; hence fights are performed – you do not win a match, you 'go over' your opponent. Fights take place along storylines, with the use of outlandish characters and costumes or 'gimmicks'. Wrestling is performed in a ring; wrestlers compete for Title Belts and trophies.

Wrestling originated in the 1800s as a sideshow attraction, where members of the public would pay to try to pin a wrestler; the wrestlers would not hurt their opponent but would always win through their skill. In the early 1900s, wrestling matches began to be shown at venues alongside boxing matches, with two star competitors being pitted against one another. In order to keep these brawls contained and provide a stage for them, the wrestling ring was introduced.

By World War I, wrestling in America had evolved to the hybrid of styles we see today – often with jumps, high kicks and showmanship being as much a part of the entertainment as the fight itself. This style was termed 'all-in' wrestling, and it was around this time that the choreographed nature of wrestling began – with fighters realising they could fight more matches and tour the country if they weren't actually damaged by the bouts.

Today, there are several 'schools' of wrestling:

- All-in or 'show' wrestling: a mixture of all styles, over the top in terms of storytelling, best characterised as the wrestling seen on the WWE.

- British technical: rather than using hard-hitting moves, wrestlers outsmart their opponent by tying them up in holds and manipulating the body's joints.

- Strong style: hard-hitting style originating in Japan, more akin to martial arts sparring than the more choreographed wrestling style of 'all-in'.

- *Lucha libre*: very flamboyant and fast paced, with emphasis on acrobatics, jumping or 'high-flying' and showmanship.

- *Joshi*: a specific type of wrestling practised by female wrestlers in Japan – high risk, very fast paced and badass.

Wrestler: sometimes called a 'worker', these are the people who train to wrestle and take part in matches. Wrestlers will all have their own characters and move sets, which might alter in order to tell a different story depending on who their opponent is or their audience are. A person usually stops being considered a 'trainee' wrestler and becomes a 'wrestler' from their first paid match.

Newer wrestlers are referred to as 'green' to denote their lack of in-ring experience; at the LSLL we refer to demonstrating a lack of experience or knowledge as being 'a strawb'. Wrestlers with ample experience are 'veterans' of the industry, and wrestling 'legends' are those whose names and skill are widely respected.

WWE: World Wrestling Entertainment, previously known as the World Wrestling Federation (WWF) until it changed its name due to confusion with a conservationist charity (the one with the panda logo). The WWE is an American company owned and run by the McMahon family, which became the most televised wrestling company in the world, thereby dictating what the world expects wrestling to look like. Like a television series, the WWE owns rights to the gimmicks that its wrestlers portray, and wrestlers are contractually forbidden to perform elsewhere, often not even in another gimmick.

The WWF started in the 1950s specifically to bring wrestling to television, moving it away from being a live spectacle. Though it was broadcast in America until the 1980s, it soon became a global phenomenon when it soared to popularity on the back of 'Hulkomania'. With high production values and segments where characters taunt each other in promos, it quickly wiped out most competition across the world and bought out several smaller promotions.

In the 1990s, its original owner, Vince McMahon Senior, passed management to his son, Vince McMahon Junior, who took WWE to an even more bombastic level. During the Attitude Era, McMahon made himself into the biggest villain as well as the general manager for the entire promotion.

The WWE continues to this day, with McMahon taking a backseat role and his daughter, Stephanie McMahon, and her husband, Triple H, running the company. Their management has led the WWE to become a brand that recruits and trains wrestlers alongside its main shows; the brand 'NXT' specifically brings in and showcases new talent, though often only some of them are on 'developmental' contracts. Recently the WWE has introduced NXT UK which is an equivalent promotion for wrestlers from Europe and Australia. Quite often wrestlers get bumped up to the 'main' WWE shows like 'Smackdown' and 'Raw' once they have demonstrated enough skill and gained a large fan base.

In the WWE, men and women do not fight one another, though this has happened in the past, and mixed gender fighting is outlawed. It justifies this with the claim it does not want to encourage domestic violence.

Other references to the **WWE**:

- The Undertaker, a wrestler from the 1990s who portrayed a dead man who wore purple leather gloves and who had a valet called Paul Behrer, a creepy, screeching man who carried an urn.

- Stone Cold Steve Austin, a likeable badass, who wore ripped shorts and shouted a lot.

- Hulk Hogan, a giant, orange superhero of wrestling nostalgia. He is still known for his blond hair, bandana and bleached horseshoe moustache. Hogan went from being an 'All American Hero' to a C-list celebrity, shamed for dropping 'the N word' in a sex tape that was leaked on the internet. He has recently returned to the **WWE**.

Acknowledgements

Ever since I can remember I've wanted to write a book. I never knew what it would be about, until the moment I stepped in the ring. So I want to say thank you, so much, to every person who has helped me get this misguided aspiration to paper. To all those who pledged to support this book; the team at Unbound; Kwaku, who initially persuaded me that I was not mad to write a book on women's wrestling; and Rosanna and Kirsty who have both, over the last few years, trawled through my awful grammar to get me anywhere near a submission.

Thank you also to those who have taken part in my bizarre fundraising exercises – particularly Mesha, Mauro, Claire, Michael, Amber, Anais, Rhia, Kim, Rhonda, Janey and Deano, who helped me run 'the Woodland Wrestling League' for one night only.

Thank you to all my friends and family who have forgiven me for every single thing I've missed during the last twelve months of trying to write this book. Thank you to my parents for drunkenly persuading your friends to buy copies – thank you for listening to me in tears over my existential crisis of wrestler-turned-writer. You have supported me and I couldn't be luckier.

Thank you particularly to Ruth and Becca; and of course Fraser, for literally propping me up while I tried to get this dream realised and fought severe illness at the same time. Thank you to Janey and everyone at Burning Hearts for helping me recover from early retirement. Thank you, Emily, Dann and Pro Wrestling: EVE for all your support and bringing more angry women to wrestling. And of course, thank you to Garry Vanderhorne and Greg Burridge for somehow, *somehow* teaching me to wrestle, and ensuring the London School of Lucha Libre remains a paradise for weird but well-meaning wrestling trainees.

And finally, thank you to wrestling. I'm sorry I sometimes say bad things about you but wrestling, you are a noble pursuit – long may you bring magic to those who need it.

Index

Unbound is the world's first crowdfunding publisher, established in 2011.

We believe that wonderful things can happen when you clear a path for people who share a passion. That's why we've built a platform that brings together readers and authors to crowdfund books they believe in – and give fresh ideas that don't fit the traditional mould the chance they deserve.

This book is in your hands because readers made it possible. Everyone who pledged their support is listed at the front of the book and below. Join them by visiting unbound.com and supporting a book today.

Martin Croser
Imogen Davies
Razzle Dazzle
Rebekah Dean
Flora Death
Anna Dobbie
Sarah Dobson
Sian Docksey
Caitlyn Downs
Louis Doyle
Taylor Doyle
Jen Duncan
Hannah Dunton
Louisa Dymond
Chris East
Jeanette Eiternes
Nazrin Elmes
Rhea Eris
Ilana Estreich
Ann Ette
Ryan Eyers
Kate Fallick
Rob Ferguson
John Field
Heidi Florence
Kim Fuggle
John Fuller
Tanya Fyans
Nick Galea
Ed Gamester
Jasmin Geiger
Kate and John Giblin
Ami Gorgoroso
Megan Graham
Laura Grint
Greg Haber-Smith
Jon Hall
Madeleine Hamey
Gerlineke Hawkins-van der Cingel
Claire Heafford
Matt Hunter
Rosanna Hutchings
Roxanne Joncas
Chloe Jones
Jen Jones
Duncan Joyce

Spencer King
David Kirby
Kirsty La Rain
Anais Lalange
Florence Lambdon
Kerstin Lammers
Ro Legg
Heather Levi
Jakob Lindhagen
Kate Lomax
Liz Macfie
Lynsay Mackay
Daniel Magson
Fade Manning
Matthew Manning
Sierra Martin
Alex Martino
Hannah Maxwell
Katie McCallum
Jamie Mcfarlane
Josh Middleton
H Mikhail
Carla Miskell
Ella Mitchell
Alison Moore
Lisa Morris
Nina Mosand
Dan Moxon
Ellie Munro
Colin Munro Seymour
Livvy Murdoch
Bahar Mustafa
Anna Nathwani
Carlo Navato
Tom and Alison Neat
Alex Nicholls
Dominica Nicholls
Megan Nolan
Jason Norris
Hugo op den Dries
Kwaku Osei-Afrifa
Marta Owczarek
Anastsiya Pachyna
Violette Paquet
Tom Phillips
Lily Pink

Brent Power
Gareth Preston
Psycho Lolita
Shajidur Rahman
Lisa Randisi
Fran Read
Nicholas Reder
Michael Reece
Patrick Reed
Kelsey Rees
Mags Reinig
Emma Reynolds
Alice Rieuneau
Jade-Louise Riley
Michael Riordan
Jessica Roberts
Bethany Robertson
DouglasDouglas Rockefeller
Alys Roe
Collette Rogers
Joe Rogers
Margaret Rooke
Rebecca Ruechel
Boris Sadkhin
Marnie Scarlet
Jack Shannon
Hannah Simmonds
M.J. Smith
Rachel Smith
Stef Smith
Hannah Smith-Yen
Travis Snyder
James Stedman
Tanya Stezhka

Christof Stieglitz
Simon Stirrat
Linda Stupart
Bex Stupples
Suicide Gaming
Arjun Taheem
Anna Thomas
James Thompson
Simon Thompson
Jen Tidman
Debbie Titley
Andrew Torstonson
Becky Traynor
Ruth Turner
George Twigg
Lord Rohul Ullah
Izzi Valentine
Garry Vanderhorne
Heena Vara
Hannah Von Roast
Vic Wakefield-Jarrett
Jordan Walsh
Emma Ward
Helena Waters
Amber Wells
Louisa Whitehead
Alex Whiteman
Sasha Wilde
Mog Wilde
Hannah Wilk
Gareth Williams
Tom Winton
Nick Yeoman
Ruth Young